C++
PROGRAMMING
EASY WAYS
Volume II

Alireza Ebrahimi, Ph.D.

STATE UNIVERSITY OF NEW YORK
COLLEGE AT OLD WESTBURY

american press
BOSTON, MASSACHUSETTS

Copyright 2002, 2003 by American Press
ISBN 0-89641-393-4

Printed in the United States of America.

www.DrEbrahimi.com

CONTENTS

CHAPTER 14 DATA STRUCTURES | 445

CHAPTER 15 POLYMORPHISM, TEMPLATE, AND ADT — 503

CHAPTER 17 CHARACTER MANIPULATIONS, STRING CLASS, AND IOSTREAM — **549**

CHAPTER 18 STANDARD TEMPLATE LIBRARY

CHAPTER 19 ERRORS, EXCEPTION HANDLING, AND SOFTWARE ENGINEERING

CHAPTER 20 POTPOURRI (MIXED BAG)

CHAPTER 14

DATA STRUCTURES

Data structures is about how data is organized, structured, and stored in memory, as well as how this data is retrieved and manipulated. Since computer programming began, many data structures have been developed, each having its own name, properties, and characteristics. Understanding the existing data structures enables a programmer to choose the proper data structures to solve a problem. The programmer has to decide if what has to be done can be accomplished by reusing or modifying existing data structures, rather than reinventing the wheel. Let us start this way, in building a program a piece of data does not stand-alone and there is a major concern as to how the data are related to each other in a program. For each kind of relationship, there is a predefined structure, which conceptually (abstraction) or functionally (implementation), expresses how the data is stored, retrieved, or manipulated. Data can be structured as an array, struct, or a file; and these are the first data structures that programmers are exposed to. However, talking about data structures is more about major concepts such as stacks, queues, trees, hashing, sets, and graphs. The understanding of different data structures enables the programmer to solve a problem efficiently (time and space), such as applying and/or reusing the existing, tested algorithms. A large library of algorithms for data structure usage has existed for many years and still developing new algorithms, or optimizations of the existing ones, is a major topic of advanced computing. Let's put it this way, in the field of computer science there are a series of important algorithms for solving certain problems, each having its own method of organizing data so that variables (objects) are created; this way of creating objects is known as *data structures*. You will observe that algorithms and data structures are very closely related and, in fact, a program is created by the combination of algorithms and data structures. In many occasions, as soon as the choice for the data structure is made, the rest of the program will easily follow. The storage for a data structures could be allocated during compile time- static data structures or during run time – dynamic data structures. The major data structures are stacks, queues, trees and graphs. However, each of these data structures can be implemented either statically, for example by arrays, or dynamically by linked lists. There are trade-offs in selecting a static data structure versus a dynamic data structure that will be discussed in detail.

DATA STRUCTURE IMPLEMENTATION: STATIC VERSUS DYNAMIC

There are two ways data structures can be implemented (built), statically and dynamically. The memory for static data structures is of a fixed size and is allocated during the compilation time, meaning that the size of the array or structure is known in advance. In dynamic data structures, the size of the data structure grows and shrinks; meaning memory space is allocated during the execution time. In dynamic data structures, an array may be built one by one. There are advantages and disadvantages in choosing either static or dynamic data structures. It all depends on the situation and the problem. That is why the study of data structures becomes important. Again, note that the static data structures are implemented by fixed sized arrays, and dynamic data structures are built with pointers and dynamic allocation of memory.

ADVANTAGES OF STATIC DATA STRUCTURES

Faster: The memory for static data is allocated during the compilation time, which makes the program run faster rather than if it had to stop and allocate the required memory each time. An array index can randomly access any element of an array.

Easier to understand: It is easier to define and to use a static data structure rather than its counter part dynamic data structure.

DISADVANTAGES OF STATIC DATA STRUCTURES VERSUS DYNAMIC

Insufficient memory space: Declaring an array with a fixed size leads to a situation where the size of the array is less than what we intended to use. In other words, there is insufficient memory for the program to run with all data. Another situation requesting a large consecutive block may not be granted

e.g. int x[5]; has 5 element but program needs 6.

Memory waste: Declaring an array with a large size winds up to be a memory waste. For example, if we declare an array of 100 and only a small portion are used.

Slow: There are algorithms that, done statically, would be slower than if it were done dynamically. How would you combine two lists? The solution with static arrays is to define a bigger array and copy the two arrays into the bigger array.

Not natural: There are algorithms that are more suitable to be implemented dynamically rather than implemented statically.

ADVANTAGES OF DYNAMIC DATA STRUCTURES

Saving memory space: The memory space for dynamical data structures is allocated at run time; you make a request for the memory and you get the space. There is no need to reserve memory ahead of time (too little or too big). It seems as if the programmer possesses the entire memory, takes a chunk of memory, uses it, and when finished, releases it so it can be used again. This use and release of memory enables the program to run larger programs without running out of memory.

Faster: Certain algorithms run faster using dynamic data structures rather than static data structures. How do you connect two lists together? Dynamically, one operation is sufficient to connect two lists versus numerous code writing if using static data structures.

Preserve naturalness: Using dynamic data structures enables the programmer to implement the algorithms as they are rather than simulating them. For example, connecting one list to another would require fewer operations –the last element of the first list would point to the first element of the second list.

DISADVANTAGES OF DYNAMIC DATA STRUCTURES

Difficult to understand: In dynamic data structures, the program has to allocate and de-allocate memory by providing the keywords new and delete and appropriate syntax. In addition, the data type must be declared properly. The knowledge of pointers is a must.
Slow: The fact that memory is allocated and de-allocated during run time makes the program slower than if the program memory was allocated during compilation time.

MOST FREQUENT DATA STRUCTURES

The most frequently used data structures are stacks, queues, trees, and graphs. Other data structures such as sets, lists, and symbol tables are important as well. However, it is possible that your data structure is not one of the above frequently used ones and you may want to build a new or customized data structure.

WHAT IS A STACK?

A stack is a data structure in which the last data stored is accessible first, in other words, last-in first-out (LIFO). An example of a stack in real life would be placing a tray or a plate on the pile and similarly removing a tray or a plate from the pile. Therefore, insertion and deletion in stacks is done at one end of the stack, which is called the top of the stack, or simply, *top*. Inserting an element into the stack is called *push* and deleting an element from the stack is called *pop*.

APPLICATION OF STACKS

The main customer of stacks is the computer itself. The compiler uses stacks to keep track of variables; in fact, machine language uses stacks to perform operations. Functions use stacks to keep track of variables and return addresses. The address of the recursion function will be pushed into a stack, which on return, will be popped out. The following is the list of where the stack is frequently used:

- Evaluation of arithmetic expressions (implying precedence rules)
- Conversion of infix notations to postfix or prefix notation
- Evaluation of postfix notations
- Implementing email or voice mail as a stack (last come to retrieve first)
- Conversion of a recursion function to its non-recursive equivalent (simulation)
- Program to balance the matches (opening and closing: windows, parenthesis, quotation)
- In Compiler design to match: braces, **else** with **if**, nested if and nested loops.

STACK AND SYSTEM PROGRAMMING

Stacks are best used in algorithms where the action needs to be delayed until certain other conditions occur. For example, to hold onto the input until some other input is reached (look ahead). Many system-programming algorithms rely on the stack concept in operating systems (memory management, CPU scheduling) and compilers (parsers and translators). At this moment you don't have to know all of these; I want to illustrate how important the knowledge of stacks could be.

HOW TO IMPLEMENT A STACK

There are a variety of ways that we can implement a stack, which all do the same job. It all depends on the purpose of the application. Here is the list of different ways you can implement a stack:

1) stack by using an array
2) stack by using a structure
3) stack by using a linked list
4) stack by using a class
5) stack by using STL(Standard Template Libraries)

Similarly, other data structures such as queues and trees can be implemented as the above. Learning how to implement one will lead to the understanding of the remaining data structures. For a beginner, the array is the easiest, but at the same time could be confusing, especially when an element is removed from the stack.

IMPLEMENTING STACKS USING ARRAYS

For the beginners who have just learned the array, now they can implement a stack by using an array. There are certain terminologies that one should know before working with stacks. Terms used when dealing with stacks are: *top*, *push*, *pop*, *empty*, and *full*. The following program implements a stack of integers using an array called **stack**. However, the naming is conventional and it can be called any other name. In addition, we could have a stack of other types such as characters, doubles, or even pointers. You may argue that the stack is nothing more than a regular array. You are right. Arrays can be used to build any data structure by restricting the way you put the data into and get the data from (access) the array. What makes an array become a stack? An array becomes a stack when we restrict access of the array to the index of the last element put into the stack. In a stack, you are not allowed to access the middle element or anywhere else except the last element you put in. The index of the last element of a stack has a special name- *top*. The stack access is done only through the top. The top of a stack is initialized to a value, usually −1 or 0, indicating that the stack is empty.

```
#include <iostream.h>
void main(){
        int stack[10];
        int top;
        top=-1;
        if (top==-1) cout<<"STACK IS EMPTY"<<endl;
}//MAIN
```

Figure 14.1a – Initializing a stack to empty

```
STACK IS EMPTY
```

Figure 14.1b – Output of Figure 14.1a

OPERATIONS ON A STACK

What are the operations on a stack? The following is a list of what can be done to a stack:

- push – insert an element into a stack
- pop - remove an element from a stack
- full – to check if stack is full so no more insertion can be done
- empty – to check if the stack is empty so no more pops can be done.

For each of the above stack operations, we are going to build a function to perform the task. However, we are going to initialize the stack by setting the top to either 0 or –1. Just remember, the above names, such as push, pop, and top, are not reserved words. The words push, pop, and top are simply used by convention since they easily identify the tasks of the stack operations. One more thing, all the operations are done through the top of the stack.

INITIALIZING THE STACK

How do you identify that the stack is empty? If you have not yet pushed any element into the stack, the stack is empty. We can set the top to –1, indicating that the stack is empty and top will be incremented as soon as we need to push an element into the stack. Since the array in C++ starts from 0, this convention is a good one. An alternative to initializing the stack is to set the top to zero, making the stack ready for a push. Which stack initialization is better, top to zero or –1? Setting top to zero makes the empty test natural, while setting the top to –1 makes the pop natural by accessing the top element instead of subtracting top by one first.

```
#include <iostream.h>
void main(){
        int stack[10];
        int top, item;
        top=0;
        cout<<"ENTER THE ITEM: ";
        cin>>item;
        stack[top]=item;
        cout<<"THE TOP OF STACK IS: "<<stack[top]<<endl;
        cout<<"VALUE OF TOP IS: "<<top<<endl;
        top=top+1;
        }//MAIN
```

Figure 14.2a – Program that initializes top to zero

```
ENTER THE ITEM: 5
THE TOP OF STACK IS: 5
VALUE OF TOP IS: 0
```

Figure 14.2b – Output of Figure 14.2a

STACK PUSH

How does the stack push work? The item is inserted into the stack array by its top index. After the assignment of an item into the stack, the top index is incremented by one. In order to push an item into the stack, it is necessary to make sure that there is room in the stack, that the stack is not full. The check has to be done before the item is pushed into the stack. Again, since top is initialized to 0 and index 0 is the first element of the array, top is incremented after the insertion of the item into the stack. The following program will illustrate how an item is inserted into a stack and check to make sure there is room before the insertion is done. For simplicity, the stack push is shown as a main program as a unit by itself, instead of a function or as part of a class, which will be examined at later time.

```
#include <iostream.h>
void main(){
        const int MAXSTACKSIZE=10;
        int stack[MAXSTACKSIZE];
        int top, item;
        top=0;
        if(top==MAXSTACKSIZE)cout<<"STACK FULL"<<endl;
        else{
                cout<<"ENTER THE ITEM: ";
                cin>>item;
                stack[top]=item;
                cout<<"THE TOP OF STACK IS: "<<stack[top]<<endl;
                cout<<"VALUE OF TOP IS: "<<top<<endl;
                top=top+1;}//ELSE
        }//MAIN
```

Figure 14.3a – Pushing one item to the stack

```
ENTER THE ITEM: 10
THE TOP OF STACK IS: 10
VALUE OF TOP IS: 0
```

Figure 14.3b – Output of Figure 14.3a

STACK POP

The only element that can be removed from the stack is the top element, which will be assigned to a variable for further use. However, the top should be decremented by one since the strategy to initialize the empty stack is 0 as an alternative to -1. You can realize that popping an element is the opposite of pushing an element. One problem for beginners in regards to pop is that the deleted element is still in the array, only the top has moved down so that it would not be accessible.

```
#include <iostream.h>
void main(){
        const int MAXSTACKSIZE=10;
        int stack[MAXSTACKSIZE];
        int top, item;
        top=0;
        stack[top]=5;
        top++;
        if(top==0) cout<<"STACK EMPTY"<<endl;
        else{
                top=top-1;
                item=stack[top];
                cout<<"THE ITEM POPPED IS: "<<stack[top]<<endl;
                cout<<"VALUE OF TOP IS: "<<top<<endl;
                }//ELSE
        }//MAIN
```

Figure 14.4a – Popping the stack

```
THE ITEM POPPED IS: 5
VALUE OF TOP IS: 0
```

Figure 14.4b – Output of Figure 14.4a

STACK EMPTY

It is important to check whether a stack is empty or not. If the stack is empty, then no popping from the stack should take place and an error message should be displayed or an exception handler should take charge. Since the stack is initialized to zero, the top of stack is checked against zero.

```
#include <iostream.h>
void main(){
        const int MAXSTACKSIZE=10;
        int stack[MAXSTACKSIZE];
        int top;
        top=0;
        if(top==0) cout<<"STACK EMPTY"<<endl;
        else cout<<"VALUE OF TOP IS: "<<top<<endl;
   }//MAIN
```

Figure 14.5a – Testing if the stack is empty

```
STACK EMPTY
```

Figure 14.5b – Output of Figure 14.5a

STACK FULL

To check whether the stack is full is important so that no insertion will take place. If someone tries to insert an item when the stack is full, there should be an error message to alert or an exception handler should activate. The top of the stack is compared to the maximum size of the array allocated for the stack. In this example, the maximum size of the stack is defined as a constant identifier, which is initialized at the beginning of the program.

```
#include <iostream.h>
void main(){
        const int MAXSTACKSIZE=10;
        int stack[MAXSTACKSIZE];
        int top;
        top=0;
        if(top==MAXSTACKSIZE) cout<<"STACK FULL"<<endl;
        else{   cout<<"STACK NOT FULL"<<endl;
                cout<<"VALUE OF TOP IS: "<<top<<endl;   }//ELSE
}//MAIN
```

Figure 14.6a – Checking if the stack is full

```
STACK NOT FULL
VALUE OF TOP IS: 0
```

Figure 14.6b – Output of Figure 14.6a

SIMPLE STACK MENU: USING ARRAYS AND FUNCTIONS

The following program puts operations of stacks together so that each function is tested separately. A main program with a menu will call to each function: **push( )**, **pop( )**, **isfull( )**, **and isempty( )**. An array is used as a static data structure to implement the stack. For efficiency, the stack and its top variable are not declared as external variables, instead they are declared as local variables within the main program and are passed through the functions by reference so that the changes on them will impact back. The function: **void push(int mystack[],int &mytop,int item);** takes three arguments, stack, top, and item to be pushed with no return value. The function: **int pop(int mystack[], int &mytop);** takes two arguments and returns the item on top of the stack. The function: **int isfull(top);** takes two arguments- top and **MAXSIZESTACK** as value parameters to determine if the stack is at its maximum size. The function **isempty(int mytop);** takes one argument -top to determine whether the stack is empty. Both functions **isfull( )** and **isempty( )** could return a *boolean value (true/false)* instead of an integer, for instance, **bool isfull(top)**. In the program, the variables stack and top are preceded with the word my to reemphasized that these names are not reserved words, they are your words and can be any legal identifier name. For simplicity, the variable names used in the function (formal parameters) and names used in the calling program (actual names) are kept the same.

```cpp
#include <iostream.h>
void push(int mystack[],int &mytop,int item){
        mystack[mytop]=item;
        mytop=mytop+1;  }//PUSH
int pop(int mystack[],int &mytop){
        mytop=mytop-1;
        int item=mystack[mytop];
        return item;  }//POP
int isempty(int mytop){
        if(mytop==0) return 1;
        else return 0; }// ISEMPTY
int isfull(int mytop,const int MAXSTACKSIZE){
        if(mytop==MAXSTACKSIZE) return 1;
        else return 0; }// ISFULL
void main(){
        const int MAXSTACKSIZE=5;
        int mystack[MAXSTACKSIZE]; int mytop,x, option;
        mytop=0; // STACK TOP INITILIZATION
        do{ cout<<"SELECT ONE OF THE FOLLOWING OPTIONS:"<<endl;
            cout<<"1-PUSH 2-POP 3-ISEMPTY 4-ISFULL 5-QUIT: ";
            cin>>option;
            switch(option){
                case 1: if (isfull(mytop,MAXSTACKSIZE))
                                cout<<"YOU CAN'T PUSH"<<endl;
                        else{ cout<<"ENTER THE NUMBER THAT WILL BE PUSHED: ";
                              cin>>x;
                              push(mystack,mytop,x);}//ELSE
                        break;
                case 2: if(isempty(mytop))
                                cout<<"YOU CAN'T POP"<<endl;
                        else{ cout<<"THE NUMBER POPPED IS: "<<pop(mystack,mytop);
                              cout<<endl;}//ELSE
                        break;
                case 3: if(isempty(mytop)==1)
                                cout<<"STACK EMPTY."<<endl;
                        else cout<<"STACK IS NOT EMPTY."<<endl;
                                break;
                case 4: if(isfull(mytop,MAXSTACKSIZE)==1)
                                cout<<"STACK FULL."<<endl;
                        else cout<<"STACK IS NOT FULL."<<endl;
                                break;
                case 5: cout<<"THANK YOU FOR USING OUR MENU!"<<endl;
                        break;
                        default: cout<<"ENTER CORRECT OPTIONS"<<endl;    } // SWITCH
            } while (option !=5);
}//MAIN
```

Figure 14.7a – Stack menu with functions

```
SELECT ONE OF THE FOLLOWING OPTIONS:
1-PUSH 2-POP 3-ISEMPTY 4-ISFULL 5-QUIT: 1
ENTER THE NUMBER THAT WILL BE PUSHED: 7
SELECT ONE OF THE FOLLOWING OPTIONS:
1-PUSH 2-POP 3-ISEMPTY 4-ISFULL 5-QUIT: 1
ENTER THE NUMBER THAT WILL BE PUSHED: 6
SELECT ONE OF THE FOLLOWING OPTIONS:
1-PUSH 2-POP 3-ISEMPTY 4-ISFULL 5-QUIT: 1
ENTER THE NUMBER THAT WILL BE PUSHED: 5
SELECT ONE OF THE FOLLOWING OPTIONS:
1-PUSH 2-POP 3-ISEMPTY 4-ISFULL 5-QUIT: 1
ENTER THE NUMBER THAT WILL BE PUSHED: 4
SELECT ONE OF THE FOLLOWING OPTIONS:
1-PUSH 2-POP 3-ISEMPTY 4-ISFULL 5-QUIT: 1
ENTER THE NUMBER THAT WILL BE PUSHED: 3
SELECT ONE OF THE FOLLOWING OPTIONS:
1-PUSH 2-POP 3-ISEMPTY 4-ISFULL 5-QUIT: 1
YOU CAN'T PUSH
SELECT ONE OF THE FOLLOWING OPTIONS:
1-PUSH 2-POP 3-ISEMPTY 4-ISFULL 5-QUIT: 2
THE NUMBER POPPED IS: 3
SELECT ONE OF THE FOLLOWING OPTIONS:
1-PUSH 2-POP 3-ISEMPTY 4-ISFULL 5-QUIT: 5
THANK YOU FOR USING OUR MENU!
```

Figure 14.7b – Output of Figure 14.7a

STACK APPLICATION: INFIX EXPRESSION TO POSTFIX EXPRESSION

One of the famous stack applications is the conversion of infix expressions to postfix expressions and also evaluation of postfix expressions. What is infix and what is postfix notation? The arithmetic we use is expressed in the infix notation where the binary operator (the sign) is placed between the two numbers (operands). However, there are other notations where the operator is not between its operands, but it is placed either at the end or at the beginning. If the operator is after its operands, it is known as postfix or polish notation (after its polish inventor). If the operator is before its operands, it is known as prefix notation. What is good about postfix or prefix notation? There is no precedence and no parentheses are needed in the expression. In postfix notation, every operator is evaluated by applying it to the two previous operands, and we don't care whether it is addition or multiplication. However, a postfix equivalent of an infix notation will evaluate to the same result. For example the 3 + 4 * 2 will be converted to:
3   4   2 * + where * will apply to its operands 4 and 2, resulting to 8, and + will apply to 3 and 8, resulting to 11. One observation in converting infix to postfix is that the position of the numbers does not change while the position of the operators can change, depending on the precedence of the two operators. A stack holds (push) the operator that has lower precedence; otherwise the operator pops from the stack and will be displayed. The algorithm is straightforward but could be lengthy. The main theme of the infix

conversion is as follows: if input is a number (operand), display it, if it is an operator that has higher precedence over the operator on top of the stack, display it, otherwise pop the operator on the stack and display it. Let's start with the evaluation of the postfix notation where the algorithm is less code.

ALGORITHM FOR EVALUATION OF POSTFIX NOTATION

To evaluate a postfix notation, we have the following strategy. If the input is a number, it is pushed to the stack, if the input is an operator, the stack is popped twice and evaluated by applying the operator and the result is pushed to the stack. When there is no more input, the stack is popped and displayed. For example, to evaluate the following postfix notation: 12 3 5 * +,which is the equivalent for the infix expression, 12 + 3 * 5, it would follow this algorithm:

- 12 is recognized as a number and therefore pushed to the stack
- 3 is recognized as a number and therefore pushed to the stack
- 5 is recognized as a number and therefore pushed to the stack
- * is recognized as an operator and therefore the stack is popped twice (5 and 3) and the operator is applied to the popped numbers (3*5) and the result (15) is pushed to the stack
- + is recognized as an operator and the stack is popped twice (15 and 12) and the operator is applied to the popped numbers (12+15) and the result is pushed to the stack (27)
- when there is no more input, the stack is popped and the result is displayed (27).

Note that the stack is only necessary for the numbers, and also for simplicity the unary operators such as -3 or +3 and exponentiation 2^3 are not considered.

POSTFIX EVALUATION PROGRAM

In the following program we need a stack to hold the numbers and each operator will be applied to the two previous numbers by popping the stack twice. The core of the program is to recognize whether the input is a number or an operator; since there is as mixture of input (numbers and operators), we have no choice but to read the data as characters. If the input character is a digit, then we know it is a number and there is a possibility that there are more digits to follow. The input digits must be converted from its ASCII value to its numeric value. For the moment, we are not using this strategy (trick), instead, after the recognition of a digit, we put back the character by **putback(t);** and use **cin>>x** to get the number.

```
#include<iostream.h>
void push(int stack[], int &top, int x){
   stack[top++]=x; }//PUSH
int pop(int stack[],int &top){
   return stack[--top]; }//POP
int evaluate(int num1, int num2, char t){
   switch(t){
      case'+':return num2+num1;break;
      case'-': return num2-num1;break;
      case'/': return num2/num1;break;
      case'*': return num2*num1;break;
   }//SWITCH
}//EVALUATE
int main(){
   int stack[10],top=0, x, num1, num2, value;
   char t;
   cout<<"PLEASE ENTER A POSTFIX NOTATION"<<endl;
   while(cin.get(t)){
     if((t>='0') && (t<='9')) {
                  cin.putback(t); cin>>x;
                  push(stack,top,x);}//IF
       else if ((t=='+') || (t=='-') || (t=='/') || (t=='*')){
          num1=pop(stack,top);
          num2=pop(stack,top);
          value=evaluate (num1,num2,t);
          push(stack,top,value);
       }//ELSE IF
                  if(t=='\n') break;
   }//WHILE
   cout<<pop(stack,top);
   return 0;
}//MAIN
```

Figure 14.8a – Postfix evaluation program

```
PLEASE ENTER A POSTFIX NOTATION
12 5 3 + *
96
```

Figure 14.8b – Output of Figure 14.8a

457

TO CONVERT ASCII DIGITS TO ITS NUMERIC VALUE

The keys on the keyboard, including numbers, are considered characters, and for each character there is an associated numerical value, e.g. ASCII value. For example, the key 0 has an ASCII value of 48, the key 1 has an ASCII of 49, and so forth. When digits are entered from the keyboard, they are characters and must be converted to their numerical equivalent before used in any arithmetic expression. Note that the C++ compiler will automatically do this conversion when using **cin**. In the following program, after a character is read by **get(c)**, it is tested to see if it is a digit by the library function **isdigit(c)**. If it is a digit, the expression **c-'0'** will convert the character to its numeric equivalent. If there is more than one digit, multiplication by 10 is applied to the conversion. For example, to convert characters 123, the following steps would take place in the loop:

$$value=0*10+1;$$

$$value=1*10+2;$$

$$value=12*10+3;$$

The following program works for only integer numbers, however, for a fixed decimal number or scientific notation, a similar program can be written with minor changes. For example 23.99 is an integer number followed by a decimal point and another integer number.

```cpp
#include<iostream.h>
#include<ctype.h>
void main(){
        char c;
        int value=0;
        cout<<"ENTER CHARACTERS: ";
        cin.get(c);
        while(isdigit(c)){
                value=value * 10 + (c-'0');
            cin.get(c);
        }//WHILE
        cout<<"THE NUMERIC VALUE IS: "<<value<<endl;
        }//MAIN
```

Figure 14.9a – Program to convert ASCII digits to numerical value

```
ENTER CHARACTERS: 9574
THE NUMERIC VALUE IS: 9574
```

Figure 14.9b – Output of Figure 14.9a

TO CONVERT DECIMAL NUMBERS TO BINARY: STACK APPLICATION

One stack application would be the conversion of a number from a decimal system to a binary system. The way the decimal to binary conversion works is each time the number is divided by two and its remainder is put into the stack. After the division, the quotient becomes the new number and the same steps will be repeated until the number is zero.

```
#include<iostream.h>
struct stack{
        int info[16];
        int top;}; //STACK
void push(stack &mystack, int x){
        mystack.info[mystack.top]=x;
        mystack.top=mystack.top+1;}//PUSH
int pop(stack &mystack){
        mystack.top=mystack.top-1;
        return mystack.info[mystack.top];}//POP
int isempty(stack &mystack){
        if(mystack.top==0) return 1;
        else return 0;} //ISEMPTY
void main(){
        int rem;
        stack mystack;
        mystack.top=0;
        int number;
        cout<<"ENTER A NUMBER\n";
        cin>>number;
        while(number!=0){
                rem=number%2;
        push(mystack,rem);
        number=number/2;}//WHILE
        while(!isempty(mystack)){
                cout<<pop(mystack)<<" ";}//WHILE
        }//MAIN
```

Figure 14-10a – Program to convert a decimal number to binary

```
ENTER A NUMBER
8
1 0 0 0
```

Figure 14-10b – Output of Figure 14-10a

HIDDEN STACK: CONVERT DECIMAL TO BINARY

The following program converts a decimal number to its equivalent binary number without the programmer declaring the stack; instead, the required stack is built in the compiler. The compiler with each call to the function uses a stack to keep track of the variables and the return addresses. With this knowledge of the hidden stack, a programmer can take advantage of this property to solve certain problems. A recursive function uses a hidden stack to push the local variables and return addresses. Upon exit from the recursion, the pushed variables and return addresses are popped out. Based on what is needed, certain variables may be involved in operations or displayed. For example, in the below program the local variables **num** and **rem** are pushed into a stack upon each call to the function. When the number becomes 0, recursion will terminate and the stack will be popped. In this case, we only need the variable **rem** to be displayed.

```
#include<iostream.h>
void tobinary(int num){
        int rem;
        if(num!=0) {
                rem=num%2;
                tobinary(num/2);
                cout<<rem;}//IF
        }//TOBINARY
void main(){
        int num;
        cout<<"ENTER A DECIMAL NUMBER: ";
        cin>>num;
        cout<<"THE BINARY NUMBER IS: ";
        tobinary(num);
        }//MAIN
```

Figure 14-11a – Using a hidden stack to convert decimal to binary

```
ENTER A DECIMAL NUMBER: 12
THE BINARY NUMBER IS: 1100
```

Figure 14-11b – Output of Figure 14-11a

DYNAMIC DATA STRUCTURE: LINKED LISTS

A data structure such as a stack can be implemented dynamically by allocating the memory for the variables as the program is running and releasing the memory when there is no more need for it, unlike static data structures where memory is requested during compilation time and the size of the data structure is fixed. Most static data structures are implemented by using fixed sized arrays. In dynamic data structures, most data structures are implemented by using linked lists and are built gradually, one node (cell) at a time. Creating a linked list is similar to creating a homemade array where a new node is added to the connected nodes. In a linked list there is no random access as there is in an array. Instead, a list is usually accessed by a pointer that points either to its beginning or to its end and from there the rest of the list can be accessed (traversed).

A HOME MADE ARRAY BY LINKING THE NODES: LINKED LIST

A request for an array, whether it is static or dynamic, is granted by providing a chunk of memory, according to its size. Each array element is indexed relative to the beginning address of the array, which is the name of the array (or the zero index of the array). A linked list, as the name suggests, is a list that is created by linking its elements (**nodes**) together. A linked list has its own terminologies: each cell of memory (self-referential cell) is called a **node** and each node has an aggregate of at least two parts, one that contains the information (info, or data) and one part that is a pointer and points to the next element which is usually called **next** or **link**. In languages that do not support pointer manipulation, a linked list can be simulated by using a two dimensional array, where one of the dimension contains the next index.

VARIETIES OF LINKED LISTS

There are different kinds of linked lists, depending on where each node points.

- A *single linked list* is a list where each node has a (single) pointer which points to the next node or NULL (end of list). The name of this pointer is commonly known as **next**. A single linked list also is known as a *one-way list*.
- A *circular linked list* is a list in which the last node points to the first node; therefore, the last node is not NULL anymore and there is no end except when there is nothing in the list.
- A *double linked list* is a list in which each node has two pointers: one pointer points to the next node (*next pointer*) and the other pointer points to the previous node (*previous pointer*). A double linked list is also known as a *two-way list*.

There are other linked lists that we are not discussing here such as a node containing an array of pointers. Usually when we talk about linked lists, we refer to a single linked list.

LINKED LIST IMPLEMENTATION OF A STACK

A linked list is built by adding one node at a time to an existing list. At the beginning, a linked list is an empty node that points to **NULL**. How would you represent a stack by a linked list? We are adding or deleting from the stack with one pointer which points to the stack. When there is no list (nodes), a stack is empty- the stack pointer has a NULL value. To push to the stack, the new node points to the top of the stack and the new node becomes the top of the stack; this is done by re-adjusting the stack pointer. To pop from the stack, take the node that stack pointer points to, name it, and re-adjust the stack pointer. Again, a stack is a linked list where the node is added to and deleted from one end. In building a stack, we need two things: a pointer and a node.

```
struct node {
        int info;
        node *next; };

node *stack;
```

LINKED LIST STACK OPERATIONS

How are the major operations on a stack defined when a stack is implemented by a linked list? The operations on stack are much easier to grasp using a linked list rather than using a fixed array. The stack is empty if no nodes exist in the linked list. To push to the stack, simply connect the node to the beginning of the list and, to pop from stack, remove the beginning node. In other words, the nodes are physically added to and removed from the stack. Finally, the only time the stack is full is when there is no memory left in the computer, rather than when a fixed number allocated by an array request is reached. The keyword **new** operator should return a valid address. A return of an invalid address-NULL by **new** operator indicates there is no more memory in the computer; and therefore, the stack is full (overflow).

PROGRAM FOR LINKED LIST - STACK OPERATIONS

The following simple program illustrates the linked list stack operations. The operations become much easier when the pointer manipulation is understood. To empty the stack, a NULL value is assigned to the stack pointer. Similarly, the stack pointer is compared with NULL to check if the stack is empty. For simplicity we call the stack pointer just **stack**, which is used as the top of the stack. The stack pointer is the only variable that has access to the stack; therefore, all the operations are done through this stack pointer. In this program, the stack operations are performed as follows:

The pushing of the node **p** to the stack is done by **p->next = stack;** which connects the **p** to the stack, and re-positions the stack by **stack = p;** to include the node **p** as well.
The popping of a node from the stack is done by assigning a new name to the stack (top node) such as **p** and then re-position the stack pointer to the next node by the statement **stack= stack->next**. Finally, the newly named **p** is disconnected physically by **p->next =NULL;** and deleted by the statement **delete p;**.

```
#include <iostream.h>
struct node{
        int info;
        node *next; };
void main(){
        node *stack, *p; int x;
        stack=NULL;
        if(stack==NULL) cout<<"UNDERFLOW-STACK EMPTY"<<endl;
        cout<<"ENTER THE VALUE TO PUSH: ";
        cin>>x;
        p=new node;
        if(p==NULL ) cout<<" NO MORE MEMORY AVAILABLE";
        else{
                p->info=x;
                p->next=stack;
                stack=p;
                cout<<"VALUE: "<<stack->info<<" HAS BEEN PUSHED "<<endl;
                cout<<"NOW READY TO POP: "<<stack->info<<endl;
                p=stack;
                stack=stack->next;
                p->next =NULL;
                cout<<p->info<<" WILL BE DELETED "<<endl; }//ELSE
        }//MAIN
```

Figure 14-12a – Stack implemented by linked list

```
UNDERFLOW-STACK EMPTY
ENTER THE VALUE TO PUSH: 10
VALUE: 10 HAS BEEN PUSHED
NOW READY TO POP: 10
10 WILL BE DELETED
```

Figure 14-12b – Output of Figure 14-12a

IMPLEMENT STACK DYNAMICALLY: STACK MENU

The following program implements a stack dynamically and the stack operations are shown in a menu. A self-referential structure is used as a user-defined type for the node, and **stack** is a pointer of this type. The function push will push a node to the stack. Note that stack is passed by reference (&stack), which indicates that the change in the function reflects back. The function pop deletes a node from the stack and returns the node to the main function and deletes the node. An option in the menu checks to see if the stack is empty, the functions pop and push do not check for underflow and overflow.

```
#include<iostream.h>
struct node{
        int info;
        node *next;    };
void push(node *&stack, node *p){
        cout<<"ENTER THE NUMBER TO BE PUSHED: ";
        cin>>p->info;
        p->next=stack;
        stack=p; }//PUSH
int pop(node *&stack, node *p){
        p=stack;
        stack=stack->next;
        p->next=NULL;
        return p->info; }//POP
void main(){
        node *p, *stack;
        stack=NULL;
        int option;
        do{
                cout<<"SELECT ONE OF THE FOLLOWING OPTIONS:"<<endl;
                cout<<"1 PUSH\n2 POP\n3 ISEMPTY\n4 QUIT\n";
                cin>>option;
                switch(option){
                case 1: p=new node; push(stack,p); break;
                case 2: cout<<pop(stack,p)<<endl; delete p;  break;
                case 3: if(stack==NULL) cout<<"STACK IS EMPTY."<<endl;
                                else cout<<"STACK IS NOT EMPTY."<<endl; break;
                case 4: cout<<"THANK YOU FOR USING OUR MENU!"<<endl;break;
                        default: cout<<"ENTER CORRECT OPTIONS"<<endl;
                }//SWITCH
        }while (option !=4);
        }//MAIN
```

Figure 14-13a – Dynamic implementation of a stack

```
SELECT ONE OF THE FOLLOWING OPTIONS:
1 PUSH
2 POP
3 ISEMPTY
4 QUIT
1
ENTER THE NUMBER TO BE PUSHED: 10
SELECT ONE OF THE FOLLOWING OPTIONS:
1 PUSH
2 POP
3 ISEMPTY
4 QUIT
1
ENTER THE NUMBER TO BE PUSHED: 5
SELECT ONE OF THE FOLLOWING OPTIONS:
1 PUSH
2 POP
3 ISEMPTY
4 QUIT
3
STACK IS NOT EMPTY.
SELECT ONE OF THE FOLLOWING OPTIONS:
1 PUSH
2 POP
3 ISEMPTY
4 QUIT
2
5
SELECT ONE OF THE FOLLOWING OPTIONS:
1 PUSH
2 POP
3 ISEMPTY
4 QUIT
5
SELECT ONE OF THE FOLLOWING OPTIONS:
1 PUSH
2 POP
3 ISEMPTY
4 QUIT
4
THANK YOU FOR USING OUR MENU!
```

Figure 14-13b – Output of Figure 14-13a

DATA STRUCTURE QUEUE: FIFO

A queue is a kind of data structure where insertion is done at one end and deletion is done from the other end. The following terminologies are used in regards to queues: *rear*, *front*, *enqueue*, *dequeue*, *isempty* and *isfull*. A queue can be thought of as a line, such as a bus line or a ticket line, where individuals arrive at the end of the line (rear) and depart (receive the service) from the front (beginning). A queue is referred to as First-In-First-Out (FIFO).

OPERATIONS ON QUEUES

The main operations on queues are as follows:

- To add an item (node) to the rear of the queue is known as *enqueue*
- To remove an item from the front of the queue is known as *dequeue*
- The function *isempty()* checks if there are no items (nodes) in the queue
- The function *isfull()* checks if there is no more room in the queue

There are other functions: *makequeueempty()* and *checkfrontqueue()* which respectively empties the queue and checks the front of the queue without removing an item from the queue.

HOW TO IMPLEMENT A QUEUE

The following is a list of ways a queue can be implemented:

- arrays
- structures
- linked lists
- classes
- STL

We can divide the implementation of the queue into two major categories: static and dynamic, referring to whether the storage is provided during compile time or run time. The majority of static queues are implemented using arrays, structures, and classes. Dynamic queues are mostly implemented by the use of self-referential structures (classes) where one node points to other node, also known as a linked list. Finally, the STL (Standard Template Library) makes the queue ready to go and frees you from implementing the queue functions; however, you have to know the syntax and semantics of each function (what does it do). Make sure to include the library name; we will discuss STL in later chapters.

ARRAY IMPLEMENTATION OF A QUEUE

The queue data structure can be simply seen as an array with two restrictions: for assigning an item (enqueue) and removing (dequeue) an item. Remember that in an array you can insert an item into or remove an item from anywhere in the array. However, to make an array a queue, you must only insert at one end and delete from the other end. Therefore, the first element of the array (e.g. **queue[0]**) is the one to be removed. Insertion is done at the end using a variable called **rear**, which is the number of items entered into the queue (counter) and is originally set to zero. For example, the code for insertion is **queue[rear] = item**. What happens if the first element of the queue is removed and we want to remove the next element? In the array implementation of a queue, after the removal of the item from the queue, the memory (cell) is still present (in the array). One solution is to shift every element to the left simulating a waiting line where everyone moves one position down. After all the shifts the queue will have one less element as demonstrated in the following code:

for (front=1; front<rear; front++) {queue[front-1]=queue[front];}//FOR
rear--;

QUEUE WITH ARRAY: PROGRAM

The following program implements a queue using an array. As each data is entered the index, known as **rear**, is incremented (enqueue). The data in the first element of the array is the one that is removed (dequeue). After each removal, the entire data is shifted so that the next data is in the first position and ready for the next removal. While this program is very simple for a small queue, for a large queue this method of shifting all the elements of the array is inefficient. Moreover, the program does not check for an empty or full queue. To check if the queue is full, add the following lines of code before inserting an element into the queue:

if(rear = = MAXSIZE) cout <<" QUEUE IS FULL: "<<endl;
else cout<<" QUEUE IS NOT FULL: "<<endl;

To check if the queue is empty, similarly add the following lines of code before removing an element:

if(rear= = 0) cout<<"QUEUE IS EMPTY:"<<endl;
else cout<<" QUEUE IS NOT EMPTY: "<<endl;

```
#include<iostream.h>
void main(){
        const int MAXSIZE=10;
        int choice,item;
        int queue[MAXSIZE], rear=0;
        cout<<"ENTER 1 TO ENQUEUE 2 TO DEQUEUE: ";
        while (cin>>choice){
        switch(choice){
        case 1: cout <<"TO ENQUEUE- ENTER THE ITEM: ";
                    cin>>item;
                    queue[rear]=item;
                    rear++;
                    break;
        case 2: cout<<"THE DEQUEUE ITEM IS: "<<queue[0]<<endl;
                    for(int front=1; front<rear;front++)
                    queue[front-1]=queue[front];
                    rear--;
                    break; }//SWITCH
        cout<<"ENTER 1 TO ENQUEUE 2 TO DEQUEUE, Q TO QUIT: ";
        }//WHILE
        }//MAIN
```

Figure 14-14a – Program implementing a queue with an array

```
ENTER 1 TO ENQUEUE 2 TO DEQUEUE: 1
TO ENQUEUE- ENTER THE ITEM: 3
ENTER 1 TO ENQUEUE 2 TO DEQUEUE, Q TO QUIT: 1
TO ENQUEUE- ENTER THE ITEM: 6
ENTER 1 TO ENQUEUE 2 TO DEQUEUE, Q TO QUIT: 1
TO ENQUEUE- ENTER THE ITEM: 9
ENTER 1 TO ENQUEUE 2 TO DEQUEUE, Q TO QUIT: 2
THE DEQUEUE ITEM IS: 3
ENTER 1 TO ENQUEUE 2 TO DEQUEUE, Q TO QUIT: 2
THE DEQUEUE ITEM IS: 6
ENTER 1 TO ENQUEUE 2 TO DEQUEUE, Q TO QUIT: 2
THE DEQUEUE ITEM IS: 9
ENTER 1 TO ENQUEUE 2 TO DEQUEUE, Q TO QUIT: Q
```

Figure 14-14b – Output of Figure 14-14a

ENDLESS QUEUE USING ARRAY

Theoretically, you can have an endless queue by declaring a large array where you can add to one end and take away from the other end by simply moving the front and rear indexes. In other words, increment each variable by 1, whether to insert (**rear=rear+1**) an item or remove an item (**front = front +1**). With a large array there is no need to shift all the elements when a front element is removed. While implementing a queue with large array is easy, a request for a large array size may be not be granted by a compiler, or if it is, there may be a lot of memory waste. One solution for the memory waste of the array implementation of an endless queue is to reuse the location of the removed item by shifting all the remaining elements of the queue one element to the front.

WRAPPING THE ARRAY: CIRCULAR QUEUE

A circular queue can be implemented using an array. There are two indexes to the queue: one to the beginning (**front**) and one to the end (**rear**). The queue also has a given **MAXSIZE** and a **counter** to keep track of the number of elements in the queue. Initially, **front** and **rear** are set to the first element of the array (index of 0). When the **counter** is equal to zero, the queue is empty; when the **counter** is equal to **MAXSIZE**, the queue is full. After an element is inserted, the **counter** is incremented and the **rear** will also be incremented. When the **rear** reaches the **MAXSIZE**, the **rear** is set to zero (circular). When one element is removed from the queue, the **counter** is decremented and the **front** advances (**front++;**) leaving the array spot for future insertion. Also, when the **front** reaches the **MAXSIZE**, it is set to zero. After the removal of an item, this array location can be reused for the insertion of another item when the queue has reached its maximum limit. In other words, this location becomes available for the **rear** value. It seems a little confusing, but it becomes easy to implement when understood.

```
if(rear = = MAXSIZE) rear=0;
else rear =rear +1;

if(front = = MAXSIZE) front=0;
else front = front + 1;
```

We can substitute the above statements with simply dividing the **rear** or the **front** by the **MAXSIZE** and then reassigning the rear the remainder.

```
rear = (rear+1)%MAXSIZE;
front = (front+1)%MAXSIZE;
```

Trying to implement the circular queue using an array without a counter presents the problem of checking if the queue is full or empty because when **front= =rear**, the queue could either be full or empty; to avoid this problem, use a counter.

CIRCULAR QUEUE

One way to implement a queue when using arrays is to make it circular so that memory is not wasted. In a circular queue that is implemented using an array after an element of the queue is used its storage can be reused for the next queue insertion. With arrays, in most cases, queues are implemented circularly to save memory. When using a linked list implementation of a queue, there is not the problem of wasting memory since after an item is removed from the queue (circular or others) that memory can be released. A circular queue is like a ring where its end is connected to its front. There are situations where there is a demand for a circular queue rather than just a queue. For example, in a multitasking environment, a circular queue can be designed to give each job (task) a fixed amount of CPU time on each round until the specific task is finished and is out of the queue (circle). One example of a circular queue used in CPU scheduling techniques is known as *round robin.*

STATIC IMPLEMENTATION OF A CIRCULAR QUEUE

The following program demonstrates the operations involved in a queue implemented by a structure using an array. A structure is used to define a queue with two variables **front** and **rear** to keep track of removal and insertion of items respectively. The program checks if the queue is empty or full by using a counter variable that counts the number of items in the queue.

```
#include <iostream.h>
const QMAX=10;
struct Queue{
        char item [10];
        int front,rear, counter;};
void enqueue(Queue &, char);
char dequeue(Queue &);
bool isfull(Queue);
bool isempty(Queue);
void main(){
        Queue myqueue;
        char choice;
        char x;
        myqueue.front=myqueue.rear=myqueue.counter=0;
        do{
        cout<<"CHOOSE ONE OF THE FOLLOWING QUEUE OPERATIONS"<<endl;
        cout<<"1 - ENQUEUE , 2- DEQUEUE 3- ISEMPTY  4- ISFULL  Q- QUIT"<<endl;
        cin>>choice;
        switch(choice){
        case '1': if(!isfull(myqueue)){ cout<< "ENQUEUE- ENTER THE ITEM:";
                                cin>>x;
                                enqueue(myqueue,x); }//IF
                else cout<<"QUEUE IS FULL"<<endl;
                break;
        case '2':  if (!isempty(myqueue)){ x=dequeue(myqueue);
```

```
                                    cout<<"DEQUEUE ITEM IS "<<x<<endl;}//IF
                else cout<<"QUEUE IS EMPTY"<<endl;
                    break;
            case '3': if(isempty(myqueue)) cout<<"QUEUE IS EMPTY"<<endl;
                    else cout<<"QUEUE IS NOT EMPTY"<<endl;
                    break;
            case '4': if (isfull(myqueue)) cout<<"QUEUE IS FULL"<<endl;
                    else cout<<"QUEUE IS NOT FULL"<<endl;
                    break;
            case 'Q': cout<<"BYE"<<endl;              }//SWITCH
            }while(choice!='Q');//DO WHILE
}//MAIN
void enqueue(Queue &myqueue, char x){
        myqueue.item[myqueue.rear]=x;
        myqueue.rear++;
        myqueue.counter=myqueue.counter + 1; }//ENQUEUE
char dequeue(Queue &myqueue ){
        myqueue.counter--;
        return myqueue.item[myqueue.front++]; }//DEQUEUE
bool isempty(Queue myqueue){
        if(myqueue.counter == 0)return true;
        else return false; }//ISEMPTY
bool isfull(Queue myqueue){
        if(myqueue.counter == QMAX)  return true;
        else return false; }//ISFULL
```

Figure 14-15a – Static implementation of a circular queue

```
CHOOSE ONE OF THE FOLLOWING QUEUE OPERATIONS
1 - ENQUEUE , 2- DEQUEUE 3- ISEMPTY  4- ISFULL  Q- QUIT
2
QUEUE IS EMPTY
CHOOSE ONE OF THE FOLLOWING QUEUE OPERATIONS
1 - ENQUEUE , 2- DEQUEUE 3- ISEMPTY  4- ISFULL  Q- QUIT
1
ENQUEUE- ENTER THE ITEM:a
CHOOSE ONE OF THE FOLLOWING QUEUE OPERATIONS
1 - ENQUEUE , 2- DEQUEUE 3- ISEMPTY  4- ISFULL  Q- QUIT
1
ENQUEUE- ENTER THE ITEM:b
CHOOSE ONE OF THE FOLLOWING QUEUE OPERATIONS
1 - ENQUEUE , 2- DEQUEUE 3- ISEMPTY  4- ISFULL  Q- QUIT
2
DEQUEUE ITEM IS a
CHOOSE ONE OF THE FOLLOWING QUEUE OPERATIONS
1 - ENQUEUE , 2- DEQUEUE 3- ISEMPTY  4- ISFULL  Q- QUIT
Q
BYE
```

Figure 14-15b – Output of Figure 14-15a

QUEUE APPLICATION: AIRPORT SIMULATION PROGRAM

One major application of the queue, besides the computer system itself, which uses queues to manage resources, is in the area of simulation. Simulation is useful for keeping track of traffic, telephone calls, and sending email, etc. The following program simulates an airport with airplanes landing and taking off. The airport has two queues: one for landing and the other for taking off. A number ranging from 1 to 4, generated by a random number generator **(1 + rand()%4)**, is used for the following queue options:

    Option 1: Arrival en-queue

    Option 2: Arrival de-queue (Landing)

    Option 3: Departure en-queue

    Option 4: Departure de-queue (Taking OFF)

You can expand the simulation to include other information such as plane identification by producing a three-digit number from a random number generator and using the **srand**() function so that **rand**( ) produces a different sequence of numbers each time the program is run. In the following simulation program, we use two queues: arrival queue and departure queue. The options 1 and 2 are for arrival and options 3 and 4 are for departure queue. In this program, the simulation terminates when both arrival and departure queues are full.

```cpp
#include <iostream.h>
#include <stdlib.h>
const QMAX=10;
struct Queue{
        int item[10];
        int front, rear, counter;};
void enqueue(Queue &portqueue, int id){
        portqueue.item[portqueue.rear]=id;
        portqueue.rear++;
        portqueue.counter++; }//ENQUEUE
char dequeue(Queue &portqueue ){
        int item;
        portqueue.counter--;
        item=portqueue.item[portqueue.front];
        portqueue.front++;
        return item;}//DEQUEUE
bool isempty(Queue portqueue){
        if(portqueue.counter == 0) return true;
        else return 0; }//ISEMPTY
bool isfull(Queue portqueue){
        if(portqueue.counter == QMAX) return true;
        else return 0; }//ISFULL
void main(){
        Queue arrqueue, depqueue;
        int option;
        int item,x;
        arrqueue.front=arrqueue.rear=arrqueue.counter=0;
        depqueue.front=depqueue.rear=depqueue.counter=0;
        cout<<"RUNNING THE AIRPORT SIMULATION"<<endl<<endl;
```

```
while(1){
option=1+rand()%4;
switch(option){
case 1: if(!isfull(arrqueue)){ cout<<"ENTER ARRIVING FLIGHT TO QUEUE: ";
                        cin>>item;  enqueue(arrqueue,item); }//IF
        else cout<<"ARRIVAL QUEUE IS FULL"<<endl;
        break;
case 2: if(!isempty(arrqueue)){ x=dequeue(arrqueue);
        cout<<"ARRIVING FLIGHT IS: "<<x<<endl;}//IF
        else cout<<"ARRIVAL QUEUE IS EMPTY"<<endl;
break;
case 3: if(!isfull(depqueue)){ cout<<"ENTER DEPARTING FLIGHT TO QUEUE: ";
                        cin>>item; enqueue(depqueue,item);}//IF
        else cout<<"DEPARTING QUEUE IS FULL"<<endl;
        break;
case 4: if(!isempty(depqueue)){ x=dequeue(depqueue);
                        cout<<"DEPARTING FLIGHT IS: "<<x<<endl;}//IF
        else cout<<"DEPARTING QUEUE IS EMPTY"<<endl;
        break;  }//SWITCH
if((arrqueue.counter==QMAX)&&(depqueue.counter==QMAX)){
        cout<<"TERMINATING SIMULATION"<<endl;
 break;}//IF
}//WHILE
}//MAIN
```

Figure 14-16a – Airport simulation program

```
RUNNING THE AIRPORT SIMULATION

ARRIVAL QUEUE IS EMPTY
DEPARTING QUEUE IS EMPTY
ENTER DEPARTING FLIGHT TO QUEUE: 1
ENTER ARRIVING FLIGHT TO QUEUE: 2
ARRIVING FLIGHT IS: 2
ENTER ARRIVING FLIGHT TO QUEUE: 3
ENTER DEPARTING FLIGHT TO QUEUE: 4
ENTER DEPARTING FLIGHT TO QUEUE: 5
ENTER DEPARTING FLIGHT TO QUEUE: 6
ENTER ARRIVING FLIGHT TO QUEUE: 7
ARRIVING FLIGHT IS: 3
ARRIVING FLIGHT IS: 7
ARRIVAL QUEUE IS EMPTY
DEPARTING FLIGHT IS: 1
ARRIVAL QUEUE IS EMPTY
DEPARTING FLIGHT IS: 4
DEPARTING FLIGHT IS: 5
...
```

Figure 14-16b – Output of Figure 14-16a

LINKED LIST IMPLEMENTATION OF QUEUE

In a linked list implementation of the queue, a node (cell) is added to the queue as an item needs to be inserted. Similarly, as the item is removed its node is deleted. A linked list implementation of the queue is more natural than an array implementation because the nodes are inserted and deleted physically. In addition when the queue is empty there are no nodes in the queue and the queue can virtually use an entire computer's memory unless there is restriction on the size of the queue. In this case a queue counter determines if the queue is full. This program implements the queue using a linked list and a self-referential struct with two pointers, one known as front that points to the beginning of the queue, and one known as rear that points to the end. Each data is inserted to the end (enqueue), an element is added by the code **rear->next=p;**. To remove an element (dequeue) isolate the first element and assign it to a name (p=front;), the front of the queue advanced and called front (front=front->next). In the **dequeue( )** function, the content of the node (x) should be saved so it can be returned to the main program, and the isolated node should be deleted. The following program demonstrates implementing a queue using a struct.

```
#include<iostream.h>
struct node{     int info;
                 node *next;};
void main(){
      node *front, *rear, *p;
      front=rear=NULL;
      int x, option;
      do{      cout<<"\t\tENTER 1-ENQUEUE, 2-DEQUEUE, 3-CHECK IF EMPTY, 4-EXIT: ";
               cin>>option;
               switch(option){
               case 1:  cout<<"ENTER VALUE: ";
                        cin>>x;
                        p=new node;
                        p->info=x;
                        p->next=NULL;
                        if(front==NULL){front=p;
                                        rear=p;}//IF
                        else {rear->next=p; rear=p;}//ELSE
                        break;
               case 2: if(front!=NULL){cout<<front->info<<" ";
                                       front=front->next;}//IF
                       else cout<<"QUEUE IS EMPTY\n"<<endl;
                       break;
               case 3: if(front==NULL) cout<<"QUEUE IS EMPTY\n";
                       else cout<<"QUEUE IS NOT EMPTY\n";
                       break;
               case 4: cout<<"BYE";}//SWITCH
               }while(option!=4);
      }//MAIN
```

Figure 14-17a – Queue implemented with linked list

```
            ENTER 1-ENQUEUE, 2-DEQUEUE, 3-CHECK IF EMPTY, 4-EXIT: 1
ENTER VALUE: 10
            ENTER 1-ENQUEUE, 2-DEQUEUE, 3-CHECK IF EMPTY, 4-EXIT: 1
ENTER VALUE: 20
            ENTER 1-ENQUEUE, 2-DEQUEUE, 3-CHECK IF EMPTY, 4-EXIT: 3
QUEUE IS NOT EMPTY
            ENTER 1-ENQUEUE, 2-DEQUEUE, 3-CHECK IF EMPTY, 4-EXIT: 1
ENTER VALUE: 30
            ENTER 1-ENQUEUE, 2-DEQUEUE, 3-CHECK IF EMPTY, 4-EXIT: 1
ENTER VALUE: 40
            ENTER 1-ENQUEUE, 2-DEQUEUE, 3-CHECK IF EMPTY, 4-EXIT: 2
10          ENTER 1-ENQUEUE, 2-DEQUEUE, 3-CHECK IF EMPTY, 4-EXIT: 2
20          ENTER 1-ENQUEUE, 2-DEQUEUE, 3-CHECK IF EMPTY, 4-EXIT: 2
30          ENTER 1-ENQUEUE, 2-DEQUEUE, 3-CHECK IF EMPTY, 4-EXIT: 2
40          ENTER 1-ENQUEUE, 2-DEQUEUE, 3-CHECK IF EMPTY, 4-EXIT: 2
QUEUE IS EMPTY

            ENTER 1-ENQUEUE, 2-DEQUEUE, 3-CHECK IF EMPTY, 4-EXIT: 4
BYE
```

Figure 14-17b – Output of Figure 14-17a

The following program shows how to implement a queue with a linked list using functions **enqueue( )**, **dequeue( )**, and **isempty( )**.

```
#include<iostream.h>
struct node{     int info;
                 node *next;};
void enqueue(node *&front, node *&rear, int x){
      node * p=new node;
      p->info=x;
      p->next=NULL;
      if(front==NULL){
              front=p;
              rear=p;}//IF
      else {rear->next=p; rear=p;}//ELSE
      }//ENQUEUE
int dequeue(node *&front){
              int x;
              x=front->info;
              front=front->next;
              return x; }//DEQUEUE
int isempty(node *front){
      if(front==NULL) return 1;
      else return 0; }//ISEMPTY
void main(){
      node *front, *rear;
      front=rear=NULL;
```

```
int x, option;
do{cout<<"\t\tENTER 1-ENQUEUE, 2-DEQUEUE, 3-CHECK IF EMPTY, 4-EXIT: ";
    cin>>option;
    switch(option){
        case 1:  cout<<"ENTER VALUE: ";
                      cin>>x;
                      enqueue(front, rear, x);
                      break;
        case 2: if(!isempty(front)) cout<<dequeue(front);
                      else cout<<"QUEUE IS EMPTY\n";
                      break;
        case 3: if(isempty(front)) cout<<"QUEUE IS EMPTY\n";
                      else cout<<"QUEUE IS NOT EMPTY\n";
                      break;
        case 4: cout<<"BYE";}//SWITCH
        }while(option!=4);
    }//MAIN
```

Figure 14-18a – Linked list implementation of queue with enqueue( ), dequeue( ), and isempty( ) functions

```
        ENTER 1-ENQUEUE, 2-DEQUEUE, 3-CHECK IF EMPTY, 4-EXIT: 1
ENTER VALUE: 4
        ENTER 1-ENQUEUE, 2-DEQUEUE, 3-CHECK IF EMPTY, 4-EXIT: 1
ENTER VALUE: 3
        ENTER 1-ENQUEUE, 2-DEQUEUE, 3-CHECK IF EMPTY, 4-EXIT: 1
ENTER VALUE: 2
        ENTER 1-ENQUEUE, 2-DEQUEUE, 3-CHECK IF EMPTY, 4-EXIT: 3
QUEUE IS NOT EMPTY
        ENTER 1-ENQUEUE, 2-DEQUEUE, 3-CHECK IF EMPTY, 4-EXIT: 2
4       ENTER 1-ENQUEUE, 2-DEQUEUE, 3-CHECK IF EMPTY, 4-EXIT: 2
3       ENTER 1-ENQUEUE, 2-DEQUEUE, 3-CHECK IF EMPTY, 4-EXIT: 2
2       ENTER 1-ENQUEUE, 2-DEQUEUE, 3-CHECK IF EMPTY, 4-EXIT: 2
QUEUE IS EMPTY
        ENTER 1-ENQUEUE, 2-DEQUEUE, 3-CHECK IF EMPTY, 4-EXIT: 4
BYE
```

Figure 14-18b – Output of Figure 14-18a

The next program implements the queue by creating a class **queue**. The advantage of using a class in this case is that the **front** and **rear** pointers do not have to be passed to the functions because they are members of the class.

476

```cpp
#include<iostream.h>
class node{ public: int info;
                node *next;};//NODE
class queue{ private: node *front, *rear, *p;
        public: queue(){ front=rear=NULL;}//CONSTRUCTOR
            ~queue(){ while(front){ p=front;
                            front=front->next;
                            delete p;}//WHILE
                }//DESTRUCTOR
            void enqueue(int x){
                p=new node;
                p->info=x;
                p->next=NULL;
                if(front==NULL){
                    front=p;
                    rear=p;}//IF
                else{ rear->next=p; rear=p;}//ELSE
                }//ENQUEUE
            int dequeue(){
                int x;
                x=front->info;
                front=front->next;
                return x; }//DEQUEUE
            int isempty(){
                if(front==NULL) return 1;
                else return 0; }//ISEMPTY
    };//QUEUE
void main(){
    queue myqueue;
    int x, option;
    do{cout<<"\t\tENTER 1-ENQUEUE, 2-DEQUEUE, 3-CHECK IF EMPTY, 4-EXIT: ";
        cin>>option;
        switch(option){
        case 1:  cout<<"ENTER VALUE: ";
                cin>>x;
                myqueue.enqueue(x);
                break;
        case 2:  if(!myqueue.isempty()) cout<<myqueue.dequeue();
                else cout<<"QUEUE IS EMPTY\n";
                break;
        case 3:  if(myqueue.isempty()) cout<<"QUEUE IS EMPTY\n";
                else cout<<"QUEUE IS NOT EMPTY\n";
                break;
        case 4: cout<<"BYE";}//SWITCH
        }while(option!=4);
    }//MAIN
```

Figure 14-19a – Program using a queue class

```
        ENTER 1-ENQUEUE, 2-DEQUEUE, 3-CHECK IF EMPTY, 4-EXIT: 2
QUEUE IS EMPTY
        ENTER 1-ENQUEUE, 2-DEQUEUE, 3-CHECK IF EMPTY, 4-EXIT: 1
ENTER VALUE: 1
        ENTER 1-ENQUEUE, 2-DEQUEUE, 3-CHECK IF EMPTY, 4-EXIT: 1
ENTER VALUE: 2
        ENTER 1-ENQUEUE, 2-DEQUEUE, 3-CHECK IF EMPTY, 4-EXIT: 1
ENTER VALUE: 3
        ENTER 1-ENQUEUE, 2-DEQUEUE, 3-CHECK IF EMPTY, 4-EXIT: 3
QUEUE IS NOT EMPTY
        ENTER 1-ENQUEUE, 2-DEQUEUE, 3-CHECK IF EMPTY, 4-EXIT: 2
1       ENTER 1-ENQUEUE, 2-DEQUEUE, 3-CHECK IF EMPTY, 4-EXIT: 2
2       ENTER 1-ENQUEUE, 2-DEQUEUE, 3-CHECK IF EMPTY, 4-EXIT: 2
3       ENTER 1-ENQUEUE, 2-DEQUEUE, 3-CHECK IF EMPTY, 4-EXIT: 4
BYE
```

Figure 14-19b – Output of Figure 14-19a

PRIORITY QUEUE

A queue behaves as a FIFO structure, meaning first come first served; this can be considered a priority in itself. However, if another property is considered for determining the priority of the items in the queue, the FIFO principle may be changed- serving a prioritized item of the queue first instead of first come first served. A priority queue can be implemented by attaching other information, such as a number to indicate priority. There are many applications for a priority queue. For example, in order to optimize a printer queue, a higher priority can be given to a person with a higher rank or with a lower number of pages to print. Hence, service will be given to the first job with the higher priority rather than just to the job that came first.

PRIORITY QUEUE IMPLEMENTATION

A priority queue can be implemented according to one of the following methods. Each of these methods has its advantages and disadvantages that one can analyze and then choose.

enqueue: Insert at the rear
dequeue: Find the highest priority, remove the item and subtract 1 from the queue counter. In an array implementation, in order to not waste memory the remaining items of the queue may be shifted on position.
enqueue: Insert at the end of the queue and increment the counter.
In a linked list implementation an item can simply be removed from the queue and its memory can be freed to the memory.

478

Another method of implementing the priority queue is to keep the queue sorted at all times. Then to enqueue, the insertion has to be in the proper place and to dequeue, the first element has to be removed.

LINKED LIST OPERATIONS

What are the operations on a linked list? Mainly there are two main operations involved in a linked list: adding to the list and removing from the list. An element can be added at the beginning, the end, or anywhere else in the list. Similarly an element can be deleted from anywhere in the list. A list can be revisited (traversed) for printing or comparison purposes. A linked list is normally initialized to NULL at the beginning of the program or operation.

LINKED LIST OPERATION PROGRAM

The following simple program demonstrates the linked list operations such as: initializing the list, and inserts nodes at the beginning, in the middle, and at the end of the list. Then the program displays the newly created list and then applies the deletion operation by deleting from the beginning, the middle, or the end. For simplicity, we have chosen **b** for the beginning node, **m** for the middle, and **e** for the last (end) node of the list. At the beginning, the program inserts three nodes **b**, **m**, and **e** (beginning node, middle node and end node respectively). After the insertion, the program removes each the middle node, end node and beginning node. You may prefer to use a function for the insertion and removal operations.

```
#include<iostream.h>
struct node {    int info;
                 node *next;};
void main(){
        node *list;
        int x;
        cout<<"INITIALIZE THE LIST:"<<endl;
        list=NULL;
        cout<<"INSERTING NODE B AT BEGINNING OF THE LIST"<<endl;
        node *b;
        b=new node;
        cout<<"ENTER THE ITEM: ";
        cin>>x;
        b->info=x;
        b->next=list;
        list=b;
        cout<<"ITEM INSERTED: "<<list->info<<endl;
        cout<<"INSERTING THE NODE E AFTER THE NODE B"<<endl;
        node *e;
        e=new node;
        cout<<"ENTER THE ITEM: ";
```

```
cin>>x;
e->info=x;
e->next=NULL;
b->next=e;
cout<<"INSERTED ITEMS IN LIST ARE: "<<list->info<<" "<<list->next->info<<endl;
cout<<"INSERTING THE NODE M BETWEEN B AND E"<<endl;
node *m;
m=new node;
cout<<"ENTER THE ITEM: ";
cin>>x;
m->info=x;
m->next=e;
b->next=m;
cout<<"INSERTED ITEMS IN LIST ARE: ";
cout<<list->info<<" "<<list->next->info<<" "<< list->next->next->info<<endl;
cout<<"REMOVE THE MIDDLE NODE FROM LIST B, M, AND E"<<endl;
b->next=e;
m->next=NULL;
delete  m;
cout<<list->info<<" "<<list->next->info<<endl;
cout<<"REMOVE THE END NODE FROM LIST B E"<<endl;
b->next=NULL;
delete e;
cout<<list->info<<endl;
cout<<"REMOVE THE FIRST ELEMENT FROM LIST B"<<endl;
b=list;
list=list->next;
b->next=NULL;
delete b;
}//MAIN
```

Figure 14-20a – Program to demonstrate linked list operations

```
INITIALIZE THE LIST:
INSERTING NODE B AT BEGINNING OF THE LIST
ENTER THE ITEM: 1
ITEM INSERTED: 1
INSERTING THE NODE E AFTER THE NODE B
ENTER THE ITEM: 2
INSERTED ITEMS IN LIST ARE: 1 2
INSERTING THE NODE M BETWEEN B AND E
ENTER THE ITEM: 3
INSERTED ITEMS IN LIST ARE: 1 3 2
REMOVE THE MIDDLE NODE FROM LIST B, M, AND E
1 2
REMOVE THE END NODE FROM LIST B E
1
REMOVE THE FIRST ELEMENT FROM LIST B
```

Figure 14-20b – Output of Figure 14-20a

DOUBLE LINKED LIST

A double linked list is a list with two ends and two beginnings, in contrast to a single linked list with one beginning and one end. In a double linked list, each node has two pointers: one pointing to the next node (element) and one pointing to the previous node. The simplest form of a double linked list has three fields (components). One field of a double linked list holds the info or data and the two other fields point to other nodes. A double linked list can be accessed from both ends. Node insertion and removal in a double linked list is much easier than in a single linked list since because from each node we can access the previous node; this is not true for a single linked list. In order to insert or delete a node in a linked list, we need the previous node.

DOUBLE LINKED LIST DECLARATION AND EXAMPLE

To declare a double linked list we need a structure with at least three fields: one for the information part, and the two others for pointing to the previous and next node. Note that the pointer variables **next** and **previous** are self-referential. For the sake of understanding the linked list operations, the following program is kept simple by not using functions and class. You may want to convert the program to include functions for the insertion and deletion operations.

```
#include<iostream.h>
struct node{      int info;
                  node *next;
                  node *previous; };
void main(){
      node *dlistbeg, *dlistend, *p, *q, *m;
      dlistbeg=dlistend=NULL; //INITIALIZE DOUBLE LIST
      cout<<"INSERT THE FIRST ELEMENT OF LIST"<<endl;
      p=new node;
      p->info=5;
      p->next=NULL;
      p->previous=NULL;
      dlistbeg=dlistend=p; //BOTH POINT TO SAME NODE
      q= new node;
      q->info=8; //INSERT  q AFTER p
      p->next=q;
      q->previous=p;
      q->next=NULL;
      dlistend=q;
      cout<<"INSERT m BETWEEN p AND q"<<endl;
      m=new node;
      m->info=6;
      m->next=q;
      q->previous=m;
      p->next=m;
      m->previous=p;
      cout<<"DISPLAY LIST INFO FROM BEGINNING: ";
```

```
    cout<<dlistbeg->info<<" "<<dlistbeg->next->info<<" ";
    cout<<dlistbeg->next->next->info<<endl;//TRAVERSE FROM BEGINNING
    cout<<"DISPLAY LIST INFO FROM END OF LIST: ";
    cout<<dlistend->info<<" "<< dlistend->previous->info<<" ";
    cout<<dlistend->previous->previous->info<<endl;
    cout<<"DELETE THE NODE m BETWEEN p AND q"<<endl;
    p->next=m->next;
    q->previous=m->previous;
    m->next=NULL;
    m->previous=NULL;
    delete m;
    cout<<"DELETE THE END NODE q "<<endl;
    dlistend=dlistend->previous;
    dlistend->next=NULL;
    q->previous=NULL;
    delete q;
    cout<<"THE FIRST NODE IS: "<<dlistbeg->info<<endl;
    }//MAIN
```

Figure 14-21a – Program to demonstrate a double linked list

```
INSERT THE FIRST ELEMENT OF LIST
INSERT m BETWEEN p AND q
DISPLAY LIST INFO FROM BEGINNING: 5 6 8
DISPLAY LIST INFO FROM END OF LIST: 8 6 5
DELETE THE NODE m BETWEEN p AND q
DELETE THE END NODE q
THE FIRST NODE IS: 5
```

Figure 14-21b – Output of Figure 14-21a

INSERTION SORT USING DOUBLE LINKED LIST

To build an insertion sort using a double linked list, each time the data is inserted, it is placed in the right spot. In other words, the program finds the place where the data is supposed to be and then connects it. The following insertion sort program uses a double linked list with a node consisting of an **info** integer and two pointers linking to the **next** and **previous** node. A function named **getnode( )** dynamically allocates the memory for each node and initialize the pointers to NULL. The functions **insertatbeg( )**, **insertinbetween( )** and **insertatend( )**, as their names suggest, insert a node at the beginning, in between, and at the end of the list respectively, upon identification of the insertion position. The function **traverse( )** goes through the list, starting from the beginning, and print the **info** of each node. The function **traverse( )** can be written to start from the end of the list and go backwards and print the list using the **previous** pointer. As an exercise, you can write the program for the backward traversal.

```
#include<iostream.h>
struct node{      int info;
                  node *next;
                  node *previous; } *dlistbeg, *dlistend, *p;
node *getnode(int x){
        p=new node;
        p->info=x;
        p->next=NULL;
        p->previous=NULL;
        return p;} //GETNODE
void insertatbeg(node *p){
        p->next=dlistbeg;
        dlistbeg->previous=p;
        dlistbeg=p; }//INSERTATBEG
void insertatend(node *p){
        dlistend->next=p;
        p->previous=dlistend;
        dlistend=p; }//INSERTATEND
void insertinbetween(node *p){
        node *t=dlistbeg;
        while(p->info > t->info) t=t->next;
        p->next=t;
        t->previous->next=p;
        p->previous=t->previous;
        t->previous=p; }//INSERTINBETWEEN
void traverse(node *t){
        while(t!=NULL){
                cout<<t->info<<" ";
        t=t->next;}//WHILE
        }//TRAVSERSE
void main(){
        int x;
        dlistbeg=dlistend=NULL;
        cout<<"ENTER A NUMBER, -1 TO QUIT: ";
        cin>>x;
        do{
        p=getnode(x);
        if(dlistbeg==NULL) dlistbeg=dlistend=p;
        else if(p->info < dlistbeg->info) insertatbeg(p);
        else if(p->info > dlistend->info) insertatend(p);
        else insertinbetween(p);
        cout<<"ENTER A NUMBER, -1 TO QUIT: ";
        cin>>x;}while(x!=-1);
        traverse(dlistbeg);
        }//MAIN
```

Figure 14-22a – Insertion sort implemented with a double linked list

```
ENTER A NUMBER, -1 TO QUIT: 5
ENTER A NUMBER, -1 TO QUIT: 9
ENTER A NUMBER, -1 TO QUIT: 1
ENTER A NUMBER, -1 TO QUIT: 7
ENTER A NUMBER, -1 TO QUIT: 3
ENTER A NUMBER, -1 TO QUIT: -1
1 3 5 7 9
```

Figure 14-22b – Output of Figure 14-22a

DATA STRUCTURE TREE

A tree is a kind of data structure where data is represented in a hierarchical and non-sequential way. In a tree, each node of the data consists of several branches where each branch contains a node that may have several branches (sub-trees). The last nodes of the tree do not have branches and are known as leaves. A tree is like a double linked list except that instead of pointing to the next and previous node, it points to the left and right node. The top node (first node) of the tree is known as the root and the bottom nodes (last nodes) of the tree are known as leaves. A node in the left branch is known as a left child and a node in the right branch is known as a right child. The top node of a left and right child is known as a parent or ancestor. You have to look at the tree upside down. A binary tree is a tree in which each node can have maximum of two branches; and a B tree is a kind of tree where each node can have more than two branches. A binary search tree is a version of a binary tree where each node is greater than the other nodes of its sub-trees. Trees have many applications in databases, games, and diagnostic systems. Note that the implementation of a binary search tree is much simpler than a B tree.

STATIC IMPLEMENTATION OF BINARY TREE

To implement a tree using an array, one node is assigned as a root or parent and two adjacent cells are considered the two children (descendents). Subsequently each child becomes a parent with two adjacent cells as its children. The following array implementation represents a tree with a parent node and two children nodes. For example, root is in index zero shown by tree[0] and its two children are tree[1] and tree[2]; similarly, the children of tree[1] are tree[3] and tree[4]. Therefore, the parent tree[i] has tree[2*i +1] and tree[2*i+2] as its children. The array representation of a tree is best suited when a binary tree is complete, meaning that each node in the tree has two children.

484

DYNAMIC IMPLEMENTATION OF BINARY TREE

A natural way to represent a tree is by a dynamic implementation where the tree grows as it receives data and shrinks as it looses data. To build a binary tree, each node consists of two self-referential pointers that point to its left and right node. For simplicity, one field is set aside to hold the data.

```
struct node{
    int info;
    node *lchild, *rchild; };
```

TREE TERMINOLOGIES

There are many terms associated with tree data structures. Knowledge of the terminology is crucial to understand how the tree is built, used, expanded, and shrunk. Listed below are some of the conventional terms used with trees:

Binary Tree - two branches -each node has at most 2 children.
Root - the first node, the only node with no parent root.
Child – a node branched off from the parent either to the right (the right child) or to the left (the left child).
Parent – a node that a child node is branched off from.
Leaf - a node without children.
Sub-tree – a branch from the tree either to the left (left sub-tree) or to the right (right sub-tree).
Level - the number of levels distanced away from the root.
Height - a number that indicates the maximum number of levels in the tree. This is known as the Depth of tree, and is the number of nodes in the longest path from the root to a leaf.

BINARY SEARCH TREE

A binary search is a version of the binary tree where each node has a higher value than its children. To build a binary tree start with the root and as the tree is built, if a node has a lower value, it is placed on the left and if the node has a higher value it is placed on the right. A binary search tree is a fast way to search through data, and is faster than a sequential search. Recall that a binary search uses arrays and the data has to be sorted, while a binary search tree is built gradually as data is inserted into the tree.

BUILDING THE FIRST LEVEL OF A BINARY SEARCH TREE

The following program illustrates how to building a binary search tree with a root and a left child and a right child. At the beginning, the root of the tree is initialized to NULL. The first data is chosen for the root and the second and third data is linked to either the left of the root as a left child or to the right of the root as a right child.

```
#include<iostream.h>
struct node{
        int info;
        node *lchild, *rchild; } *root;
void main(){
        int x;
        root=NULL; //TREE INITIALIZATION
        for(int i=0; i<3; i++){
        node* p=new node;
        cout<<"ENTER THE ITEM"<<endl;
        cin>>x;
        p->info=x;
        p->lchild=NULL;
        p->rchild=NULL;
        if(root==NULL) root=p;
        else if (p->info < root->info) root->lchild=p;
        else if (p->info > root->info) root->rchild=p; }//FOR
        cout<<"ROOT: "<<root->info<<endl;
        cout<<"ROOT LEFT CHILD: "<<root->lchild->info<<endl;
        cout<<"ROOT RIGHT CHILD: "<<root->rchild->info<<endl;
}//MAIN
```

Figure 14-23a – Building the first level of a binary search tree

```
ENTER THE ITEM
2
ENTER THE ITEM
1
ENTER THE ITEM
3
ROOT: 2
ROOT LEFT CHILD: 1
ROOT RIGHT CHILD: 3
```

Figure 14-23b – Output of Figure 14-23a

486

BINARY SEARCH LOOKUP

A binary search tree is an excellent data structure to search through large amounts of data, especially when data is in some hierarchical order such as taxonomy, a family tree, or diagnostic cases. A binary search tree is created gradually with the insertion of each node to the existing tree. The tree is initially set to NULL. The first node is considered the root and the other nodes are inserted after the root, depending on their values, at the leaf level. When the node's value is less than its parent, it is inserted in the left sub-tree; and similarly, when the node's value is more than its parent, it is inserted in the right sub-tree. A search must take place before insertion to a binary search tree (creation). The only time a node is added is if it does not already exist in the tree. For every node insertion, there must be a search through the tree, starting from the root down the tree until the proper place is located by reaching a NULL. To locate a proper place to insert a node in the tree, several left and right or right and left traversals maybe required.

BINARY SEARCH TREE INSERTION PROGRAM

The following program illustrates how a binary search tree is created node by node. At first, the root is initialized to NULL. For the first item, the memory is allocated dynamically for the node and the data is assigned to the info of the node and both left child and right children are set to NULL. Since the tree is empty, the first node is assigned to the root. For insertion of the other items we need to traverse the tree by introducing a temporary pointer variable to the root because we don't want to alter the root. The tree traversal is done with a **while** loop and the **if** statements control the left and right traversals based on the insertion value. In the case where a left child points to a NULL, the insertion is done with the code **t->left = p;**. Similarly, if a right child points to a NULL, the insertion is done with the code **t->right = p;**. After insertion of the new node, a **break** statement terminates the **while** loop. During the duration of the loop, if the left child has not reached NULL, the next left value is assigned to the traversed node (visiting node) with the code **t=t->left;**. Similarly, if the right child has not reached NULL, the next right value is assigned to the traversed node by **t = t -> right;**. Note that if the value to be inserted is neither to the left nor to the right of the node, it is already in the tree.

```
#include<iostream.h>
struct node{
        int info;
        node *lchild, *rchild;}*root,*p,*t;
void main(){
        int x;
        root=NULL;
        cout<<"ENTER THE ITEM, CTRL/D TO STOP: ";
        while (cin>>x){
        node* p=new node;
        p->info=x;
        p->lchild=NULL;
        p->rchild=NULL;
        if (root==NULL) root=p;
        else{   t=root;
                while(t!=NULL){
                        if(x < t->info) if (t->lchild==NULL){
                                                t->lchild=p;
                                                cout<<"INSERTED LEFT"<<endl;
                                                break;}//IF
                                        else t=t->lchild;
                        else if (x > t->info) if(t->rchild==NULL){
                                                        t->rchild=p;
                                                        cout<<"INSERTED RIGHT"<<endl;
                                                        break;}//IF
                                        else t=t->rchild;
                        else {cout<<"REDUNDANT-NO INSERTION NECESSARY " <<endl; break;}
                }//WHILE T
        }//ELSE
        cout<<"ENTER THE ITEM: ";
        }//WHILE CIN
}//MAIN
```

Figure 14-24a – Creating a binary search tree

```
ENTER THE ITEM, CTRL/D TO STOP: 5
ENTER THE ITEM: 4
INSERTED LEFT
ENTER THE ITEM: 6
INSERTED RIGHT
ENTER THE ITEM: 6
REDUNDANT-NO INSERTION
NECESSARY
ENTER THE ITEM: □
```

Figure 14-24b – Output of Figure 14-24a

488

RECURSIVE BINARY SEARCH TREE

Recursion is a good tool when it comes to manipulating a tree since on each call, the tree shrinks to another sub-tree and the problem becomes smaller sub-problems. An understanding of recursion makes the problem much simpler than its iterative version and most of the tree operations can be done in a few recursive calls. The following recursive binary search tree is written in the same way it would have been solved without writing a program, solving it the way you are saying it. Recall that insertion is tied to the search of the tree and before every insertion the tree must be searched first. For the sake of focusing on the search, the insertion part is done separately.

```cpp
#include<iostream.h>
struct node {    int info;
                 node *lchild, *rchild; } *root,*p,*t;
int binsearchtree(node* t, int x){
    if(t==NULL) return -1;
    if(x==t->info) return 1;
    else if(x < t->info){ binsearchtree(t->lchild,x);}
    else binsearchtree(t->rchild,x); }//BINSEARCHTREE
void main(){
        int x;
        root=NULL;
        cout<<"ENTER THE ITEM: ";
        cin>>x;
        for(int i=0; i<5; i++){
        node* p=new node;
        p->info=x;
        p->lchild=NULL;
        p->rchild=NULL;
        if (root==NULL) root=p;
        else{    t=root;
                while(t!=NULL){
                if(x < t->info) if(t->lchild==NULL){
                                t->lchild=p;  cout<<"INSERTED LEFT"<<endl;  break;}//IF
                            else t=t->lchild;
                else if (x > t->info) if(t->rchild==NULL){
                                t->rchild=p;  cout<<"INSERTED RIGHT"<<endl;  break;}//IF
                            else t=t->rchild;
                    else{ cout<<"REDUNDANT-NO INSERTION NECESSARY " <<endl; break;}
                }//WHILE T
        }//ELSE
        cout<<"ENTER THE ITEM: ";
        cin>>x; }//FOR
        cout<<"ENTER ITEM TO SEARCH: ";
        cin>>x;
        if (binsearchtree(root, x)==1) cout<<"ITEM FOUND: "<<x<<endl;
        else cout<<"ITEM NOT FOUND"<<endl;
}//MAIN
```

Figure 14-25a – Recursive binary search tree

```
ENTER THE ITEM: 5
ENTER THE ITEM: 4
INSERTED LEFT
ENTER THE ITEM: 6
INSERTED RIGHT
ENTER THE ITEM: 3
INSERTED LEFT
ENTER THE ITEM: 7
INSERTED RIGHT
ENTER THE ITEM: 2
ENTER ITEM TO SEARCH: 3
ITEM FOUND: 3
```

Figure 14-25b – Output of Figure 14-25a

TREE WITH DIFFERENT TRAVERSALS

To go through the tree, you must start from the tree's root (parent node) and traverse the left sub-tree or right sub-trees visiting the other nodes. While visiting a node, it may be desirable to do an operation such as printing the node (process it) or increasing its value. However, a specific operation on the nodes of a tree may take place in some order relative to the processing of the root or the root of a sub-tree. Processing a node relative to the root node can be categorized in three forms: *pre-order*, *in-order,* and *post-order*. In a *pre-order* traversal, a root node is processed before visiting the left and right sub-trees. In an *in-order* traversal the left sub-tree is traversed all the way before the corresponding root is processed. In a binary search tree, an in-order traversal would result in ascending order. In a *post-order* traversal the left and right sub-trees are traversed all the way and then the root (node) is processed. Note that each of the above traversals is done recursively with two recursive calls to traverse the left and right sub-trees. For ease of explanation, we use the root each time to indicate the root of the sub-tree, not the root of the whole tree. The naming of the different traversals can be traced relative to the position of the processing node. When the processing node is placed before the two traversing calls, this is named *pre-order*. When the processing node is placed between the two traversing calls, this is named *in-order*. And finally, if the processing node is placed after the traversing calls, this is named *post-order*.

```
#include<iostream.h>
struct node {    int info;
                 node *lchild, *rchild; }*root,*p,*t;
void preordertraversal(node *t){
      if (t!=NULL) { cout<<t->info<<" ";
                          preordertraversal(t->lchild);
                          preordertraversal(t->rchild); }// IF
      }//PREORDER
void inordertraversal(node *t){
      if (t!=NULL) { inordertraversal(t->lchild);
                          cout<<t->info<<" ";
                          inordertraversal(t->rchild); }//IF
      }//INORDER
void postordertraversal(node *t){
      if (t!=NULL) { postordertraversal(t->lchild);
                          postordertraversal(t->rchild);
                          cout<<t->info<<" "; }//IF
      }//PREORDER
void main(){
      int x;
      root=NULL;
      for(int i=0; i<5; i++){
      cout<<"ENTER THE ITEM: ";
      cin>>x;
      node* p=new node;
      p->info=x;
      p->lchild=NULL;
      p->rchild=NULL;
      if (root==NULL) root=p;
      else{
      t=root;
      while(t!=NULL){
              if(x <t->info) if(t->lchild==NULL){ t->lchild=p; break;}
                  else t=t->lchild;
                if (x> t->info) if(t->rchild==NULL) {t->rchild=p; break;}
                            else t=t->rchild;
              else {cout<<"REDUNDANT-NO INSERTION NECESSARY " <<endl; break;}
                }//WHILE
      }//ELSE
      }//FOR
      cout<<"\nPREORDER TRAVERSAL "<<endl;
      preordertraversal(root);
      cout<<"\nINORDER TRAVERSAL "<<endl;
      inordertraversal(root);
      cout<<"\nPOSTORDER TRAVERSAL "<<endl;
      postordertraversal(root);
      }//MAIN
```

Figure 14-26a – Program to demonstrate preorder, inorder, and postorder traversal of a tree

```
ENTER THE ITEM: 8
ENTER THE ITEM: 5
ENTER THE ITEM: 9
ENTER THE ITEM: 3
ENTER THE ITEM: 12

PREORDER TRAVERSAL
8 5 3 9 12
INORDER TRAVERSAL
3 5 8 9 12
POSTORDER TRAVERSAL
3 5 12 9 8
```

Figure 14-26b – Output of Figure 14-26a

ANALYSIS OF BINARY SEARCH TREE

A binary search tree that has n nodes takes O(Log2n) to search for or insert an item. To delete a node may require an adjustment to the following sub-tree. What can go wrong with a BTS that is skewed left or right? This means the entire tree is tilted to the left or to the right. In this case, the order-of magnitude becomes O(n). The solution to this problem is to keep the BTS balanced at all times. How? If you start with a root that divides the data equally to the left and the right, this will keep the tree in balance.

B TREE

A B tree is a kind of tree where a node can have more than one entry (key) and as a result more than two branches (sub-trees) and still stay **B**alanced. Recall that in the binary tree each node has one entry and at most two branches (sub-trees). What if you want to build a tree that has more than two branches and more than one item in a node?

To build a B tree the following rules have to be considered:
- What is the minimum and maximum numbers of entries (items) per node?
- The entries on each node must be sorted, let us say from smallest to largest.
- How many sub-trees a non-leaf node must have and what is the order of the tree?
- All the leaves are at the same depth.

ADVANTAGE OF B TREE OVER BINARY SEARCH TREE

Insertions, deletions, and searches in a binary search tree are calculated as *O(n)* for *n* items because the binary search tree is not balanced and the tree can be completely skewed left or right. The average case for a binary search tree is *log2n*. However, a B tree is a balanced tree by its nature and may have *m* branches (sub-trees). Therefore, to search for an item in a B tree with *m* branches, it takes $O(log_m n)$ which is less the than average case $O(log_2n)$ for a binary search tree. A B tree is an ideal data structure in situations where all the data cannot reside in RAM (primary memory) and the data is stored in secondary memory. Keep in mind that insertion and deletion of an entry to a B tree can be complex because the tree has to be balanced at all times and must comply with the other rules of a B tree.

GRAPH DATA STRUCTURES

A graph is a non-linear data structure where connectivity between the items (nodes) is a major concern. A graph is made up of several nodes (vertices) and several links (edges or arcs) that connect the nodes together. Let us not confuse the idea of a graph with what you have in your mind, such as chart and curves. A graph is like a road map with cities as its vertices and the roads from a city to other cities as the edge. Another example of a graph is an airline route that travels through several cities to arrive at its final destination. Graphs resemble trees in that they both have nodes and branches. Recall that in a tree one node is designated as the root and the other nodes branch off from the root. A graph can be viewed as a kind of tree where its sub-trees can connect to one another. However, the graph should be viewed as a separate concept with its own terminologies. There are two kinds of graphs: directed and undirected. In a directed graph, the order of the two connected vertices is important. One vertex is the source and the other is the destination. An edge (arc) connects two vertices in one direction or another edge connects the same vertices in the other direction. In an undirected graph, the direction is unimportant and there is no source or destination vertex. Either vertex can be a source or destination. Two vertices can be linked by multiple edges both in a directed and an undirected graph. In summary, a graph is a set of vertices and a set of edges connecting the vertices

GRAPH TERMINOLOGIES:

The following are some of the main graph terminologies:

Vertex: Each object (node) of graph is known as a vertex, e.g. a city like New York or a computer like Server.

Edge: The line (link) that connects two vertices is known as an edge.

Weight: A value (Numeric) that is associated (labeled) with an edge is called weight. A weight can be the distance, cost, or time it takes to get from one vertex to another vertex.

Directed graph: Is a kind of graph where the order in which two vertices are visited is important. In a directed graph, there is a first vertex and a second vertex. A pointed arrow is used to show the intended direction. An edge between New York and Los Angeles is different than an edge from Los Angles to New York.

Undirected graph: Is a kind of graph where the order in which two vertices are visited are not important. An edge between New York and Los Angeles simply identifies the connection and the direction is unimportant.

Path: A sequence of edges from the source vertex to the destination vertex.

APPLICATION OF GRAPH

Graphs have a wide variety of applications in areas where there are many relationships between the entries (vertices). An example of a graph is an airline's flight plans that connect network of cities. A major operation on a graph is to find an existing path between two vertices; e.g., "is there a flight from New York to Miami?" A graph operation may include weight criteria, such as distance, cost, or time; e.g., "what is the minimum cost from New York to Los Angles?"

Other examples of graphs:

> Computer network design
> Neuron systems
> Chemical components
> Family relationships
> Diagnostic systems
> City map and emergency services
> Telephone system lines
> Satellites

ADJACENCY MATRIX REPRESENTATION OF A GRAPH

A square grid (matrix) with n rows and n columns represents a graph on n vertices. Each row and column of a matrix represents a vertex. When there is an edge between two indices, it is represented by an integer value 1 or a Boolean value true. Similarly, when there is no connection between two vertices, the entry of grid (matrix) is filled by 0 or a false value. A two dimensional array with its memory allocated statically or dynamically can be used to implement an adjacency matrix. For example, **int matrix[5][5]** represents a graph with five vertices and the assignment **matrix[2][4]=1;** indicates there is an edge between vertex 2 and vertex 4. Similarly, the assignment **matrix[1][2]=0;** indicates that there is no edge between vertex 1 and vertex 2. Finally, the adjacency matrix is a square grid filled with entries of zero's and one's representing a direct connection of two vertices.

ADJACENCY LINKED LIST OF A GRAPH

For each vertex in a graph, a linked list is designated to show its connection (edges) to other vertices. If a vertex is not connected to any other vertices, the list is assigned NULL. For example, when vertex 1 has an edge to vertex 3 and vertex 5, the linked list for vertex 1, list 1, will be linked to two elements, vertex 3 and vertex 5. Similarly, vertex 3 can have edges to vertex 1, vertex 2, and vertex 5; and in this case list 3 will have three elements vertex 1, vertex 2, and vertex 5. Adjacency linked lists can be summarized as an array of linked lists containing all the vertices and their connecting vertices.

SHORTEST PATH

If more than one path exists between two vertices, how do you determine the shortest path? Obviously the shortest path between two vertices is the path with the lowest total cost. The cost could be the distance between two vertices in mileage, time in hours and seconds, or cost in term of money. Finding the shortest path is not only a concern in the computer science community but in the business world and other fields as well. Much research has been done in this area and many algorithms have been developed. A problem known as the traveling salesman is a shortest path problem where a salesman wants to travel to several cities and return with minimum spending (e.g. airline traveling cost).

ALGORITHM FOR FINDING SHORTEST PATH

How would you find an efficient way to determine the shortest path from a given vertex to another vertex in a graph? A path from one vertex, as a starting point, to another vertex, as a destination point, may pass over other vertices. We need to choose the minimum distance along this path. One way is to keep track of all the distances and pick the minimum cost by comparing with the next edge and reassigning the minimum (so far). At the end of all comparisons, the shortest path will be found. One solution is to keep an array with the size of the vertices and the first location of the array is 0 and the next location is the smallest of all edges going to the vertex 1. And, similarly, location 2 is the shortest value kept from vertex 0 to vertex 2, and so on. At the end, all the minimum distances are added to give the total cost.

HASHING WITH NO COLLISION

In the previous chapter, we discussed hashing as a fast search with an order of constant O(c). The ideal situation is for c to have a value of one, so that you find what you want in one attempt. This is not the case in most situations. However for a compiler symbol table, we might explore ways to achieve this goal. The following hashing program has no collisions and uses C++ reserved words as its data file. The program uses the bit-wise operations left shift and exclusive or. It is simple to understand and creates an output file with the keys and shows that there are no collisions. This hash uses the number 1031; as you know, prime numbers are best to use in a hash, and you can also try the numbers 9574 and 9575.

```
#include <fstream.h>
const int size=1031;
int hash(char *a){
        char *c=a;
        unsigned n=*c;
        for(int i=0;*c!='\0';i++)
                    n^=(*c++<<i)<<6;
        return n % size; }//HASH
void main(){
        char input[25];
        bool collide=false;
        int a[size],v=0,x=0;
        for(int j=0;j<size;j++) a[j]=0;
        ifstream fin("reserve.txt");
        ofstream fout("output.txt");
        while(fin>>input){
                v=hash(input);
                x++;
                if(x%10==0)
                        fout<<endl;
                fout<<v<<" ";
                a[v]+=1;
                if(a[v]>1){
                        fout<<endl<<"Collision occurred at "<<v<<endl;
                        collide=true;}//IF
        }//WHILE
        if(collide==false)
                fout<<endl<<"No collisions"<<endl;
        }//MAIN
```

Figure 14-27a – Program using hashing

```
asm auto bool break case catch char class const const_cast continue default delete
do double dynamic_cast else enum explicit extern false float for friend goto if inline int
long mutable namespace new operator private protected public register reinterpret_cast
return short signed sizeof static static_cast struct switch template this throw true
try typedef typeid typename union unsigned using virtual void volatile wchar_t while
```

Figure 14-27b - reserve.txt

```
28 954 863 220 39 1 125 827 152
206 138 608 416 663 93 403 290 69 912
884 331 154 972 60 839 227 944 143 1022
103 322 461 240 11 316 319 127 979 235
303 891 151 23 994 574 516 414 341 801
618 211 139 67 367 829 15 999 855 648
441 410 745
No collisions
```

Figure 14-27c - output.txt

TOPICS NOT COVERED HERE

The topic of data structures covers many areas, including the common algorithms that apply to them. The topic of stacks and queues is less complicated than the topic of trees and graphs. While the data structure *set* is not implemented in this chapter, it would be a good exercise to develop it and set operations such as union, intersection, difference, and membership. There are a variety of trees, each with its own algorithms: such as the one having a maximum of two siblings (binary sub-trees always have two children) which may happen to be unbalanced, or a tree with multiple siblings such as the B tree which is balanced. A heap tree is a kind of binary tree, but a complete one where an entry in any node is never less than its children's entries. Every interior node of a heap tree has two children. An efficient way to implement a priority queue is to use a heap tree. Many solutions of artificial intelligent (AI) problems are expressed in the form of trees. The graph introduces another complex dimension; while the data structure can be expressed as a connected tree (closed tree), the algorithms that apply to graphs become difficult to grasp and the computer has a hard time finishing them in real time (unsolvable). The *shortest path* and *minimum cost* algorithms are among the most difficult algorithms to understand. In fact, you can look at the whole Internet as a graph: one node is connected to another. Searching a tree or a graph can be done level-by-level, which is known as *breath first search*, or through the depth of each path, known as *depth first search*.

There are situations and problems like a game tree, like for chess, where it is not realistic to represent all branches of a tree or a graph, but the program can generate certain levels of branches as it tries to reach its goal states. Game trees are very interesting problems of AI where there is more than one solution to a problem. Nowadays, almost all of the data structures and their algorithms are pre-written and packaged in libraries known as STL (Standard Template Libraries) and are provided through the C++ compilers and programmers can easily use them without creating them. The question may then arise, why bother to learn or program data structures when the effort has been done and we should not reinvent the wheel.

For users that are already familiar with data structures, STL is a great choice and time saver. For users who do not know what data structures are and want to learn through STL, it may be difficult since you do not see how it is done and what ingredients are used to build it and for that reason things may go wrong. One may argue that it is like automatic programming, so that we do not have to program. While STL is an important topic to be discussed here, because of its lengthy coverage I have decided to delay the topic to further chapters.

CLOSING REMARKS AND LOOKING AHEAD

Data structure is a way of organizing data. It is seen as a collection of values and its operations. For years, data structures have been developed and certain algorithm have been tested and proven to work. Among the common algorithms we can name stacks, queues, trees, and graphs. Depending on how we want to implement the data structures, they are divided into the two categories of static and dynamic. Static data structures allocate space during compile time and dynamic data structures allocate space during run time as the program is executing. Whether the data structure is implemented statically or dynamically, one must use reasoning and analyze which is better to solve the problem. There are advantages and disadvantages for static and dynamic data structures, and it depends on what you want to do.

Stack is a LIFO data structure that has a top variable and operations such as push, pop, isempty, and isfull. Queue is another common data structure, its operations are enqueue and dequeue and its variables are front and rear. Trees represent a hierarchical data structure where there are subdivisions.

Graphs are used where connectivity and networking is the concern. Interestingly, we can implement stacks, queues, trees, and graphs or we could even simulate linked lists with arrays. After understanding the data structures and the common existing algorithms, the programmer is in a better position to decide what to do. In designing a system, as soon as the choice of the data structures is determined, the rest follows. Due to the limitations of programming languages, it forced certain styles in dealing with data structures. For example, Fortran did not have pointers, structures, or classes; and therefore, programmers could only use arrays with other variables to form logical connections between those isolated entities. The notion of Structure in C language allows the related components of one entity to bundle together (encapsulate) and as a result enables the programmer to build its own *user defined type* (abstract data type) such as a stack or queue. The language C++ added functions (methods) to the structure of C and improved the C structure with the class, and making C++ an object-oriented programming language, a better tool for the design of data structures where abstraction can be viewed to its fullest extent so far. The notion of class in data structures is where functions are added to the attributes and defining the data structure as a whole. The user, by the looking at the class, can expect is suppose to expect. The idea of encapsulation in information hiding becomes more apparent with the application of classes.

To print a list is the same whether it is implemented by linked list or by array. In the next two chapters we will focus on classes and what makes the class reusable and interesting, the concept of polymorphism (many form for a name), and inheritance to avoid redundancy by carrying down the properties of a class.

Let us end the chapter this way; data structure terminology plays an important role in understanding the whole concept. For example, you are not physically (forcefully) pushing a stack (simple assignment) or building a tree, forest or jungle. These naming conventions may resemble a little bit of what these words actually are all about. This conceptual abstraction helps us to build a concept that we can picture rather than using words to explain them, and from then on it becomes our own abstraction. Our data structure tree is not a natural tree; it has branches and leaves, but its root is at the top and there is no color to it. So we are going to use this abstraction that overrides the existing abstraction. After you use these terms and become comfortable with them, they become a very good way to communicate.

SELF TEST CHAPTER 14: DATA STRUCTURES TRUE / FALSE

__1. Data structures deals with how data is stored, retrieved, and manipulated.

__2. Major data structures are stacks, queues, trees, and graphs.

__3. The stack is useful to evaluate the postfix notation.

__4. * 5 3 is Postfix (Polish) Notation of 5 * 3.

__5. FIFO is queue and LIFO is the stack.

__6. In Postfix (Polish) Notation, there is no precedence of operators.

__7. Airport Simulation is a good application of a stack.

__8. Dynamic data structures use fixed arrays and static data structures use pointers.

__9. Some applications of queues are e-mail and printer.

__10. Pop and push are the two functions of stacks.

__11. A circular linked list is a list in which the last node points to the first node.

__12. A priority queue can be used in operating systems to give service to the job with highest priority.

__13. In a double linked list, you can access the next and previous nodes.

__14. A tree is a data structure where data is represented in a sequential way.

__15. In a binary tree, each node may have more than two children.

__16. A binary search tree is a binary tree where the data on the left is less than the data on the right.

__17. In an in-order traversal of a tree, the root node is processed first.

__18. A binary search tree with n nodes takes $O(n^2)$ to search for or insert an item.

__19. In a B tree, the leaves are at the same depth and there is a min and a max number of entries per node.

__20. A graph is a linear data structure made up of several nodes.

__21. In a directed graph, the order in which two vertices are visited is important.

__22. One advantage of dynamic data structures is that memory is not wasted.

__23. Often static data structures perform faster than dynamic data structures, due to random access.

__24. An adjacency matrix can be used to represent a graph.

__25. A linked list is used to implement a queue dynamically.

CHAPTER 14 DATA STRUCTURES ASSIGNMENTS

Q14a) What are data structures? Give 4 examples of data structures.

Q14b) What is the advantage of dynamic data structures versus static data structures?

Q14c) What is a pointer and how are pointers used in data structures?

Q14d) Define the following terms and include a diagram to demonstrate each:
   Stack: push, pop
   Queue: enqueue, dequeue

Q14e) Write the following function for a static stack using arrays:
   push(mystack,x);
   x=pop(mystack);

Q14f) Use structure or class to implement a stack called STACK. Declare an object called mystack. The class' data members are: stkinfo[MAXSIZE] and stktop. The member functions of STACK are: stkpush( ), stkpop( ), stkempty( ), and stkfull( ). For stkfull( ), return true or 1 if the stack is full, else return false or 0. For stkempty( ), return true or 1 if the stack is empty, else return false or 0.

Q14g) Explain how the following infix expression is converted to postfix 2 + 7 * 4, and how the postfix expression (after conversion) is evaluated. Write a program to convert infix to postfix and then evaluate the postfix expression. Include the following functions:
   push( ) : push either operator or operand onto the stack
   pop( ) : returns the top of the stack
   ishigher(stktop,operator) : returns true if top of stack is higher than the current operator
   evaluate(operandl,operand2, operator) : returns the numeric result after applying the operator

Q14h) Build a queue program (using an array) with a menu that uses only the following variables: x, option, myqueue[100], rear, and front. The menu's choices are:
   1 to enqueue
   2 to dequeue
   3 to check if queue is empty
   4 to check if queue is full
   Q to quit

Q14i) Write the following functions for a queue using a linked list:
   enqueue(myqueue,x);
   x=dequeue(myqueue);

Q14j) Write a program that will implement a priority queue to determine which students will get a scholarship. There are only a limited amount of scholarships and the students with the highest gpa are considered. Implement a priority queue that will dequeue the student with the highest gpa. Hint: To find which student to dequeue, traverse through the entire queue to find the student (node) with the highest gpa.

Q14k) You are to build an Insertion Sort using double linked list with the following: insertatbegining( ), insertatmiddle( ), and insertatend( ). Use the following data in the order given: 20 10 45 8 25 12.
a) Write the function insertatbeginning(node *q, node *p) { // p about to insert at beginning }
b) Write the function insertatmiddle(node *q, node *p) { // p about to insert after q }
c) Write the function insertatend(node *q, node *p) { //p will be inserted at the end }
d) Write an insertion sort function that calls proper function upon the decision of where x is to be inserted.
e) Write the main program to test the functions.

Q14l) Define the following terms. Choose three of the terms and show their declaration and how they could be accessed in a tree structure: root, left child, right child, parent, leaf.

Q14m) Draw a diagram to represent how a binary search tree would be structured, given the following data: 20 45 10 8 25 12. Explain how the numbers get to their final position in the tree.

Q14n) Write a recursive function for binsearchtree(node *p, int x) that starts at the root and searches the tree for x. Use the following structure:
```
struct node{
        int info;
        node *lchild, *rchild; } *root, *p;
```

Q14o) Explain the difference between pre-order, post-order, and in-order tree traversals. Give an example when it would be best to use each one.

Q14p) What is the advantage of B tree over Binary Search tree? What is a disadvantage?

Q14q) You are to network five computers known as A, B, C, D, and E accordingly. The Computer A is connected to All computers in both ways (bidirectional). Each computer is connected to its adjacent computer (letter wise).
   a) Show the Graph with a diagram.
   b) Show the Adjacency Matrix with a diagram.
   c) Show the data structure representing the matrix .
   d) Show the data structure using the linked list (array of pointers).
   e) What are three ways a message can be sent from Computer B to all the computers (according to above Graph)? Which path is the fastest? Why? Assuming the cost of a message is the difference between two letters (A is 1, B is 2, C is 3, D is 4 and E is 5), the cost of a message from A to D (4 - 1) is 3 and the cost of a message from B to C (3 - 2) is 1.

Q14r) What is a vertex, and how does an edge relate to? Similarly, how does a path relate to an edge? What is the different between a directed graph and an undirected graph?

Q14s) a) What is hashing and what does a hash function do?
       b) What are the advantages and disadvantages of hashing?
       c) Give two ways to hash social security numbers.
       d) Write a hash function for SSN. The size of the hash table is 100.

Q14t) Many operating system CPU schedulers use data structures that you have learned such as first come first serve, shortest job first, last come first serve, and queue with priority. With these data structures, simulate the tasks of an operating system.

CASE STUDY –PAYROLL SYSTEM PHASE 14: DATA STRUCTURES

a) Implement a search function that uses hashing to find an employee by social security number.

b) Implement an insertion sort, using a double linked list, in order to sort the data according to the last name of employees, as they are entered.

c) For employee wage cuts, use a stack to determine who gets cut first. The last employee that was hired would be the first to get a wage cut (LIFO).

CHAPTER 15

POLYMORPHISM, TEMPLATE, AND ADT

Polymorphism consists of two words: *poly,* which means *"many,"* and *morph,* which means *"form."* In programming, polymorphism is the ability to have many forms for the same name. An example of polymorphism is when different functions do a similar task and have the same function name or similarly when using many forms for the same operator. Polymorphism, encapsulation, and inheritance are three important features of object-oriented programming. Function overloading and operator overloading are two examples of polymorphism. A user function or a built-in operator can be overloaded while performing what it was originally designated to do. A computer teacher can become overloaded by teaching an additional math or other course. One form of polymorphism is function overloading. For example, the same function name: *print( )* prints the list of items in a queue or a stack, regardless if they were created statically or dynamically. Another example of polymorphism is operator overloading which adds a new meaning to most of the C++ operators. C++ operators are defined for the basic data types; with operation overloading, the same operators can be applied to user-defined types, keeping the operation in the same form as it is applied to the basic types. The goal of operator overloading is to allow user defined types (classes) to behave in the same way as built-in types. Polymorphism contributes to the concept of abstraction by providing a meaningful name that can be used differently for several similar functions and operations. Therefore, a programmer can focus on the function's and operator's work rather than getting involved in the overwhelming details of the implementation. As long as the same interface is exposed, the implementation is irrelevant. Finally, for a language to be considered an object-programming language, it must support the features of polymorphism. C++ templates allow programmers to code and reuse code regardless of the specific data type. When the type of data is defined, the compiler will generate the code as if it was written for that specific data type.

FUNCTION OVERLOADING

A function is overloaded when the same function name is used to perform different tasks depending on the data type. Function overloading is one of the simplest forms of polymorphism. In the following program, there are three versions of **findsmaller( )**; each version of the function takes and returns a different data type. The function **findsmaller( )** is referred to as an overloaded function. Without the use of function overloading, the same program would require three different function names to perform the same task.

```
#include<iostream.h>
int findsmaller(int x, int y){ if(x<y) return x;  else return y; }
double findsmaller(double x, double y){ if(x<y) return x; else return y; }
char findsmaller(char x, char y){ if(x<y) return x; else return y; }
void main(){
        int a,b;   double c,d;   char e,f;
        cout<<"ENTER TWO INTEGER VALUES: ";
        cin>>a>>b;
        cout<<"ENTER TWO DOUBLE VALUES: ";
        cin>>c>>d;
        cout<<"ENTER TWO CHARACTER VALUES: ";
        cin>>e>>f;
        cout<<"THE SMALLER OF TWO INTEGERS IS: "<<findsmaller(a,b)<<endl;
        cout<<"THE SMALLER OF TWO DOUBLES IS: "<<findsmaller(c,d)<<endl;
        cout<<"THE SMALLER OF TWO CHARACTERS IS: "<<findsmaller(e,f)<<endl;
        }//MAIN
```

Figure 15-1a – Example of function overloading

```
ENTER TWO INTEGER VALUES: 9 10
ENTER TWO DOUBLE VALUES: 5.50 7.75
ENTER TWO CHARACTER VALUES: a z
THE SMALLER OF TWO INTEGERS IS: 9
THE SMALLER OF TWO DOUBLES IS: 5.5
THE SMALLER OF TWO CHARACTERS IS: a
```

Figure 15.1b – Output of 15.1a

HOW DOES FUNCTION OVERLOADING WORK: FUNCTION SIGNATURE

How does the compiler determine which function to call when there are several functions with the same name? A C++ complier uses the function's signature to determine which function to call. A function's signature consists of the function name and the parameter (argument) list. Note that in the function's signature, the return type is not needed because it is necessary in the function's prototype. If there is not an exact match in the argument list, the C++ compiler tries to use a standard type conversion such as converting an integer to a double if necessary. The following program swaps different data types; the compiler is able to figure out the correct function call by using the actual types from the arguments. The number of the arguments and their type may vary in each function.

```
#include<iostream.h>
#include<string.h>
void swap(char * str1, char * str2){
        char temp[80];
        strcpy(temp,str1);
        strcpy (str1,str2);
        strcpy(str2,temp); }//SWAP
void swap(double x, double y){
        double temp;
        temp=x;
        x=y;
        y=temp; }//SWAP
void main(){
        char password[30],newpassword[30];
        double x,y;
        cout<<"ENTER YOUR PASSWORD: ";   cin>>password;
        cout<<"ENTER YOUR NEW PASSWORD: ";  cin>>newpassword;
        swap(password,newpassword);
        cout<<"ENTER A VALUE: ";   cin>>x;
        cout<<"ENTER THE NEW VALUE: ";   cin>>y;
        swap(x,y);
        cout<<"YOUR PASSWORD IS: "<<password<<endl;
        cout<<"THE VALUE IS: "<<y<<endl;
        }//MAIN
```

Figure 15.2a – Program using overloaded swap function

```
ENTER YOUR PASSWORD: windows
ENTER YOUR NEW PASSWORD: linux
ENTER A VALUE: 500
ENTER THE NEW VALUE: 1000
YOUR PASSWORD IS: linux
THE VALUE IS: 1000
```

Figure 15.2b – Output of 15.2a

DEFAULT PARAMETER

In a function, a default value for a parameter can be assigned if the function call does not provide one. Default parameters are listed last in the parameter list. When one parameter is assigned a default value, the following parameters should be set to their default values as well otherwise there will be a problem. In the following main program, the function call to **temporary.findgrosspay(1234);** only passes one parameter, the **id**; therefore, the default values will be set for **hoursworked** and **hourlywage**. Default parameters can be very useful in constructors to initialize member data.

505

```
#include<iostream.h>
class employee{
private: int employeeid, hoursworked;
        double hourlywage, grosspay;
public:  void findgrosspay(int id, int hoursworked=35, double hourlywage=25.00){
            employeeid=id;
            grosspay=hoursworked * hourlywage;
            cout<<"GROSSPAY FOR EMPLOYEE #"<<employeeid;
            cout<<" is: "<<grosspay<<endl;   }//FINDGROSSPAY
        };//EMPLOYEE
void main(){
        employee temporary;
        temporary.findgrosspay(1234);   }//MAIN
```

Figure 15.3a – Program using default parameters

```
GROSSPAY FOR EMPLOYEE #1234 is: 875
```

Figure 15.3b – Output of 15.3a

OPERATOR OVERLOADING

Defining more than one operation for an existing operator is called *operator overloading.* In C++, there are a variety of operators: arithmetic operators such as **+, -, * , /** and **%**, bit wise operators such as **& | ^ , <<,** and **>>**, etc.. With the exception of a few operators, most of the C++ operators can be overloaded. The C++ compiler has already overloaded some of its operators, such as operator + to add an integer as well as a double; and << bit wise left shift operator for the insertion operator (output). In addition, a C++ programmer can overload an existing operator and give it a new meaning. Operator overloading can extend the C++ language and an overloaded operator can be used to overload other operators. The purpose of overloading operators is to make the program easy to read and to apply an operation naturally. In reality, people do not have a problem understanding conventional operators because they are self-explanatory; therefore, the task is to mimic conventional operators and with this in mind, the new overloaded operator should be consistent with the original purpose of the operator.

OPERATOR OVERLOADING EXAMPLES

For example, the operator plus + that adds integers and floating decimals can be overloaded to concatenate two strings. A benefit of overloading is that it makes programming code natural and readable. In the following example, the + operator is overloaded to concatenate the two strings BUTTER and FLY.

    string3 = string1 + string2;

506

Also, without overloading, the concatenation of two strings can be done as follows:

string3= concatenate (string1, string2);

Note that you have to write the function for **concatenate( )**;

Another example of the overload operator is the multiplication of two arrays such as matrix multiplication or finding the intersection of two sets. In the statement A=B * C; where A, B and C are matrixes, the multiplication operator * is overloaded for matrix multiplication and the assignment operator = is overloaded to assign the result of the matrix multiplication.

OPERATORS THAT CANNOT BE OVERLOADED

The following C++ operators cannot be overloaded:

?: Conditional expression operator such as **x>y?max=x :max =y;**
. Class (structure) member operators such as **employee.name.**
.* Pointer to member operator such as **employee.*name.**
:: Scope resolution operator such as **stack::top;**
sizeof( ) to determine the size of a type such as **sizeof(int);**

OVERLOAD RESOLUTION RULE

How does the compiler know which function or operator to use now that several exist? The C++ compiler applies a set of rules such as matching the exact type from the argument list or the type of operands. A resolution rule may have to apply a conversion rule. It is possible that one function call (overloaded) matches more than one function's definition; this may cause an ambiguity that may lead to a problem for the compiler that should have been handled properly.

Also, when you overload an operator you cannot change the order of the operator's precedence and you cannot change operator's associativity. In the following example, a- b* c + d, the order of precedence for multiplication is higher than addition, and subtraction is performed first before addition due to its associatively (left to right). Note that when two operators have the same precedence, they work according to their associatively: either from left to right or from right to left.

HOW TO OVERLOAD AN OPERATOR

In order to overload an operator you must write a function for that operator so that C++ will call the function to do the process when the operator is used. The overload function definition is the same as ordinary functions except that the keyword **operator** is used before the parenthesis of the function's argument list. One thing you must realize when you are making an overloaded operator is that you are calling a function except that you do it with a class object. Ask yourself what kind of parameters the function needs and what the function will return. Obviously the overloaded operator will be used in the same manner as the ordinary operator is used. The following illustrates the general syntax of an overloaded operator prototype with one sample example:

returntype **operator** op (parameters);

OVERLOADING MATH OPERATORS: BINARY + OPERATOR

The binary operator + is used to add two numbers whether they are integers, floats, doubles, or even characters. In fact the C++ compiler has overloaded all these operations under one operator +. The question is how to add more operations to existing operators. C++ allows overloading by simply writing the function for what the overloaded operator should do. After the function is written, the operator will be used in the same way it has been used normally. For example, an employee may have two sources of income, one from a full time job and one from a part time job. Therefore to compute the total salary we have to compute the full time as well as part time salary. Overloading allows the use of the operator + as it is used in the normal addition of numbers, but here + is applied to a user data type which results in self-explanatory programming code.

totalsal= fulltimesal + parttimesal;

Let's not forget that we have to write the function to take care of the above overloading. Once the function is written, then naturally the operator can be used over and over. If we did not want to use overloading, our statement would look like the following, possibly with several parameters.

totsalary = findfulltimesal(…..) + findparttimesal(….);

OVERLOADING BINARY + OPERATOR: PROGRAM

The following program illustrates overloading the + operator to add two objects of the **employee** class known as **fulltime** and **parttime**. This allows us to calculate the total salary of an employee whose income comes from two different sources.

```
#include<iostream.h>
class employee{
private: long int id;
        double salary;
public:  employee(const long int empid, const double empsal);
        double operator+(const employee &emp); };
employee::employee(const long int empid, const double empsal){
        id=empid;
        salary=empsal; }//CONSTRUCTOR
double employee::operator+(const employee &emp){
        double totsalary;
        totsalary= salary + emp.salary;
        return totsalary; }//OP+
void main(){
        employee fulltime(1234599,70000.00), parttime(1234599, 10000.00);
        double totsalary=fulltime+parttime;
        cout<<"Total Salary: "<<totsalary;   }//MAIN
```

Figure 15.4a – Example of overloaded binary operator

Total Salary: 80000

Figure 15.4b – Output of 15.4a

PREFIX AND POSTFIX OPERATOR OVERLOADING

Prefix or postfix operators, ++ (increment operator) and -- (decrement operator), can be overloaded for use with user defined types in a similar way as other operators. Again the idea of overloading is to make the program more understandable and not to make it confusing. You do not want to overload ++ to decrement or overload -- to perform increment. The following simple program illustrates the overloading of the increment operator ++ for a type known as a date. The program keeps track of the working day by adding one to each day with a range of 1 to 5. The same program can be extended to add one to the day of the month.

The general form of an increment overloading is:

classtype &operator++(classtype &obj)

```
#include<iostream.h>
class date{
public:
        date(){ wday=1; }
        int getwday(){ return wday;}
        void operator ++ ( ){
                if(wday>5) wday=1;
                else ++wday;}
private:
        int wday; };//DATE

void main(){
        date workday;
        ++workday;
        cout<<"WORK DAY IS: "<< workday.getwday()<<endl;
}//MAIN
```

Figure 15.5a – Example of increment operator overloading

WORK DAY IS: 2

Figure 15.5b – Output of 15.5a

FRIEND FUNCTION

A friend function is not a member of a class but it has access to the class's private and protected members. A friend function is declared in the class that grants the access. To recall every member function implicitly has a pointer to its object known as **this** pointer. However a friend function does not have a **this** pointer and for this reason all of the necessary objects need to be passed explicitly to the friend function. For example, using a friend function to overload a binary operator. To declare a function as a friend of a class, you must precede the function prototype in the class definition with the keyword friend.

WHAT IS this POINTER?

Every member function has an implied parameter, called **this** pointer. The value of **this** points to the class-object (class argument) of the member function. In order to refer to the implicit argument that is passed to the member function, the keyword **this** preceded by an asterisk is used.

The following three statements perform the same task and show how **this** pointer is used within a member function. In the first version the keyword **this** is implied.

```
print( ){ cout<<findgrosspay(); }
print ( ){cout <<(*this).findgrosspay();
print( ){cout<<this->findgrosspay();
```

Friend functions and **this** pointers are further discussed in a later chapter.

OVERLOADING INPUT AND OUTPUT OPERATORS: >> AND <<

In C language the operators >> and << are used as right-shift and left-shift, respectively. However in C++ these operators are overloaded for input (extraction) and output (insertion). You can also overload these operators to work with your own abstract data type (class object). The function that does the overloading **operator <<( )** is a friend function since it is not a class member. This function returns a reference to **ostream**; this is done by placing an **&** in the function header. The two arguments are a reference to an **ostream** object and a reference to the object that is to be output.

The general prototypes for >> and << overloading can be shown as follows:

```
istream& operator >> (istream& parameter1, datatype& parameter2);
ostream& operator <<(ostream& parameter1, datatype& parameter2);
```

EXAMPLE OF I/O OVERLOADING

How is it possible to input or output a long list of information for an employee class in one instance without going through field by field? One solution is to overload the input or output operators so that when they are used in the program they can input and output all the data. In fact, you can customize the output the way you want to and for beginners I/O overloading is a meaningful example of how overloading can be useful. In the following example the >> extraction and << insertion operators have been overloaded.

```cpp
#include<iostream.h>
#include<string.h>
class employee{
private: char name[20];
         int hw;
         double hr,taxrate;
         double grosspay,taxamount,netpay;
public: void compute(){
         taxrate=0.15;
         grosspay=hw*hr;
         taxamount=grosspay*taxrate;
         netpay=grosspay-taxamount; }//COMPUTE
         friend  istream& operator >>(istream& cin , employee& individual );
         friend ostream&  operator << (ostream& cout, const employee& individual);
         };//EMPLOYEE CLASS
istream& operator >>(istream& cin , employee& individual){
         cout<<"ENTER NAME, HOURS WORKED, HOURLY RATE: ";
         cin>>individual.name>>individual.hw>>individual.hr;
         return cin; }// >>
ostream& operator <<(ostream& cout, const employee& individual){
         cout<<"EMPLOYEE NAME: "<<individual.name<<endl;
         cout<<"GROSS PAY: $"<<individual.grosspay<<endl;
         cout<<"TAX AMOUT: $"<<individual.taxamount<<endl;
         cout<<"NET PAY: $"<<individual.netpay<<endl;
         return cout; }//<<
void main(){
         employee regularemp;
         cin>>regularemp;
         regularemp.compute();
         cout<<regularemp;
         }//MAIN
```

Figure 15.6a – Example of I/O overloading

```
ENTER NAME, HOURS WORKED, HOURLY RATE: Ebrahimi 45 18
EMPLOYEE NAME: Ebrahimi
GROSS PAY: $810
TAX AMOUT: $121.5
NET PAY: $688.5
```

Figure 15.6b – Output of 15.6a

OVERLOADING ASSIGNMENT OPERATOR =

The operator = is used for assignment meaning the value of the right hand side is placed into the content on the left hand side. In the following example: int x,y=5; x=y; the assignment places 5 in x. What happens when you assign one object to another object? For example, in: date x,y; x=y; the object y is copied to object x and the memory is overwritten. An object may have more than one value and the overloaded assignment operator will assign all the values of the object on the right hand side to the values of the object on the left hand side.

The general form of the = overloading is shown as follows:

classtype &operator=(classtype &object);
classtype x,y;
x=y;

The above function takes a reference to the object and returns a reference from the object. An example where an overloaded assignment operator could be used is to copy an employee's information such as name, hours worked, and hourly wage into another object such as:

class employee{   string name;
                   double hoursworked, hourlywage;
                   . . .
                   }//EMPLOYEE
employee manager, ebrahimi;
manager=ebrahimi;

OVERLOADING THE EQUALITY OPERATOR = =

The equality operator = = can be overloaded so that it can be applied to class objects, for example comparing the time of two objects known as time1 and time2. Note that after the = = operator is overloaded the following statement could be used:

if (time1= =time2) cout<<" BOTH TIME ARE EQUAL";

To overload the = = operator we have to write a function that takes an argument of the class type and compares its data members with the data members of the passed object (right side) and returns a Boolean value (true or false). The following is the function to overload the equality operator for the time class; it compares two time objects to see if they are equal by testing the hours, minutes, and seconds.

bool time::operator= =(const time& appointment){
if ((hour==appointment.hour)&&(minute==appointment.minute) &&
                              (second==appointment.second)) return true;
else return false; }// END= =

OVERLOADING AN INDEX OPERATOR [ ]

The index or subscript operator is used to index arrays; an integer number ranging from zero to one less than the maximum size of the array indicates the position. By overloading an index operator, the index can be a basic data type such as integer or a user defined type (class objects). The overloaded index operator is not restricted to work with arrays only but with any other collection of items (containers). By overloading [ ], we can mimic the linked list to work like an array. One example of index overloading is to find the frequency of an object's occurrence, such as the frequency of each word in a document. The function to handle the index operator takes two parameters: the first is a reference to an object of the class that is going to be used as an array, and the second argument may be of any type such as an integer or class of an object to be used as the index.

int & operator[](const str& s);

Note that in the following statement that uses overloaded [ ], the string s is used as an index.

freq[s]=freq[s]+1;

OVERLOADING ISSUES AND LIMITATIONS

Most of the C++ operators can be overloaded, but there are few that cannot be overloaded. Keep in mind, operator overloading should make the program easier and the programmer should be able to use the operator in a natural way and eventually overloading should lead to reusability and less programming code. Improper usage of operator overloading can result in programming chaos. For example, overloading ++ to perform subtraction instead of addition would lead to confusion. Depending on what you want to do, you may want to overload an operator. Among the more frequently used overloaded operators we can name +, >>, <<, =, = =, and ++. Notice that while you can add additional meaning to the existing operators, you cannot create a new operator even though it is highly desirable such as exponentiation (**). Moreover, you cannot change the required number of operands; for example, a unary operator cannot have more than one operand.

CONSTRUCTOR OVERLOADING

A constructor is a member class that initializes an object and is called automatically as the object is created. Remember, a constructor has the same name as its class and does not return a value. Moreover, a constructor that has no parameters is known as a default constructor.

A constructor can be overloaded with different data types. For example, a stack class can have more than one constructor to initialize the stack with character type numbers or to initialize the stack with integer type numbers.

BINARY + OPERATOR OVERLOADING: TIME CLASS PROGRAM

The following program overloads the binary operator + for adding two objects of the class **time** known as **begintime** and **durationtime** and assigns the result into a third object, **finishtime**. Keep in mind, the overloaded + operator adds the elements of objects, not two values of basic data types such as integer.

```cpp
#include<iostream.h>
class time{
private: int hour, minute, second;
public: time(){ hour=0; minute=0; second=0; }
        time(int hr, int mn, int sec){
                hour=hr; minute=mn; second=sec; }
time operator+(const time& t){
        time totaltime;
        totaltime.hour = hour + t.hour;
        totaltime.minute = minute + t.minute;
        totaltime.second = second + t.second;
        return totaltime; }//+
friend ostream& operator<<(ostream&, const time&); };//TIME
ostream& operator<<(ostream& cout, const time& t){
        cout<<t.hour<<":"<<t.minute<<":"<<t.second<<endl;
        return cout; }//<<
void main(){
        int hr, mn, sec;
        cout<<"ENTER HOUR, MINUTE, AND SECOND: ";
        cin>>hr>>mn>>sec;
        time begintime(hr,mn,sec);
        cout<<"ENTER HOUR, MINUTE, AND SECOND: ";
        cin>>hr>>mn>>sec;
        time  durationtime(hr,mn,sec);
        time finishtime= begintime + durationtime;
        cout<<"FINISH TIME: "<<finishtime;  }//MAIN
```

Figure 15.7a – Example of overloading the + operator

```
ENTER HOUR, MINUTE, AND SECOND: 1 15 10
ENTER HOUR, MINUTE, AND SECOND: 1 11 20
FINISH TIME: 2:26:30
```

Figure 15.7b – Output of 15.7a

ABSTRACTION

Abstraction is the process of focusing on the essential and relevant aspects of an object or a task (function) without getting bogged down in their unnecessary details (molecular structure). Abstraction means to generalize an object and hide its details. To apply abstraction to objects, one must classify the objects according to their similarities as to what they do and what they have. One method of abstraction is to classify objects according to the domain of the problem as to the requirements at the moment, the characteristics of the objects, and how these objects interact with each other. An abstraction can have many layers of abstraction itself. Abstraction is around us daily, we express and represent ideas in abstract terms. We should not confuse abstraction with impossibilities (e.g. painting); however, some abstractions are difficult to figure out depending on the situation. You can think of abstraction as a box, and within the box is another box, and so on. How would you use abstraction to classify the following objects? Lion, tiger, cat, mouse, horse, rooster, bat, fish, frog, lobster, snake. Can you categorize the objects around you in any of the four elements of air, earth, fire, and water?

DIFFERENT LAYERS OF ABSTRACTION

The world around us is made of objects and each object has a name that represents an abstraction. For example: car, book, and computer each represent an abstract concept that can each be overwhelmingly described. An object or a thought can be represented in many layers of other objects and thoughts. Depending on what is important at each stage, the detail is either hidden or revealed. To understand what abstraction is and how it is used, look at the following example. A computer is an abstract object which itself is made of other abstract objects such as a mouse, keyboard, CPU, memory, and programs. A program is an abstract object that is made of other programs or statements. Similarly, a statement is made of identifiers (names) that may each represent a memory and the operations that are applied. Each operation is made of instructions and each instruction is made of microinstructions. Can you imagine if we reveal all the above interactions each time a user types a word? It is overwhelming and undesirable. Let us not forget that while the details of how a word is stored and how it interacts with other words is not important to a word processor, that same information is crucial for a compiler writer or a computer architect. What we want to do is classify each concept and wrap it (encapsulate) like a box under a name and provide an interface to deal with the box when it is necessary. To wrap it up, abstraction allows a programmer to look at the big picture and to focus only on important parts of problem that need to be solved. You should realize that there are two parts to an abstraction: interface and implementation. For example, a computer itself is an abstraction and when we are using it through an interface we are not concern about its detail. In programming, the abstraction concept is everywhere and has evolved into two main categories from procedural to data abstraction. For example, use of functions in the main program is the procedural abstraction and use of objects is a data abstraction. An example of procedural abstraction would be a function called **sort( )** and an example of data abstraction would be a class called **employee**. An abstract data type (ADT) is a higher level of abstraction than what C++ data types provide. Some important examples of abstract data types are stacks, queues, and trees.

ABSTRACT DATA TYPE (ADT)

The concepts of hiding detail (information hiding) and encapsulation are related to abstract data types. ADT emphasizes the work that is to be done rather than how it is done. The term ADT refers to the classes with information hiding that can be implemented by a programmer and then used by another programmer without knowing the details of how these classes have been implemented. Note again, the programmer that uses the class is not concerned (doesn't care) with how the class is implemented, but what the class is going to do. Therefore any detailed information can have a negative impact and can be misused. For experienced programmers terms such as stack, queue, tree, and graph have special meaning. In fact these terms are ADTs, each with its own data and operations. When these ADTs are implemented, they are ready to be used and the user should focus on how to use them rather than getting involved in the details of how they are designed. An important step in software engineering is creating an efficient ADT initially; this ADT becomes a pioneer tool for further expansion of the program. ADTs allow us to separate the interface (program interaction) from any particular data structure and algorithm implementation.

CLASS AND OBJECT

The world around us is composed of objects like book, mouse, and window. Each object comes from a class or blueprint (pattern). Classes correspond to categories (classifications) and are general terms while objects correspond to individuals (instances) and what you are dealing with at the moment. You can say a class is a blueprint and an object is an instance of the class. Think of a house blueprint and your own house. The kind of house is the class and your particular house is an object. Every object is an instance of a class. For example, date is a class and my birthday is an instance of class date.

INFORMATION HIDING (DATA HIDING)

Information hiding is applying an access restriction on data that the user should not be exposed to. Data hiding helps prevent errors that result from intentional or inadvertent changes in data. Keep in mind that by applying abstraction we are hiding and encapsulating data and vise versa. Think of your computer as an object of a computer class where internal components (details) are hidden in a box and communication is done through an interface (keyboard, mouse, or screen).

MODULE

A group of several related functions with the data they manipulate is known as a module. In a modular programming, a program (large program) is divided into several modules where in each module its data is hidden. Each module is placed into separate namespaces or files, which can also be compiled separately.

How the module works (user interface) is kept separate from how the module is implemented. Separating the user interface from the implementation enables a user to change the implementation without changing the interface.

HOW TO MAKE AN INCLUDE FILE

By this time you are fully aware that every C++ program requires an include file ranging from I/O to math and standard libraries. In fact one reason the C/C++ language is a compact, and as result, fast language is that you only include what you need in a program. Even **cin** and **cout** are not part of the C++ language itself, you have to include the library for them. For example, if you need to do a variety of mathematical functions, you place **#include <math.h>** in your program. The C++ compiler keeps the program and data for these libraries in separate files (modules) and when needed you can add them to the head (top) of your program. Do you know why these files are called header files? Using these modules contributes to information hiding and a programmer can make their own header files and include them in a program when needed. Commonly the class and function prototypes are kept in a header file. To make a header file, just as making any ordinary file, type the information and save it under a filename with extension **.h** (for example **employee.h**). To use your own include file, instead of angle brackets, surround the file name in double quotations as shown below.

> **#include "employee.h"**

ENCAPSULATION

Encapsulation is a way to put together (to enclose in a capsule) data (attributes) and the functions (behavior) that manipulate the data into one self-contained unit (package) and safeguard it from outside misuse. In object-oriented programming the encapsulation concept is achieved by means of a class where data and functions can be either private or public to the object. The private data members and member functions are hidden from the class user; they are encapsulated within the class and they are not accessible from outside of the class. However, through the public parts (as an interface) of a class, the private elements can be accessed.

HOW ABSTRACT DATA TYPES (ADT) ARE IMPLEMENTED

In C++, abstract data types (ADT) are implemented by having a class where the member variables are declared as private and some of the member functions are public. These public member functions are used as an interface to access the private members. Putting an access restriction on the data in a class will maintain data integrity and consistency. The definition of class can be placed in a separate file and then be compiled; and whenever it is needed it can be included in different programs. Similarly the class implementation can be placed in a different file that can be included with other programs that need them.

TEMPLATE

How would you write a program that searches for a number like salary or for an employee's name? How would you write a stack program where you can push either a number or a string? You may respond quickly that you would write a separate program for each data type. By using **template**, a C++ programmer can design generic algorithms and generic classes. With a template your algorithm can work for integers as well as floating-point numbers. In C++, you specify what type of data to work with by the function call or when an object is declared (instantiated). One advantage of the template is that it promotes program reusability and in the long run programming becomes easier.

TEMPLATE FUNCTION

A template function is a function that works with a generic data type such as writing one function that works with any type of data, whether it is a built-in or user-defined type. In a template function the actual data type is not specified; rather, the generic data type is used. On a function call with the arguments (actual data types), the compiler will substitute the parameters for the actual data type such as: integer, character, or other data type. The actual value type parameter can also be used for local variables as well as the return value of the function. A template function includes a template definition followed by a function definition. The function template starts with the keyword template following by an angle bracket enclosing the keyword class with a parameterized data type (generic type) name.

After the template definition the function definition would be the same except the generic type name would be used for the parameterized data type. The general syntax of a template function is shown below:

```
template  < class generictypename>
generictypename  functionname (generictypename parametername){
       functionbody;
       return functionvalue; }
```

TEMPLATE FUNCTION: PROGRAM

The following program finds the smaller of two values whether they are integers, characters, or floating decimal numbers. The template function will take care of the different data types. The generic data type in the template function will be substituted with the actual data type provided by the calling function. Note that GT is an identifier name and as a convention I used capital letters to represent it. Other conventions have used identifier names such as T and Type.

```
#include<iostream.h>
template <class GT>
GT smaller (GT x, GT y){
        if (x < y) return x;
        else return y; }//SMALLER
void main(){
        int i,j;
        cout<<"ENTER TWO INTEGERS: ";
        cin>>i>>j;
        cout<<"THE SMALLER OF THE TWO IS: "<<smaller(i,j)<<endl;
        char  c, d;
        cout<<"ENTER TWO CHARACTERS: ";
        cin>>c>>d;
        cout<<"THE SMALLER OF THE TWO IS: "<<smaller(c,d)<<endl;
        float f,g;
        cout<<"ENTER TWO FLOATING POINT NUMBERS: ";
        cin>>f>>g;
        cout<<"THE SMALLER OF THE TWO IS: "<<smaller(f,g)<<endl;
        }//MAIN
```

Figure 15.8a – Example of a template function

```
ENTER TWO INTEGERS: 10 5
THE SMALLER OF THE TWO IS: 5
ENTER TWO CHARACTERS: a c
THE SMALLER OF THE TWO IS: a
ENTER TWO FLOATING POINT NUMBERS: 2.75 12.50
THE SMALLER OF THE TWO IS: 2.75
```

Figure 15.8b – Output of 15.8a

TEMPLATE WITH MULTIPLE TYPES

It is possible for a template to have more than one type. For instance, in computing gross pay, the hours worked is an integer, however the hourly rate and gross pay are doubles. The general syntax of a template function having multiple types is as follows:

template <class T1, class T2>
T2 computegrosspay (T1 hoursworked, T2 hourlyrate){
**   T2 grosspay;**
**   grosspay=hoursworked * hourlyrate; return grosspay; }//GROSS**

T2 computetotalprice (T1 quantity, T2 unitprice){
**   T2 totalprice;**
**   totalprice=quantity * unitprice; }//TOTALPRICE**

In the above two examples, T1 and T2 are the type identifiers that will be replaced by the two different actual data types.

OVERLOADED FUNCTIONS VERSUS TEMPLATE FUNCTIONS

Function overloading becomes useful when performing similar operations on different data types. In function overloading we use only one function name with several different versions of the function even though the whole operation is identical. However when using template functions, we have one function name with one version of the function that is parameterized and the compiler generates different versions of the function based on the data type provided by the function call. For example we could have a function called sort to be overloaded so it will cover a variety of sorting algorithms (generic algorithms) with many different swaps. One disadvantage of function overloading is that if one function needs to be changed, all the functions must be changed. It should be noted that a template function could be overloaded in the same way as a regular function.

CLASS TEMPLATE

A class template is a class that can have a generic data type instead of an actual data type. The actual data type for a class will be provided as the class is instantiated and the compiler will generate the proper code by substituting the generic type with the actual type.

The general syntax for a class template is the same as a function template, which starts with the keyword template followed by the keyword class and its parameterized type enclosed in angle brackets.

The class definition is done in the same way as an ordinary class, except that the generic type (parameterized type) is used in place of an actual type. Remember to place the actual data type in angle brackets when the object is instantiated. One good usage of class templates is to build a generic stack, queue, or tree. You can define a generic stack with an unspecified data type. Remember that every time you use a template class or its member functions, the template definition must precede the class definition or function definition. For clarity you may want to place the template definition on a separate line.

```
#include<iostream.h>
template <class T>
class employee{
private: T hoursworked, hourlyrate, grosspay;
public: employee (T hw, T hr ){ hoursworked=hw; hourlyrate=hr; }
        void resetdata( T hw, T hr ){ hoursworked=hw; hourlyrate=hr; }
        T computegrosspay( ){ grosspay= hoursworked * hourlyrate; return grosspay; }
}; //EMPLOYEE
void main(){
        employee <double>  manager(40.5, 100.0);
        cout<<"SALARY IS "<<manager.computegrosspay()<<endl;
        manager.resetdata(30.0, 50.0);
        cout<<"SALARY IS "<<manager.computegrosspay()<<endl;    }//MAIN
```

Figure 15.9a – Example of a class template

```
SALARY IS 4050
SALARY IS 1500
```

Figure 15.9b – Output of 15.9a

CLASS TEMPLATE: GENERAL SYNTAX

When you are using a class template, make sure to distinguish between the general syntax for the class itself, its members, and when the object is instantiated. The following example demonstrates each of the above cases:

template <class typeidentifier>
class classname{
        ......
        typeidentifier ...variablename.
        typeidentifier functionname (typeidentifier....);
        }; //CLASS

template <class typeidentifier>
typeidentifier classname <typeidentifier>:: functionname (typeidentifier...){
        .....
        return ....; }//FUNCTION
main(){
        .....
        classname <actualtype> objectname
        ..... }//MAIN

STACK WITH TEMPLATE: GENERIC CLASS PROGRAM

A stack is a data structure and an ADT where items are added and removed from one end. The function **push( )** inserts a new item to the stack and **pop( )** removes the item that was most recently inserted. To summarize the stack ADT, items are removed according to the last-in-first-out discipline. The functions **isempty( )** and **isfull( )** check the stack to determine whether it is empty or full, respectively. The following program defines a generic class called **stack** with a maximum of 5 items, including double and character values. The operand stack is used to hold the numbers while the operator stack holds the character operators. The stack can be extended to hold other different data types as well.

```cpp
#include <iostream.h>
const int MAXSIZE=5;
template <class T>
class stack{
public: stack(void);
        bool isempty() const;
        bool isfull() const;
        void push(T x);
        T pop();
private: int top;
        T items[MAXSIZE];  };  //STACK
template<class T>
stack< T > :: stack(){  top = -1;}
template<class T>
bool stack <T> :: isempty() const{ return(top == -1); }//ISEMPTY
template<class T>
bool stack <T> :: isfull() const{ return(top == (MAXSIZE-1));  }//ISFULL
template<class T>
void stack<T> :: push (T x){
     if (isfull())  cout<<"YOU CAN'T PUSH"<<endl;
     else { top++; items [top] = x; } }//PUSH
template<class T>
T stack <T>:: pop(){
     if (isempty()){cout<<"YOU CAN'T POP"<<endl;   return 0; }//IF
     else return items [top--];  }//POP
void main( ){
     stack<double> operandstack;
     operandstack.push(3.00);   operandstack.push(12.5);    operandstack.push(1.2);
     cout<<"STACK VALUE IS:"<< operandstack.pop()<<endl;
     operandstack.push(8.00);   operandstack.push(2.00);    operandstack.push(5.4);
     while (! operandstack.isempty()) cout<<"STACK VALUE IS:"<< operandstack.pop()<<endl;
     stack <char> operatorstack;
     operatorstack.push('+'); operatorstack.push('*');
     operatorstack.push('-');operatorstack.push('/');
     while (! operatorstack.isempty()) cout<<"STACK VALUE IS:"<< operatorstack.pop()<<" "<<endl;
}//MAIN
```

Figure 15.10a – Stack template program

```
STACK VALUE IS:1.2
STACK VALUE IS:5.4
STACK VALUE IS:2
STACK VALUE IS:8
STACK VALUE IS:12.5
STACK VALUE IS:3
STACK VALUE IS:/
STACK VALUE IS:-
STACK VALUE IS:*
STACK VALUE IS:+
```

Figure 15.10b – Output of 15.10a

QUEUE WITH TEMPLATE

A queue is a data structure or an abstract data type (ADT) where insertion is done on one end and removal is done on the other end. The following example implements a queue with a template, enabling the queue to work with a variety of data types. The following template queue is tested with **int** and **char** types, however one can extend the template queue to work with other data types and include overloading, making it more powerful and complex.

```cpp
#include <iostream.h>
const int MAXSIZE = 10;
template <class T>
class queue {
private: int front, rear,size;
        T info[MAXSIZE];
public:  queue(int);
        void enqueue(T x);
        T dequeue( );
        bool isempty( ) const;
        bool isfull() const;  };//CLASS QUEUE
template<class T>
queue <T>::  queue(int s=MAXSIZE){
        front = 0;
        rear = 0;
        size=s+1;   }//CONSTRUCTOR
template<class T>
bool queue <T>:: isempty() const{   return (rear == front); }
template<class T>
bool  queue <T>:: isfull() const {   return ((rear + 1) % size == front);  }//ISFULL
template<class T>
void queue <T>::enqueue(T  x){
        if(isfull()) cout<<"QUEUE FULL:"<<endl;
        else{  rear = (rear +1) % size;
```

523

```
                  info[rear] = x; }  }//ENQUEUE
template<class T>
T queue <T>::dequeue( ){
        if( isempty() ){cout<<"QUEUE EMPTY"<<endl;
                   return -1;}//IF
        else{ front = (front + 1) % size;
                return info[front];}//ELSE
}//ENQUEUE
void main(){
    queue <int> myintqueue(5);
    for (int i=0;  i<=5; i++){
    myintqueue.enqueue(i); }//FOR
    while(!myintqueue.isempty()){ cout<<myintqueue.dequeue()<<" "<<endl;}//WHILE
    queue <char> mycharqueue(4);
    for (char c='A';  c<='E'; c++){
    myintqueue.enqueue(c); }//FOR
    while(!myintqueue.isempty()){ cout<<char(myintqueue.dequeue())<<" "<<endl;}//WHILE
}//MAIN
```

Figure 15.11a – Queue template example

```
QUEUE FULL:
0
1
2
3
4
A
B
C
D
E
```

Figure 15.11b – Output of 15.11a

TOPICS NOT COVERED HERE

The topic of overloading, especially operator overloading, can become tedious and error prone. When an operator is overloaded, there are many versions of its function and, on top of the ambiguity as to which function to pick, conversion of one type to another must take place. Type conversion by itself needs lengthy coverage as well as how to deal with passing an object as a parameter or returning an object from a function, e.g. passing a large object versus small one. Controversial issues surrounding the friend function are not discussed here. Virtual functions need their own attention as to how C++ chooses the correct overridden functions during run-time, creating run-time polymorphism. Virtual functions become a very interesting subject when they work with a pointer to the base class and then each derived class calls its own function although the function name remains the same. The advantage of templates is that the programmer can design generic algorithms and classes. However, templates have time and space overhead, which may not be ideal for real-time applications. The use of templates can become more complicated by introducing nested templates with multiple parameters. The topic of polymorphism with virtual functions requires knowledge of inheritance and will be discussed in the next chapter.

CLOSING REMARKS AND LOOKING AHEAD

Whether you want to apply brakes on a bike, car, van, or truck, they all have one task in common; the result is the vehicle coming to a stop. Also, the process of finding the area of a geometric shape is similar whether the area is of a rectangle, triangle, or circle. The same is true for printing, regardless of whether you are printing a list, queue, or stack. One benefit of overloading is the ability to give one meaningful name to several functions that have the same task, rather than giving a different name to each function. For example, in a payroll system many functions with the same name, such as payment( ), can be used for hourly paid or salaried employees as well as for consultants and managers. Another example, double-clicking on an icon may provide different results depending on whether the icon is a word processor, e-mail application, or an executable file.

Polymorphism allows an entity (for example a variable, function, or object) to take on a variety of representations. Function overloading allows us to reuse the same name for functions (or methods) as long as the parameter list differs.

Many operations on newly defined user data types share a common ground with the operations on existing basic data types. Therefore, it is desirable that new user data types use the same operator in the same manner. The process of enabling C++ operators to work with objects is called overloading. In operator overloading, a function is written for the operator so that it can be used normally with the class object. One example is to define a complex number data type and use the same operators such as +, -, *, and / to perform the operations on complex numbers as they would perform on a real number. Another example of overloading operator is to apply it to the object of class date, time, and polynomial. With the use of a template, a C++ programmer is able to write functions and classes regardless of their specific data types.

The next chapter will cover the last aspect of object-oriented programming known as inheritance: when one object carries the properties of one or more other objects. Inheritance is one of the key concepts of object-oriented programming where member variables in one class automatically become part of objects belonging to another class. One class is considered the base class, and the class that inherits from the base class is considered the derived class.

Inheritance, in addition to encapsulation (class) and polymorphism, is a key element of object-oriented programming and enhances programming by reusing and sharing code; in the long run, inheritance is cost effective and minimizes programming errors.

SELF-TEST TRUE / FALSE CHAPTER 15: POLYMORPHISM

___1. Polymorphism is the ability to have many forms for the same name.

___2. An example of polymorphism is when different functions that do a similar task have different names.

___3. Polymorphism, encapsulation, and inheritance are important features of object-oriented programming.

___4. Operator overloading is an example of polymorphism.

___5. When a function is overloaded, the same function name is used to perform different tasks.

___6. The compiler uses the function signature to determine which function to call.

___7. A default value for a parameter will be assigned if its value is specified in the function call.

___8. An overloaded operator should be used so that is consistent with the original purpose of the operator.

___9. The + operator is overloaded since it is used to add integers, floats, and doubles.

___10. A friend function does not have access to the private and protected members of a class.

___11. By overloading the insertion operator, you can output all the information of a class in one statement.

___12. To assign one object to another, the assignment operator is overloaded to assign all data in the class.

___13. There is no need to overload the equality operator when testing the equality of two objects of a class.

___14. The index operator can be overloaded to take a class object as the index.

___15. A constructor can be overloaded to initialize members of a class with different data types.

___16. Abstraction means generalizing an object and hiding its detail.

___17. ADT (Abstract Data Type) emphasizes the work that is to be done rather than how it is done.

___18. Objects refer to general categories while classes refer to specific instances.

___19. Information hiding is a means of applying abstraction.

___20. In modular programming, the user interface is kept separate from the implementation.

___21. The following is an example of how you would include your own header file: #include<person.h>.

___22. A class is a means of encapsulation since data and functions are contained in one unit.

___23. Templates are used to design specific algorithms and classes and they work for only one data type.

___24. A template function uses a generic data type that is substituted with the actual data type.

___25. Using a class template, you can define a generic stack for multiple data types.

CHAPTER 15 POLYMORPHISM ASSIGNMENTS

Q15a) What is the main idea behind polymorphism in object-oriented programming? An example of polymorphism is when two functions have the same name but different implementations. For example, the function printlist( ) can be used to print the contents of an array or a linked list.

Q15b) Write an overloaded function for sorting that uses an overloaded swap function.

Q15c) Explain one advantage of default parameters. What is the restriction on default parameters?

Q15d) How does a compiler resolve overloading?

Q15e) What is the idea behind operator overloading? Give an example.

Q15f) Write an overloaded binary operator + for the intersection of two sets and an overloaded – operator for the difference of two sets. Use arrays to represent each set. Display the result using cout<<A+B; and cout<<A-B;

Q15g) What is a friend function? What is an advantage and a disadvantage of having friend functions?

Q15h) How are templates different from function overloading? Give an example of a template using sort with a swap function.

Q15i) What does the following template class do?

```
#include <iostream.h>
const int MAXSIZE=5;
template <class T>
class stack{
public: stack(void);
        bool isempty() const;
        bool isfull() const;
        void push(T x);
        T pop();
private: int top;
        T items[MAXSIZE];  }; //STACK
template<class T>
stack< T > :: stack(){  top = -1;}
template<class T>
bool stack <T> :: isempty() const{ return(top == -1); }//ISEMPTY
template<class T>
bool stack <T> :: isfull() const{ return(top == (MAXSIZE-1)); }//ISFULL
template<class T>
void stack<T> :: push (T x){
    if (isfull())  cout<<"YOU CAN'T PUSH"<<endl;
    else { top++; items [top] = x; } }//PUSH
template<class T>
T stack <T>:: pop(){
    if (isempty()){cout<<"YOU CAN'T POP"<<endl;  return 0; }//IF
```

```
        else return items [top--];  }//POP
void main( ){
        stack<double> operandstack;
        operandstack.push(3.00);   operandstack.push(12.5);   operandstack.push(1.2);
        cout<<"STACK VALUE IS:"<< operandstack.pop()<<endl;
        operandstack.push(8.00);   operandstack.push(2.00);   operandstack.push(5.4);
        while (! operandstack.isempty()) cout<<"STACK VALUE IS:"<<
operandstack.pop()<<endl;
        stack <char> operatorstack;
        operatorstack.push('+'); operatorstack.push('*');
        operatorstack.push('-');operatorstack.push('/');
        while (! operatorstack.isempty())
                cout<<"STACK VALUE IS:"<< operatorstack.pop()<<" "<<endl;
}//MAIN
```

Name one advantage of template function as well as template class.

Q15j) What is abstraction? Where does the word come from? What are the similarities between an art abstraction and a programming abstraction?

Q15k) What is the idea behind the ADT? How does ADT hide detail? How has abstraction evolved in programming?

Q15l) Write an abstract data type known as date with its own attributes and its own function members. Write a simple program to involve the operations and data.

Q15m) Write an abstract data type known as time with its own data members and member functions. Write a simple program to support the operations defined for the type time.

Q15n) Create an individual universal abstract data type. Start from date of birth, infant, child, teenager, adult, senior, and finally date of rest.

Q15o) Create an abstract data type for employee. Include salary, commission, bonus, and calculate overtime pay. Set the data members and member functions. Test your ADT with a simple program.

CASE STUDY –PAYROLL SYSTEM PHASE 15: POLYMORPHISM

a) Write an overloaded search function for your employee class. This will allow you to use the same function name to search for an employee by either a last name or id number. You will need to write two implementations for the search function, one takes a string as a parameter and the other takes an integer.
b) Overload the insertion operator << to display all the employee information.

CHAPTER 16

INHERITANCE:
REUSABILITY AND EXTENDABILITY

The world around us is made of objects that share many similarities. These similarities can be classified into common groups. For example, in biology taxonomy organisms are classified into a hierarchy of group, from general to specific. In C++, objects are created from classes; and a class may share (inherit) some common data members and member functions that belong to another class or classes. As a result, a new class can be created based on an existing class rather than creating it from scratch. An inherited class can have its own data and function members and can modify or override the inherited members. Inheritance is an important tool of Object-Oriented Programming (OOP), because it promotes reusability and ease of extensibility by building on what is already there and customizing it as desired. A programmer can build a hierarchy that goes from a general class to a specific class by incorporating inheritance. With class hierarchy a program is easier to follow, debug, and modify. With inheritance, a class is built on an existing class that has already been tested; therefore, inheritance reduces the time and the cost of development as well as minimizes errors in the program. Inheritance is also known as *derivation* or *specialization*. In fact, inheritance is not something new. For example, humans have organized knowledge into hierarchical structures such as the animal kingdoms.

CLASS INHERITANCE: GENERAL SYNTAX

The general form of a class inherited from another class is shown in fig 9.1. The access specifier (access control) can be **public**, **private** or **protected**. The syntax for class inheritance is the same as a regular class except that after the class name (derivedname) there is a single colon, the derivation access type (accessspecifier), and the name of the class (baseclassname) from which it is derived.

```
class derivedname : accessspecifier  baseclassname{
    accessspecifier: memberdata;
    accessspecifier: memberfunctions; };
```

Figure 16.1 – Class inheritance syntax

EXAMPLE OF INHERITANCE

Take a moment and categorize yourself as an object. For example, are you a full time employee, a part time student, or both? Do you have a bank account? Do you own a car? As human beings we categorize the objects around us into hierarchical structures. For example, livings things are divided into five kingdoms (plant, animal, fungi, etc.). Furthermore, these kingdoms are divided into smaller subcategories. Humans belong to the kingdom Animilia, the phylum Chordata, and the class Mammilia. These classes all share some commonality such as attributes (data) and behaviors (functions) that can be factored out.

EMPLOYEE CLASS: An employee can belong to a *base class* of person and several derived classes such as a salaried or hourly paid class both of which inherit from the person class. An employee can be full time or part time. Moreover, an employee can be a consultant, manager, or executive.

STUDENT CLASS: There may be different kinds of students in a college that all share common characteristics.
The student class is the *base class* and students can be further categorized into the following classes:

> Undergraduate
> Graduate
> Full time
> Part time
> Freshman, sophomore, junior, senior
> Exchange
> International student

For example, Jane Doe is a part time, freshman, undergraduate, exchange student.

EXAMPLE OF INHERITANCE: COMPUTE AREA OF CIRCLE

The following program computes the area of a circle by providing the x and y coordinates of two given points. The program finds the radius using the distance formula. The program begins by defining the class **point** and class **circle**. The **circle** class inherits from the **point** class. The class **point** has two member functions: **setpoints( )**, which initializes the coordinates, and **distance( )**, which computes the distance between the given the points. The class **circle** inherits the **distance( )** function in order to compute the area.

```
#include <iostream.h>
#include <math.h>
class point{
public: int xstartpoint,ystartpoint;
        int xendpoint, yendpoint;
        void setpoints(int x1, int x2, int y1, int y2){
                xstartpoint = x1, xendpoint = x2;
                ystartpoint = y1, yendpoint = y2;}
        double distance(){
                return  sqrt((pow(xendpoint-xstartpoint,2))+(pow(yendpoint-ystartpoint,2)));}
    };//POINT
class circle: public point{
public: double radius;
        double area(){
                radius = distance() ; //function belongs to base class
                return radius * radius * 3.14;} };//CIRCLE
void main(){
        int x1coord = 2, y1coord = 12, x2coord= 6,y2coord = 15;
        circle mycircle;
        mycircle.setpoints (x1coord,x2coord,y1coord,y2coord);
        cout<<"CIRCLE AREA IS "<<mycircle.area()<<endl;   }//MAIN
```

Figure 16.2a – A program showing single inheritance

```
CIRCLE AREA IS 78.5
```

Figure 16.2b – Output of 16.2a

BASE CLASS, DERIVED CLASS-GENERALIZATION TO SPECIALIZATION

In building inheritance, the existing class is called the **base class** and the class that inherits from the base class is called the **derived class.** In the above example class **point** is the base class and class **circle** is the derived class. To determine a base class we factor out the common attributes (data) and behaviors (functions) from other classes. The factoring can continue until you get to a specific class and you want to focus and instantiate (create) an object. This leads from generalization to specialization.

```
class D : public B {
                //.........
                //.........
                        };
```

In the preceding example, **D** is the **derived class** (or **subclass**) and **B** is the **base class** (or **super class**). Note that class **D** inherits the data and functions from class **B**, therefore class **B** must exist before **D** can inherit from it.

PROTECTED MEMBERS INSTEAD OF PRIVATE

Recall, the access controls for a member class are: **private**, **public**, and **protected**. In the base class, instead of private, the keyword **protected** is used so that the subclasses can access it while not making it public to every other class. When an access control is specified as protected in the base class, it suggests that there will be a derived class (subclass) whose members can access the base class members as if it were private only to that derived class. Remember that in a class, the private members are only accessible directly by its members; however, the **friend** of the class, though not a member of the class, can access the private members. Friends of classes will be further discussed. However, by making a member of a class protected, its derived class can also access the protected member, as it is private to both the base class and the derived class.

```
#include <iostream.h>
class B {
protected: int bm; };

class D: public B {
public: accessbm(int x){ bm=x+2;} };

void main(){
        D ob;
        cout<<"bm VALUE IS "<<ob.accessbm(5)<<endl;
        }//MAIN
```

Figure 16.3a – Protected base class member example

```
bm VALUE IS 7
```

Figure 16.3b – Output of 16.3a

In the above example, what would happen if the access control became private instead of protected? The data member **bm** would be inaccessible.

DEFAULT INHERITANCE ACCESS TYPE: PRIVATE

The default inheritance access for a derived class is private, which means the non-private base class members become private for the derived class; note that the private members of the base class are not accessible in the derived class. Public and protected members of the base class become accessible by the derived class member functions when the derived access modifier is private. However, once the public and protected members of the base class become private in the derived class, these members are inaccessible to the outsider. This means that if you create an object of the derived class in the main program, it cannot access any of the members in the class. Private inheritance, though it is the default, might seem useless. Setting the inheritance access type (control) to anything other than public, such as private or protected, will downgrade the accessibility of the base class members. For example, if the inheritance access type is private and the access type of the base class member is public, it forces it to become private and therefore accessible only to the members of the derived class. Note that just because private members of the base class are accessible inside the derived class, it does not mean that objects of the derived class can access the members of the base class directly. The members are only accessible through the public utility functions in the derived class or friend. To summarize and settle the confusion when dealing with members of the base class in the derived class, visualize the derived class as a new class in which the base class members are included in the derived class (except private base members) but now with new access permission types from the impact of the derived class access modifier. For example, in the following program, think that the protected member **bm** in class **B** is physically present in the derived class **D** as private **bm**.

```
#include <iostream.h>
class B {
protected: int bm; };

class DPV: private B {
public: accessbm(int x){ bm=x+2;} };

void main(){
    DPV ob;
    cout<<"bm VALUE IS "<<ob.accessbm(5)<<endl;
    }//MAIN
```

Figure 16.4a – Private inheritance example

```
bm VALUE IS 7
```

Figure 16.4b – Output of 16.4a

PRIVATE INHERITANCE

In the following example, the class **DPV** is privately derived from the base class **B**, making the base members that are public and protected to private. Therefore, the members of the derived class can access these inherited members. However, since these inherited members become private in the class **DPV**, they are no longer accessible to any other classes or any classes derived from **DPV**.

```
#include <iostream.h>
class B {
protected: int bm; };

class DPV: private B {
public: accessbm(int x){ bm=x+2;} };

class DDPV: public DPV {
public: accessbmdpv(int x){accessbm(x); } };

void main(){
        DDPV ob;
        cout<<"bm VALUE IS "<<ob.accessbmdpv(5)<<endl;
        }//MAIN
```

Figure 16.5a – Private inheritance example

bm VALUE IS 7

Figure 16.5b – Output of 16.5a

DERIVATION TYPE (INHERITANCE ACCESS): PUBLIC OR PROTECTED

How does a derived class access the base class members when the default inheritance access is private? A derived class member can only access the public and protected members of the base class. Therefore, the inheritance access has to be either public or protected for the derived class to access base class members. It is common practice to have inheritance access as public despite its default private access.

INHERITANCE ACCESS CONTROL (MODIFIER)

An inheritance access type modifier or access specifier can be private, protected, or public. Each of these access modifiers determines the accessibility of the derived members as well as how the derived members can access the base members. A private modifier will force the access to become private, while a protected modifier will force the access to become protected. However, the public modifier leaves the access as it is set in the base class. In another words, the modifier can make the access more restricted than defined in the base class. Keep in mind, members of the base class with private access become inaccessible in derived classes. By default the inheritance access is private forcing all members of the base class to be treated as private in the derived class and as a result, the other classes and the program cannot to access them.

```
class B {
public: //...
private: //...
protected: //...   };

class D: public B {
public: //...
private: //...
protected: //...   };
```

If data or functions are declared as public in a base class and the base class access is defined as public in a derived class, its access is public in the derived class. In summary, if the base class is inherited as public the access in the derived class will be the same. If the base class is inherited as protected, it will force the access in the derived class to become protected. And finally, if the base class is inherited as private, it forces the access in the derived class to become private.

USING CONSTRUCTORS WITH INHERITANCE

In a class, a constructor is used to initialize the data members. A base class and a derived class can have their own constructors. When an object of a derived class is created, which constructor will be called first? The constructor for the base class is called first and then the constructor for the derived class will follow.

```
#include <iostream.h>
class B {
public:
        B() { cout<<"BASE CLASS CONSTRUCTOR IS CALLED"<<endl; }  };//B

class D: public B {
public:
        D(){ cout<<"DERIVED CLASS CONSTRUCTOR IS CALLED"<<endl; } };//D

void main(){
        D dob;
        }//MAIN
```

Figure 16.6a – Constructors with inheritance

```
BASE CLASS CONSTRUCTOR IS CALLED
DERIVED CLASS CONSTRUCTOR IS CALLED
```

Figure 16.6b – Output of 16.6a

535

USING DESTRUCTORS WITH INHERITANCE

In a class, a destructor is used to de-initialize the data members. The destructor for the derived class is called first and then the destructor for the base class will follow. The order in which the destructors of derived class and base class are called is the opposite of constructors.

```cpp
#include <iostream.h>
class B {
public:
        ~ B() { cout<<"BASE CLASS DESTRUCTOR IS CALLED"<<endl; }  };//B

class  D: public B {
 public:
        ~ D(){ cout<<"DERIVED CLASS DESTRUCTOR IS CALLED"<<endl; } };//D

void main(){
        D dob;
        }//MAIN
```

Figure 16.7a – Destructors with inheritance

```
DERIVED CLASS DESTRUCTOR IS CALLED
BASE CLASS DESTRUCTOR IS CALLED
```

Figure 16.7b – Output of 16.7a

MULTIPLE INHERITANCE

Like a child that inherits from both parents, a derived class in a multiple inheritance can have more than one base class. Most inheritance in C++ is single inheritance with a derived class inheriting from one base class. In several situations, it is desirable to use multiple inheritances. In fact we have been using multiple inheritance in our programs since we started learning how to program in C++. For example, whenever we use **#include <iostream.h>**, we are indirectly using multiple inheritance. The class iostream is inherited from two base classes: **istream** as well as **ostream.** One example of multiple inheritance is to create a new class such as studentemployee that inherits from both the student class and the employee class. Despite its power many object-oriented programming languages such as Java do not support multiple inheritance. There are ambiguities with multiple inheritance and casting a pointer from a subclass to a base class can create confusion for a programmer as well as more work for a compiler writer. Figure 16.8 is a program that demonstrates multiple inheritance; the derived class D inherits from two base classes, B1 and B2.

```
#include<iostream.h>
class B1{
public:   int x;
          B1(){}
          B1(int a){x=a;}
          int getx(){ return x;}   };//B1
class B2{
public:   int y;
          B2(){}
          B2(int b){y=b;}
          int gety(){ return y;}   };//B2
class D: public B1, public B2{
public:   int z;
          D(int a, int b, int c):B1(a),B2(b){
                         z=c;}
          int getz(){return z;}   };//D
void main(){
      D ob(1,2,3);
      cout<<ob.getx()<<endl;
      cout<<ob.gety()<<endl;
      cout<<ob.getz()<<endl;
      }//MAIN
```

Figure 16.8a – Multiple inheritance example

```
1
2
3
```

Figure 16.8b – Output of 16.8a

The next example uses multiple inheritance to relate to parents and a child. The two base classes are the father and mother classes and the child class inherits from both. The program tries to guess the child's eye color based on the eye color of the parents.

```
#include<iostream.h>
class mother{
public:
        int eye;
        mother(){eye=0;}
        mother(int x){eye=x;}
        int getmothereye(){return eye;}
};//MOTHER
class father{
public:
        int eye;
        father(){eye=0;}
        father(int y){eye=y;}
        int getfathereye(){ return eye;}
};//FATHER
class child: public mother,public father{
public:  int eye;
        child(){eye=0;}
        child(int a,int b):mother(a),father(b){
                        if(a==b)
                                eye=a;
                        else
                                eye=2;}
                int childeye(){return eye;}
};//CHILD
void main(){
        int mcolor, fcolor;
        cout<<"Enter the color of mother's eyes."<<endl;
        cout<<"(1 for blue, 2 for brown): ";
        cin>>mcolor;
        cout<<"Enter the color of father's eyes."<<endl;
        cout<<"(1 for blue, 2 for brown): ";
        cin>>fcolor;
        child harry(mcolor, fcolor);
        cout<<"Mother's eyes: "<<harry.getmothereye()<<endl;
        cout<<"Father's eyes: "<<harry.getfathereye()<<endl;
        cout<<"Child's eyes: "<<harry.childeye()<<endl;
}//MAIN
```

Figure 16.9a – Determining eye color using multiple inheritance

```
Enter the color of mother's eyes.
(1 for blue, 2 for brown): 1
Enter the color of father's eyes.
(1 for blue, 2 for brown): 2
Mother's eyes: 1
Father's eyes: 2
Child's eyes: 2
```

Figure 16.9b – Output of 16.9a

538

VIRTUAL FUNCTION

A virtual function is a member function that is defined in one class (the base class) and will be redefined by subsequent classes (derived classes). In order to create a virtual function, precede the function's declaration with the keyword **virtual** in the base class. The subsequent classes (derived classes) can implement the virtual function depending on the object they are dealing with, and there is no need for the keyword virtual. In classes with virtual functions, the function name is the same but there are several different implementations- one interface with many implementations is the concept of polymorphism. Another kind of polymorphism can be established during run-time is to use a pointer to the base class, this is known as run-time polymorphism. To assign the address of an object of a derived class to a pointer pointing to the base class is the essence of polymorphism. For example, you may want to send a different message in each derived class.

PURE VIRTUAL FUNCTION

A pure virtual function is a function that is in an abstract base class and does not have implementation in its class and instead its body has =0 like an assignment, as shown below. A pure virtual function must be preceded by the keyword **virtual**, however, this is optional in its subclasses, but it is a good practice to include the word **virtual** in the declaration.

```
class employee {
    virtual double computesalary()=0;  };
```

Different versions of the pure virtual function's implementation are written in the subclasses. The following example computes the area of a given shape. Whether the area is computed for a circle, square, or rectangle depends on the object that calls the function in the main program.

```cpp
#include<iostream.h>
class shapearea{
 public:   virtual int computearea()=0;
          };//SHAPEAREA
class circle: public shapearea {
 private:  int radius;
 public:   int computearea(){
                    radius=20;
                    cout<<"The area of the circle is: "<<3.14*radius*radius<<endl;
                    return 0; }
          };//CIRCLE
class square: public shapearea{
 private: int side;
 public:  int computearea(){
                    side=12;
                    cout<<"The area of the square is: "<<side*side<<endl;
                    return 0; }
          };//SQUARE
class rectangle: public shapearea{
private:  int length;
          int width;
public:   int computearea(){
                    length=5;
                    width=10;
                    cout<<"The area of the rectangle is: "<<length*width<<endl;
                    return 0; }
          };//RECTANGLE
void main(){
          circle a;
          square b;
          rectangle c;
          a.computearea();
          b.computearea();
          c.computearea();
          }//MAIN
```

Figure 16.10a – Pure Virtual Function Example

```
The area of the circle is: 1256
The area of the square is: 144
The area of the rectangle is: 50
```

Figure 16.10b – Output of 16.10a

OVERRIDING BASE CLASS MEMBERS

In a derived class, you can modify or change the way a function of a class works by redefining it; this is called overriding a base class function. If the function is a virtual function it is known as overriding while for a non-virtual function, the redefinition is called redefining.

EARLY BINDING VERSUS LATE BINDING

The association of the function's name with the starting address of the function's code (entry point) is known as binding. A function's name should bind to the code that implements the function. Early binding is also known as compile-time binding, when the compiler determines which function (code) will be executed. An alternative to early binding is late binding, or run-time binding. In late binding the function to be executed is determined during run time, not during compile time.

RUN-TIME POLYMORPHISM

Polymorphism means many forms, using one name throughout the program for a function but this function has several definitions. In other words, associating multiple meanings to one function name. Run-time polymorphism (late binding) is when a function to be called finds its associated definition during the program execution rather than normal compiling time. For runtime polymorphism, a different version of a virtual function may be used in a base or other derived classes. In addition, a pointer or a reference to a base class is used to refer to each virtual function after being assigned by the object.

```
#include <iostream.h>
class B {
public: virtual vm( ){cout <<"HERE IS THE BASE FUNCTION "<<endl;}
        };//B
class D : public B {
public: virtual  vm( ){ cout <<"HERE IS THE DERIVED FUNCTION "<<endl;}
        };//D
void main(){
        B obb;
        D obd;
        B* obp;
        obp= &obb;
        obp->vm();
        obp=&obd;
        obp->vm();
        }//MAIN
```

Figure 16.11a – Program to demonstrate run-time polymorphism

```
HERE IS THE BASE FUNCTION
HERE IS THE DERIVED FUNCTION
```

Figure 16.11b – Output of 16.11a

ABSTRACT CLASS AND PURE VIRTUAL FUNCTIONS

A class with at least one pure virtual function is known as an *abstract base class*. A *pure virtual function* does not have implementation in its class but will be overridden at later time in a derived class. It is important to know that you cannot create an object from the abstract base class.

FRIEND ACCESS RIGHTS AND INHERITANCE

A class can make all of its private members accessible to another class by a friend declaration. A friend function is not a member of the class but has access to the class's members. The friend declaration is placed inside the class and is preceded by the keyword **friend** and its definition is treated as a regular non-member function. In the friend function definition the keyword **friend** does not has to be included. Friend functions may violate the concept of encapsulation. Just to recall, in inheritance the private members of a base class are not accessible by the derived class.

WHAT WOULD NOT BE INHERITED

A derived class inherits all members except the friend functions and the overloaded operators. The constructor, destructor, copy constructor, and assignment operator of the base class are not inherited but can be used by the derived classes in conjunction with their own.

WHERE DOES ABSTRACTION COME FROM

The word abstraction comes from the Latin word *abs* meaning *"away from"* and the word *trahere* meaning to *"draw"*. The idea is to take away the unnecessary detailed characteristics and reduce it to a form so that it can be used efficiently with less complexity, yet is identifiable. In programming, abstraction is a word often used these days. It is related to encapsulation, meaning putting data and its related functionality together under a name (known as class). Abstraction hides data (details) and restrains unwanted access. This will emphasize the separation of implementation from the interface. The notion of Abstract Data Type (ADT) is to build user defined types in a similar way as system data types which encompasses necessary data and operations and from which objects are instantiated and then used. For example, an employee class that is a user-defined type should behave the same way as built in types such as int (integer).

IS-A RELATIONSHIP AND HAS-A RELATIONSHIP

When a class inherits another class, the relationship is **is-a**. For example, when having a student class and a part-time student class that inherits the student class, the relationship is **is-a**. Inheritance is based on is-a relationship; a part time student **is a** student and similarly a salaried employee **is an** employee. When a class is nested inside another class

542

the relationship would be **has-a**. For example, there are two classes such as class employee and class date, and the class date is a member of the class employee.

TOPICS NOT COVERED HERE

There are certain member functions such as overloaded operators that cannot be inherited. Multiple inheritance can pose its own problems as to which base class the derived members belong to especially if there are generations of inheritance. Similarly, the constructor initialization of a base class whether there is a default constructor or not can become complicated. Conversion of one type to another can also become troublesome. A constructor cannot be virtual but a destructor can be virtual. Assigning one object of a inherited class to another can pose a problem due to type compatibility and, instead, pointer assignment may be a solution. Many people argued that single inheritance is sufficient and that multiple inheritance will cause errors for programmers due to the ambiguity of the members and the complexity in regards to initializing the objects by their constructors and cleaning them up by destructors. However, Microsoft's Foundation Classes (MFC) use multiple inheritance.

CLOSING REMARKS AND LOOKING AHEAD

Inheritance is a powerful feature of Object-Oriented-Programming that promotes code reusability and extensibility. By inheritance a new class can be created by extending the existing classes and by doing so, you do not reinvent the code but rather you reuse the proven and tested code which in a long run will saves time and cost. In addition, in a complex situation an object can be categorized by a hierarchical classification, progressing from a general class to a specific class. There are three different types of derivations: public, protected, and private. The choice of derivation indicates how the derived class receives the members of the base class. A private member of a base class is inaccessible to the derived class but a function of a derived class can call the non-private functions of base class to access the private data members.

A new class can be derived from one base class (single inheritance) or multiple base classes (multiple inheritance). Before a program is written the hierarchy of classes should be set, this includes the relationship of classes and sharing of the data and member functions. However, it is a common practice to reorganize a class hierarchy by factoring out the common parts of the two classes by creating a new base class and two subclasses. Inheritance can become intense when an object of one class, such as base class, is used instead of an object of the derived classes, or vice versa. Keep in mind that the derived classes have more than what the base class has and as a result a conversion becomes necessary. Moreover, by using the base class pointer it is possible to point to the derived classes. Doing so enables a programmer to access a collection of objects of different classes.

SELF-TEST TRUE / FALSE CHAPTER 16: INHERITANCE

__1. A class may inherit some common data members and member functions that belong to another class.

__2. Inheritance promotes reusability and extensibility and is one of the three pillars of OOP.

__3. The use of inheritance increases the time and cost of development as well as program errors.

__4. Inheritance has been used to organize knowledge into hierarchical structures, such as in biology.

__5. In the following: class animal: private bird{   bird is the derived class.

__6. The access specifier determines the accessibility of the base class members.

__7. The inheritance access control modifier can be private, public, or protected.

__8. The base class inherits from the pre-existing derived class and the base class is more specific.

__9. When the access specifier is protected, subclasses cannot access base class members.

__10. The default inheritance access type is public when the access control is not specified.

__11. In private inheritance, the non-private base class members become private for the derived class.

__12. Objects of a derived class can directly access private members of the base class.

__13. With public inheritance, the access in the derived class will remain the same as in the base class.

__14. If the base class is inherited as private, the access in the derived class will become public.

__15. When an object of a derived class is created, the constructor for the base class is called first.

__16. A destructor is used to initialize data members of a class.

__17. The destructor for the derived class is called before the base class destructor.

__18. The class iostream.h is not an example of multiple inheritance.

__19. If a class inherits from more than one class, it is considered multiple inheritance.

__20. Virtual functions are defined in the base class and redefined in derived classes.

__21. A pure virtual function is a function that is in an abstract base class and is implemented in subclasses.

__22. In a derived class you cannot override or redefine a base class function.

__23. In late binding, the function to be executed is determined during run time, not during compile time.

__24. A friend function is not a member of a class, but has access to the class' members.

__25. A derived class inherits all members except friend functions and overloaded operators.

CHAPTER 16 INHERITANCE ASSIGNMENTS

Q16a) What would be an advantage of inheriting from an existing class rather than creating a new class from scratch? In building a hierarchical inheritance, how do you go from base class (super class) to the derived class (subclass)? How do you determine steps from generalization to specification?

Q16b) Explain how a geometric shape like a cube is inherited from square and how square is inherited from line and how line inherited from point.

Q16c) Write the general syntax of a class inheritance in C++. What are the access specifiers (access controls)?

Q16d) Why is the access control **protected** used for a member data or a member function in a base class? What would happen to a derived class if protected is changed to private?

Q16e) Explain how a friend of a class can access the member of a class, even the private members. Do you find any problem with this kind of access?

Q16f) What would be the output of the following program?
```
#include <iostream.h>
class B {
protected: int bm; };

class D: public B {
public: accessbm(int x){ bm=x+1;} };

void main(){
        D ob;
        cout<<"bm VALUE IS "<<ob.accessbm(5)<<endl;
        }//MAIN
```

Q16g) What would be the output of the above program after changing the protected to private? How about changing it to public? What would be the drawback?

What would be the output of the following program?
```
#include <iostream.h>
class B {
protected: int bm; };

class DPV: private B {
public: accessbm(int x){ bm=x+1;} };

void main(){
        DPV ob;
        cout<<"bm VALUE IS "<<ob.accessbm(8)<<endl;
        }//MAIN
```

Is there any advantage to making the inheritance access type to private? Explain.

Q16h) What would be the output of the above program after changing the protected to private? How about changing it to public? Can you explain all the different situations of inheritance access type?

Q16i) Which constructor in the following program will be called first?

```
#include <iostream.h>
class B {
public:
        B() { cout<<"BASE CLASS CONSTRUCTOR IS CALLED"<<endl; }  };//B

class  D: public B {
public:
        D(){ cout<<"DERIVED CLASS CONSTRUCTOR IS CALLED"<<endl; } };//D

void main(){
        D dob;
        }//MAIN
```

Q16j) Before running the below program, which desstructor is called first?
```
#include <iostream.h>
class B {
public:
        ~ B() { cout<<"BASE CLASS DESTRUCTOR IS CALLED"<<endl; }  };//B

class  D: public B {
 public:
        ~ D(){ cout<<"DERIVED CLASS DESTRUCTOR IS CALLED"<<endl; } };//D

void main(){
        D dob;
        }//MAIN
```

Q16k) Illustrate the control flow in the following multi-heritance program. Run the program and change the value of each member data from base class to the derived class.
```
#include<iostream.h>
class B1{
public:   int x;
        B1(){}
        B1(int a){x=a;}
        int getx(){ return x;}  };//B1
class B2{
public:   int y;
         B2(){}
        B2(int b){y=b;}
         int gety(){ return y;}  };//B2
class D: public B1, public B2{
public:   int z;
        D(int a, int b, int c):B1(a),B2(b){
                        z=c;}
        int getz(){return z;}  };//D
```

```
void main(){
        D ob(8,7,6);
        cout<<ob.getz()<<endl;
        cout<<ob.getx()<<endl;
        cout<<ob.gety()<<endl;
        }//MAIN
```

Q16l) Using multi-inheritance, simulate the eye color of a child by providing the mother and father eye colors.

Q16m) Explain how a virtual function is used to create run-time polymorphism.

Q16n) What is the difference between a virtual function and a pure virtual function?
What is an abstract class? Define a simple abstract class in program.
Write a program using a pure virtual function to compute the salary of different employees, such as hourly paid with commissions, salaried with overtime, and executive with a fixed bonus.

Q16o) What is early binding and late binding? Give one example where late binding is used.

Q16p) Using late binding and virtual functions, illustrate run-time polymorphism with a program that prints the contents of a stack or the contents of a queue. Similarly, build a stack or a queue.

Q16q) How did the word **abstract** come to exist? Rediscover it.

Q16r) What may go wrong when multiple inheritance is used? What is the reason that languages like Java do not support multiple inheritance?

Q16s) Knowing the concept of inheritance, give an example for encapsulation, information hiding, and abstract data type.

Q16t) Create a universal class for living beings, including their chemistry from atoms to molecules. Use a similar inheritance structure to define the elements of the universe.

Q16u) Design an employee class that supports inheritance. Employees can be full-time or part-time and each can be hourly paid or salaried. You should include manager and department, executive, commission, bonus, overtime pay, and even temporary employee.

CASE STUDY –PAYROLL SYSTEM PHASE 16: INHERITANCE

In this phase, you are to use inheritance to allow your program to accommodate both full-time and part-time employees. Create two subclasses of the class employee, one for full-time employees and the other for part-time employees. The gross pay will be computed differently in each of the subclasses. The part-time employee class includes the number of hours worked and hourly rate, while the full-time employee class includes a set salary and any bonuses the employee may receive.

CHAPTER 17

CHARACTER MANIPULATIONS, STRING CLASS, AND IOSTREAM

Each strike or multiple strikes on the keyboard represents a character: a letter, a digit, or a symbol. However, some characters are not labeled on the keyboard and some of them are not printable. Each character is represented by a numeric code that was agreed upon and standardized by a committee and this is known as ASCII code. Characters are the building blocks of any data in a computer, whether they are integers, doubles, or strings. In fact, one of the first jobs of a system programmer is to convert a sequence of characters to its intended meaning. For example, 1, 2, and 3 (one, two, three) becomes 123 (one hundred twenty three). Similarly, a sequence of characters represents a word, several words form a sentence, and a combination of sentences generates a story.

A C–style string is an array of characters that terminates with a null as its last element. While you can initialize an array to a constant string such as **char name[]="ebrahimi"**, you cannot treat the string as other built-in types such as **int** or **double** by using = for assignment or comparison (relational) operators such as > between two strings. Library functions **strcpy( )** and **strncpy( )** are used to copy (assign) one string to another. Similarly, library functions **strcmp( )** and **strncmp( )** are used to compare two strings for equality, less than or greater than. Originally in C, string-handling functions were introduced in **string.h** and later on in C++, in **cstring**, include directive (header file). Upon the introduction of string as STL in 1994, strings are now treated as other basic data types as a class with many more capabilities. String class provides a rich set of members for string manipulation that surpasses the traditional C-style null-terminated string. However, let us not forget that when it comes to speed, some of the C-style functions supersede the functions of string class. With the string class, operations are done in the same way as other operation on integer or float data types. Since string class is a STL container, many other components like iterators and algorithms work and makes string manipulation and pattern matching easier because you don't have to built the function from scratch.

STRIPPING THE WHITE SPACE WITH CONSOLE INPUT - cin

White space is considered a space, a tab, a vertical tab, or a new line. When receiving input using **cin** (an object of istream, which is also known as console input), the leading white space to an input is ignored. In several situations, ignoring white space is useful, but there are cases where white space is part of the data, such as a street address, where we do not want to break the address into separate units. One solution is to replace the white space with punctuation such as a dot (.) as demonstrated by the program below. Additional characters to replace blank spaces can be cumbersome; you may argue that this is not a desirable solution and wish to know an alternative.

```
#include<iostream.h>

void main(){
char streetaddress[50];
cout<<"ENTER STREET ADDRESS: ";
cin>>streetaddress;
cout<<"STREET ADDRESS IS: "<<streetaddress<<endl;
}//MAIN
```

Figure 17.1a – Program to take in a street address

```
ENTER STREET ADDRESS: 71.charles.street.2c
STREET ADDRESS IS: 71.charles.street.2c
```

Figure 17.1b – Output of Figure 17.1a

TESTING FUNCTIONS OF ISTREAM

An istream has four state variables: **goodbit**, **eofbit**, **failbit**, and **badbit** that internally would be set based on the operation performed to the stream. Each of these state variables has an access function: **good( )**, **eof( )**, **fail( )**, and **bad( )** respectively that returns the value of the state variable. In the following program, **failbit** is set when the invalid input is entered. The member function **clear( )** resets the state variables.

```
#include<iostream.h>
#include<stdlib.h>

void main(){
    double hourlyrate;

    cout<<"Please enter your hourly rate: ";
    do {cin>>hourlyrate;
      if(cin.fail())
          {
           cout<<"Error\n";
           exit(1);
           }//IF
      else{cout<<"Please enter your hourly rate: ";
           }//ELSE
    }while(1);//DO WHILE
}//MAIN
```

Figure 17.2a – Example of cin.fail( )

```
Please enter your hourly rate: 5
Please enter your hourly rate: 6
Please enter your hourly rate: seven
Error
```

Figure 17.2b – Output of Figure 17.2a

PRINTING ASCII VALUES

The character A is 65 and character B is 66; can you figure out what character Z is? If you cannot figure it out, the following program demonstrates the ASCII code. You may not have figured out why NULL has an ASCII value of 0 and zero is 48, or why lower case character a is 97 which is larger than upper case A (65). I myself could not figure it out, but one could reason that in the early stages of computing only upper case letters were used and lower case was introduced later. The difference between lower and upper case letters is 32 and magically 32 is the ASCII code for blank space. Between upper case and lower case letters there are six special characters including bracket and backslash.

Moreover, the ASCII value for © is 169 and ½ is 189. You might want to try to print the extended ASCII characters and their values on your computer. This program displays the characters for the ASCII values 65 to 90 and displays the ASCII values for the lower case alphabet 'a' through 'z'.

```cpp
#include<iostream.h>

void main(){
    for (char c=65; c<=90 ; c++)
    cout<<c<<" ";

    cout<<endl;
    for (int i='a'; i<='z'; i++)
    cout<<i<<" ";
}//MAIN
```

Figure 17.3a – Example using ASCII values

```
A B C D E F G H I J K L M N O P Q R S T U V W X Y Z
97 98 99 100 101 102 103 104 105 106 107 108 109 110 111 112 113
114 115 116 117 118 119 120 121 122
```

Figure 17.3b – Output of Figure 17.3a

THREE VERSIONS OF GET( ) MEMBER FUNCTION

Any input data, whether it is from a keyboard or an input file, is a combination of characters. In order to extract each character, this member function of input stream **istream** is used in three ways. The member function **get( )** with a character parameter stores the character being read in the parameter variable. Another version of **get( )** has no parameter, its return value is the character being read. Finally, the third version of get has an array of characters as its parameter where a string can be read.

> **cin.get**(c);   fin.**get**(c);
>
> c=**cin.get**( );   c=fin.**get**( );
>
> **cin.get**(str);   fin.**get**(str);

Recall, fin is an object of the class **ifstream**; it stands for "file in" and is a nice user-convention as shown below:

> **ifstream** fin ("input.dat");

HOW TO BUILD A STRING CHARACTER BY CHARACTER

In order to build a string, the function **get( )** extracts one character at a time and assigns it to an array location. For example, the first character is assigned to the zero element of the array, and similarly the next character is assigned to the next element of the array. After the last character is assigned to the array, a NULL character is assigned to terminate the string. As a result, you can conclude that a string is an array of characters terminated by a NULL. It is important to note that an array of characters without NULL is not a string. Moreover, the difference between "A" and 'A' is that "A" is an array of two characters consisting of 'A' and '\0' while 'A' consists of a single character.

BUILDING A STRING USING get( ) AND A CHARACTER AS PARAMETER

The following program demonstrates how a string is created by using a **get( )** function which gets a character and passes it as a parameter. For example, parameter **c** passes the character back in **get**(c). The **eof( )** function checks for the end-of-file.

```
#include<stdlib.h>
#include<fstream.h>
void main(){
 char c;
 const int MAXSIZE=5;
 char str[MAXSIZE];
 int n = 0;
 do {cin.get(c);
     if(cin.eof()){
                    cout<<"BYE"<<endl; break; }//IF
         else{ str[n] = c;  n++; }//ELSE
 }while (n!=MAXSIZE);
str[n]='\0';
 cout<<"STRING IS :"<<str;
}//MAIN
```

Figure 17.4a – Building a string using cin.get( )

```
abc
STRING IS :abc

abcde
STRING IS :abcde
```

Figure 17.4b – Output of Figure 17.4a

get( ) MEMBER WITH IMPLICIT END-OF-FILE

In the following: **cin.get**(c), the function reads a character to variable **c** and returns a nonzero value. However, at the end-of-file it returns a zero that is used as the loop terminator.

```
#include<stdlib.h>
#include<fstream.h>
void main(){
 char c;
 const int MAXSIZE=5;
 char str[MAXSIZE];
 int n = 0;
 while(cin.get(c)){
        if(n==MAXSIZE){str[n]='\0';break;}//IF
        str[n] = c; n++;}//WHILE
        cout<<"STRING IS :"<<str<<endl;
}//MAIN
```

Figure 17.5a – Using cin.get( ) with implicit end-of-file

```
abc
STRING IS :abc

abcd
STRING IS :abcd
```

Figure 17.5b – Output of Figure 17.5a

int get() FUNCTION WITH NO PARAMETER RETURNS END OF FILE FLAG

Another version of the **get**( ) function does not carry any parameter but its return value is the character and also the end-of-file indicator. Since the end-of-file is –1, the return value is of type integer and not type character. This version is similar to the C version and can be used in situations when we want to count the number of characters or number of lines.

```
#include<iostream.h>
void main(){
    int c;
    while ((c=cin.get())!=EOF){
    cout<<" ECHO "<<char(c)<<endl;
        }//WHILE
    cout<<" END OF FILE IS REACHED "<<endl;
}//MAIN
```

Figure 17.6a – Program using the int get( ) function

```
hello
 ECHO h
 ECHO e
 ECHO l
 ECHO l
 ECHO o
 ECHO
```

Figure 17.6b – Output of Figure 17.6a

SKIPPING WHITE SPACE WITH get( )

Recall, the use of **cin>>c** without setting **cin>>noskipws** causes the white space before an input to be skipped. In contrast, the **get( )** function reads the white space and to skip the white space, you must exclude the white space whenever you do not need it.

```
#include<iostream>
using namespace std;
void main(){
        char c ;
        cin>>noskipws;
        while(cin>>c)
                cout <<c;
}//MAIN
```

Figure 17.7a – Using cin>>noskipws

```
#include<iostream.h>

void main(){
        char c ;
        while(cin.get(c))
                cout <<c;
}//MAIN
```

Figure 17.7c – Using cin.get( )

```
AB  CD
AB  CD
  ABCD
  ABCD
```

Figure 17.7b – Output of Figure 17.7a

```
AB  CD
AB  CD
  ABCD
  ABCD
```

Figure 17.7d – Output of Figure 17.7c

COUNT THE NUMBER OF CHARACTERS: EXCLUDE THE WHITE SPACE

The following program counts the number of characters without counting the white space character (blank, new line, tab and vertical tab).

```
#include<iostream>
using namespace std;
void main(){
        char c;
        int nc=0;
        while(cin.get(c)){
        if((c==' ')||(c=='\t')||(c=='\v'));
        else if(c=='\n') break;
        else nc++;}//WHILE
  cout<<"YOU ENTERED "<<nc<<" CHARACTERS"<<endl;
}//MAIN
```

Figure 17.8a – Counting the number of input characters

```
A    B CD
YOU ENTERED 4 CHARACTERS
```

Figure 17.8b – Output of Figure 17.8a

ACCESSING ENTIRE LINE OR PORTION OF LINE

The function **get( )** can access a portion of a line or an entire line of input accordingly and store it into a string variable. The general syntax for the **get( )** function is **get**(stringvariable, maxsize, delimiter). The function **get**(str,5,'\n') will read up to 5 characters of input or read up to the new line character, whichever comes first. In the following example: **get**(str,5,','); the delimiter is coma (,) instead of new line. It is important to observe that the **get( )** function does not extract or store the new line or any delimiter. To solve this problem either use another **get( )** function, **ignore( )** function, or **getline( )** function to handle the delimiter.

ignore() MEMBER FUNCTION

The **ignore()** function of input stream reads and discards up to a specified number of characters provided by its argument or stops and discards the delimiter, such as a new line. If a delimiter is not specified, the EOF is considered the delimiter by default.

> **cin.ignore**(20,'\n');

In the above example, the **ignore( )** function reads and discards up to 20 characters or stops when \n is reached and discards the new line. If the data is less than 20 characters long, all its characters are read. Two common uses of **ignore( )** are after the **get( )** string and if only certain fields of the data stream need to be extracted from the rest of the stream.

PORTION OR ENTIRE LINE: FUNCTION getline()

The function **getline( )**; can read a portion of a line or the entire line depending on the argument setting. The general form of the **getline( )** function is: **getline**(stringvariable, maxsize, delimiter). The delimiter is a new line by default but others such as coma (,) can be used as well. Normally, maxsize is the size of the string but any other number less than maxsize can be used. The **getline( )** function stops reading either when the maxsize characters is put into the array, including the null character, or upon encountering the new line, which ever comes first. It is important to note that **getline( )** will extract the new line or delimiter and not save it (discards it).

DIFFERENCE BETWEEN getline( ) and get( )

The function **getline( )** extracts the new line from the input stream and discards it while the function **get( )** leaves the new line in the input stream and makes it the first character for the next input operation. It seems very confusing, but after some practice you will overcome this obstacle. Just remember, **getline( )** gets the line and throws the delimiter out while the function **get( )** stops with the delimiter.

```
#include<iostream.h>

void main(){
        char streetaddress[100];
        cout<<"ENTER STREET ADDRESS: ";
        cin.getline(streetaddress,100);
        cout<<"STREET ADDRESS IS: "<<streetaddress<<endl;
}//MAIN
```

Figure 17.9a – Program demonstrating the cin.getline( ) function

```
ENTER STREET ADDRESS: 7 charles street 2c
STREET ADDRESS IS: 7 charles street 2c
```

Figure 17.9b – Output of Figure 17.9a

put() FUNCTION

You have used an **ostream** object such as **cout**<<c to display a character. However, a member of an output function like **put**(c) produces the same output. The **put**( ) function is used to display (output) a character, **cout.put**(ch) displays to the console while fout.**put**(ch) writes a character to the file, assuming fout is the object of **ofstream**. Although the **put**( ) function is the opposite of the **get**( ) function, **put**( ) is used less than the **get**( ) function because using **cout** alone does the same job.

```
#include<fstream.h>
#include<conio.h>
void main(){
        char c;
        ofstream fout("data.out");
        do{
                cout<<"ENTER A CHARACTER, ESC TO STOP: "<<flush;
                c=getch();
                if(c==27) break;
                else{
                cout.put(c);
                cout<<endl;
                fout.put(c);}}
        while(1);
}//MAIN
```

Figure 17.10a – Using the put( ) function to write to the screen and a file

ENTER A CHARACTER, ESC TO STOP: e
ENTER A CHARACTER, ESC TO STOP: b
ENTER A CHARACTER, ESC TO STOP: r
ENTER A CHARACTER, ESC TO STOP: a
ENTER A CHARACTER, ESC TO STOP: h
ENTER A CHARACTER, ESC TO STOP: i
ENTER A CHARACTER, ESC TO STOP: m
ENTER A CHARACTER, ESC TO STOP: i
ENTER A CHARACTER, ESC TO STOP:
Press any key to continue

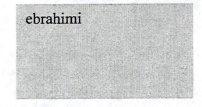

ebrahimi

Figure 17.10c - data.out file

Figure 17.10b – Output of Figure 17.10a

CHARACTER FUNCTIONS #include <ctype.h>

C/C++ provides several character manipulation functions that are defined in the **type.h** or **ctype.h** header file and must be included in your program by using **#include<type.h>**. Each function takes in a character to be tested and returns either a non-zero value (true) or zero value (false).

isalpha(c)   is c alphabetic ('A'- 'Z' or 'a'-'z')

isupper(c)   is c upper case ('A'-'Z')

islower(c)   is c lower case ('a'-'z')

isdigit(c)   is c digit ('0'- '9')

isalnum(c)   is c alpha numeric ('A'- 'Z' ,'a'-'z' or '0'-'9')

ispunc(c)   is c punctuation (, . ; etc.)

isspace(c)   is c blank space, tab, new line, or vertical tab.

The following case conversion functions take a character as a parameter and returns the resulting character.

toupper(c)   converting to uppercase if c is lowercase.

tolower(c)   converting to lowercase if c is uppercase.

CONVERTING TO UPPERCASE: PROGRAM - toupper(c)

The following program converts a lower case letter to its corresponding upper case. While the **toupper( )** function is in the **ctype** include, this function can be written simply with an if statement. Note that the difference between **isupper**(c) and **toupper**(c) is that the former returns true if the character is upper case while **toupper**(c) converts the character if it is not uppercase.

```
#include<iostream.h>
#include<ctype.h>
void main(){
        char c;
        cin>>c;
        if(isupper(c)) cout<<c;
        else {c=toupper(c);cout<<c;}
}//MAIN
```

Figure 17.11a – Using isupper( ) and toupper( )

```
t
T
```

Figure 17.11b – Output of Figure 17.11a

WRITING YOUR OWN CHARACTER FUNCTION: mytoupper(c)

The following program takes input of characters from the keyboard and converts them to upper case if they are lower case. Note that the lower case has a higher ASCII value than its corresponding upper case. Interestingly, the difference between a lower case and its upper case letter is the number 32, which is the ASCII code for a blank space.

```
#include<iostream.h>
char mytoupper(char);
void main(){
        char c;
        while(cin>>c)
        cout<<mytoupper(c);
 }//MAIN

char mytoupper(char c){
 if((c>='a')&&(c<='z')) return(c-('a'-'A'));
 else return c;
}//MYTOUPPER
```

Figure 17.12a – Writing a mytoupper( ) function

```
Ebrahimi
EBRAHIMI
```

Figure 17.12b – Output of Figure 17.12a

WRITING YOUR OWN ISUPPER FUNCTION: myisupper(c)

The **myisupper( )** function checks to see if the character is capital by checking if it is greater or equal to 'A' and less than or equal to 'Z'; it returns 1 if the character passed is upper case and 0 if it is not.

```cpp
#include<iostream.h>

int myisupper(char);
void main(){
        char c;
        cin>>c;
        if(myisupper(c))
                cout<<"UPPERCASE";
        else
                cout<<"NOT UPPERCASE";
}//MAIN

int myisupper(char c){
        if((c>='A')&&(c<='Z')) return 1;
        else return 0;
}//MYISUPPER
```

Figure 17.13a – Writing a myisupper( ) function

```
e
NOT UPPERCASE
```

Figure 17.13b – Output of Figure 17.13a

putback(c) VERSUS peek( )

The **putback( )** function puts back the last character read by the **get( )** function to the input stream. The **peek( )** function which examines the next character from the input stream without advancing, can be used instead of **get( )** and **putback()**.

WRITING A LEXICAL ANALYZER WITH C/C++

The C/C++ language is known as a language for writing systems such as compilers. One reason for selecting C/C++ as a language for system programming is the way in which characters are handled. For example, the following program shows how through simple character manipulation it is possible to write a lexical analyzer for a programming language that extracts and tokenizes (identifies) the words of a language. The program below distinguishes words from numbers by using ASCII values.

```
#include<iostream.h>
#include<string>

void main(){
       char c;
       int number;
       char identifier[100];

       c=cin.peek();
       if ((c>='0')&&(c<='9'))
       {cin>>number;
        cout<<"NUMBER IS: "<<number<<endl;}
       else if (((toupper( c )>='A' ) && (toupper(c ) <='Z')) || (c=='_'))
       {cin>>identifier;
        cout<<"IDENTIFIER IS: "<<identifier<<endl;}
}//MAIN
```

Figure 17.14a – Program that determines whether the input is a word or a number based on ASCII values

```
name
IDENTIFIER IS: name
```

Figure 17.14b – Output of Figure 17.14a

The following program duplicates the above program except that it uses built-in functions **isdigit( )** and **isalpha( )**.

```
#include<iostream.h>
#include<string>

void main(){
        char c;
        int number;
        char identifier[100];

        c=cin.peek();
        if (isdigit(c))
        {cin>>number;
         cout<<"NUMBER IS: "<<number<<endl;}
        else if (isalpha(c)||(c=='_'))
        {cin>>identifier;
         cout<<"IDENTIFIER IS: "<<identifier<<endl;}
}//MAIN
```

Figure 17.15a – Using isdigit( ) and isalpha( )

```
1234
NUMBER IS: 1234
```

Figure 17.15b – Output of Figure 17.15a

CHARACTER DIGITS TO A NUMBER

A digit, like other characters, is represented by a code (ASCII code). For example, digit 0 ASCII code is 48 and character 1 ASCII code is 49 and so on. A number consists of a sequence of character digits that must be parsed (evaluated) to its value upon entry or file access. In fact, one job of **cin**>>number is to convert the characters to its proper data type such as integer. The following program illustrates the evaluation of characters 123 (one two three) to its numeric value 123, which is read as one hundred twenty three.

```
#include<iostream.h>
#include<ctype.h>
void main(){
        char c;
        int value=0;
        c=cin.get();
        if(isdigit(c)) value=c-48;
         while(isdigit (c=cin.get())){
                value=value *10 +(c-48);
         }//WHILE
        cout<<"THE VALUE IS: "<<value<<endl;
}//MAIN
```

Figure 17.16a – Converting characters to their numerical value

```
123
THE VALUE IS: 123
```

Figure 17.16b – Output of Figure 17.16a

BUILT-IN FUNCTIONS TO CONVERT NUMERICAL STRING TO ITS NUMERICAL VALUE

The following program demonstrates how a string is converted to its numerical value using the **atoi( )** (alpha to integer) function.

```
#include<iostream.h>
#include<stdlib.h>

void main(){
        char str1[] = "1234";
        char str2[] = "5678";
        int sum = atoi(str1) + atoi(str2);
        cout << "SUM OF TWO NUMBERS IS: "<<sum<<endl;
}//MAIN
```

Figure 17.17a – Using the atoi( ) function

```
SUM OF TWO NUMBERS IS: 6912
```

Figure 17.17b – Output of Figure 17.17a

STRING FUNCTIONS TO MANIPULATE: #include <string.h>

In C/C++, a string is not a data type; it is a null-terminated array of characters. String manipulation is done through a series of functions provided by #include <string.h>. Depending on your compiler, you may need to include <cstring.h> or simply <cstring> (the newer version of <string.h>). In the standardization of C/C++, STL string was added to the language and will be discussed in a later chapter. The following is a list of common functions used to handle strings:

strcmp(s1,s2); compares two string for s1<s2 ,s1==s2; s1> s2 returning negative, zero or a positive number respectively.

strcpy(s1, s2); copies (assigns) one string to another string, the s2 is assigned to s1.

strlen(s); finds the length of a string, the null character,'\0', is not counted.

strcat(s1, s2); concatenates (appends) one string to another string, s2 is concatenated to s1.

strncmp(s1,s2,n); partially compares two strings only up to a certain number of characters(n). It is the same as **strcmp**( ) except that the whole string is not compared, the strings are compared up to n characters.

strncpy(s1,s2,n); partially copies one string to another by providing the number of characters(n).

stricmp(s1,s2); compares two strings regardless of whether they are lower case or upper case.

STRING COMPARISON: strcmp( )

The **strcmp**( ) function compares two strings and returns a positive number if the first string is greater than second string, returns a negative number if the first string is less than the first string, and returns 0 if they are equal. **strcmp**( ) compares the strings according to the ASCII values of their characters, starting with the first character of each. If the first two are equal, then the next two are compared, and so on, until a difference is found. If the first two characters of each string are different, the return value of **strcmp**( ) is based on their values. If no difference is found between the two strings, **strcmp**( ) returns 0.

```
#include<iostream.h>
#include<string.h>
void main(){
        char str1[100];
        char str2[100];
        cout<<"ENTER A STRING: ";
        cin>>str1;
        cout<<"ENTER ANOTHER STRING: ";
        cin>>str2;
        if(strcmp(str1,str2)==0)
                cout<<"THE TWO STRINGS HAVE THE SAME ASCII VALUE";
        else if(strcmp(str1,str2)>0)
                cout<<"THE FIRST STRING HAS A GREATER ASCII VALUE";
        else if(strcmp(str1,str2)<0)
                cout<<"THE SECOND STRING HAS A GREATER ASCII VALUE";
}//MAIN
```

Figure 17.18a – Program using strcmp( ) to compare two input strings

```
ENTER A STRING: ABC
ENTER ANOTHER STRING: abc
THE SECOND STRING HAS A GREATER ASCII VALUE
```

Figure 17.18b – Output of Figure 17.18a

This example uses the **stricmp**(s1,s2) function to compare two strings, independent of the case of the letters.

```
#include<iostream>
#include<string.h>
using namespace std;
void main(){
        char str1[10];
        char str2[10];
        cout<<"ENTER STRING: ";
        cin>>str1;
        cout<<"ENTER ANOTHER STRING: ";
        cin>>str2;
        if(stricmp(str1, str2)==0)
                cout<<"THE STRINGS ARE EQUAL"<<endl;
        else
                cout<<"THE STRINGS ARE NOT EQUAL"<<endl;
}//MAIN
```

Figure 17.19a – Comparing two strings using stricmp( )

```
ENTER STRING: EBRAHIMI
ENTER ANOTHER STRING: ebrahimi
THE STRINGS ARE EQUAL
```

Figure 17.19b – Output of Figure 17.19a

CUSTOMIZING YOUR OWN STRING COMPARE FUNCTIONS

You can create your own functions to compare strings as shown in the following program with the **mystrcmp**(char *s, char *t) function. This function compares two strings according to the ASCII values of the corresponding characters starting with the first character, in the same manner as the built-in **strcmp** function.

```cpp
#include<iostream>
#include<string>
using namespace std;
int mystrcmp(char *s, char *t){
        while(*s!='\0'){
                if(*s!=*t)return *s-*t;
                ++s; ++t; }//WHILE
        return *s-*t;  }//MYSTRCMP
void main(){
        char str1[10],str2[10];
        int result;
        cout<<"ENTER FIRST STRING :";
        cin>>str1;
        cout<<"ENTER SECOND STRING:";
        cin>>str2;
        result=mystrcmp(str1,str2);
        if(result<0)       cout<<"FIRST STRING IS LESS."<<endl;
        else if(result>0) cout<<"FIRST STRING IS LARGER."<<endl;
        else               cout<<"BOTH ARE EQUAL."<<endl;    }//MAIN
```

Figure 17.20a – Example of a customized string compare function

```
ENTER FIRST STRING    :alireza
ENTER SECOND STRING:ebrahimi
FIRST STRING IS LESS.

ENTER FIRST STRING    :ebrahimi
ENTER SECOND STRING:alireza
FIRST STRING IS LARGER.

ENTER FIRST STRING    :ebrahimi
ENTER SECOND STRING:ebrahimi
BOTH ARE EQUAL.
```

Figure 17.20b – Output of Figure 17.20a

566

The program below utilizes another customized string compare function:
mystrequal(char s[],char t[]), it returns 1 if the strings are equal and 0 if they are not.

```cpp
#include<iostream>
#include<string>
using namespace std;

int mystrequal(char s[],char t[]){
        int i=0;
        while(s[i]==t[i]){
                if(s[i]==NULL) return 1;
                s[i]++;t[i]++;
                i++;  }//WHILE
        return 0; }//MYSTREQUAL

void main(){
        char pass1[6],pass2[6];
        int result;
        cout<<"PLEASE ENTER YOUR NEW PASSWORD        :";
        cin>>pass1;
        cout<<"PLEASE RE-ENTER YOUR NEW PASSWORD :";
        cin>>pass2;
        result=mystrequal(pass1,pass2);
        if(result==0)
                cout<<"YOUR PASSWORD DOES NOT MATCH."<<endl;
        else
                cout<<"YOUR PASSWORD IS ACCEPTED."<<endl; }//MAIN
```

Figure 17.21a – Writing a function to test the equality of two strings

```
PLEASE ENTER YOUR NEW PASSWORD        :secret
PLEASE RE-ENTER YOUR NEW PASSWORD :secret
YOUR PASSWORD IS ACCEPTED.
```

Figure 17.21b – Output of Figure 17.21a

The next program demonstrates a condensed version of the **mystrequal**(char *s,char *t) function. It uses pointers rather than array notation.

```
#include<iostream>
#include<string>
using namespace std;

int mystrequal(char *s,char *t){
        while(*s==*t){
                if(*s==NULL) return 1;
                s++;t++; }//WHILE
        return 0;  }//MYSTREQUAL

void main(){
        char pass1[6],pass2[6];
        int result;
        cout<<"PLEASE ENTER YOUR NEW PASSWORD      :";
        cin>>pass1;
        cout<<"PLEASE RE-ENTER YOUR NEW PASSWORD :";
        cin>>pass2;
        result=mystrequal(pass1,pass2);
        if(result==0)
                cout<<"YOUR PASSWORD DOES NOT MATCH."<<endl;
        else
                cout<<"YOUR PASSWORD IS ACCEPTED."<<endl; }//MAIN
```

Figure 17.22a – mystrequal( ) written in pointer notation

```
PLEASE ENTER YOUR NEW PASSWORD      :password
PLEASE RE-ENTER YOUR NEW PASSWORD :pword
YOUR PASSWORD DOES NOT MATCH.
```

Figure 17.22b – Output of 17.22a

STRING COPY: strcpy(string2, string1)

The following program demonstrates how one string is copied to another using the **strcpy(str2, str1)** function; string str1 is copied to str2. The program below uses the **strcpy** function to swap two strings with the use of a temporary string.

```
#include<iostream.h>
#include<string.h>

void main(){
 char str1[10], str2[10], temp[10];
 cout<<"ENTER STRING 1: ";
 cin>>str1;
 cout<<"ENTER STRING 2: ";
 cin>>str2;

 strcpy(temp,str1);
 strcpy(str1,str2);
 strcpy(str2,temp);

 cout<<"AFTER SWAP"<<endl;
 cout<<"STRING 1: "<<str1<<endl;
 cout<<"STRING 2: "<<str2<<endl;
}//MAIN
```

Figure 17.23a – Swapping two strings using the strcpy( ) function

```
ENTER STRING 1: alireza
ENTER STRING 2: ebrahimi
AFTER SWAP
STRING 1: ebrahimi
STRING 2: alireza
```

Figure 17.23b – Output of Figure 17.23a

569

CUSTOMIZING YOUR OWN STRING COPY FUNCTIONS

Customized functions can also copy one string to another. The following example implements **mystrcopy**(char **s, char t**) using compact pointer notation.

```
#include<iostream>
#include<string>
using namespace std;
void mystrcopy(char *s,char *t){ while(*s++=*t++); }//MYSTRCOPY
void main(){
        char pass1[6], pass2[6];
        cout<<"PLEASE ENTER YOUR NEW PASSWORD: ";
        cin>>pass2;
        mystrcopy(pass1, pass2);
        cout<<"COPIED TO PASSWORD: "<<pass1<<endl;  }//MAIN
```

Figure 17.24a – mystrcopy( ) function in compact pointer notation

```
PLEASE ENTER YOUR NEW PASSWORD: secret
COPIED TO PASSWORD: secret
```

Figure 17.24b – Output of Figure 17.24a

This program shows another version of a function to copy a string, **mystrcopy**(char s[], char t[]) which uses explicit array notation.

```
#include<iostream>
#include<string>
using namespace std;
void mystrcopy(char s[], char t[]){
        int i=0;
        while(s[i]=t[i])
                i++;  }//MYSTRCOPY
void main(){
        char pass1[6], pass2[6];
        cout<<"PLEASE ENTER YOUR NEW PASSWORD: ";
        cin>>pass2;
        mystrcopy(pass1, pass2);
        cout<<"COPIED TO PASSWORD: "<<pass1<<endl;   }//MAIN
```

Figure 17.25a – mystrcopy( ) function in array notation

```
PLEASE ENTER YOUR NEW PASSWORD: secret
COPIED TO PASSWORD: secret
```

Figure 17.25b – Output of Figure 17.25a

PARTIAL COMPARISON: strncmp(str1, str2, n)

The following program shows how strings can be compared partially using **strncmp(str1, str2, n)**. This function matches **n** characters of the strings rather than the entire string.

```
#include<iostream.h>
#include<string.h>

void main(){
 char names[5][6]={"JOHN","JACK","JAKE","JANET","JILL"};
 for(int i=0;i<4;i++){
        if(strncmp(names[i],"JAKE",2)==0)
        cout<<names[i]<<" ";}//FOR
}//MAIN
```

Figure 17.26a – Partial string comparison using strncmp( ) function

```
JACK JAKE JANET
```

Figure 17.26b – Output of Figure 17.26a

STRING CONCATENATION: strcat(s1,s2)

Use the **strcat(s1,s2)** function to concatenate two strings as shown below.

```
#include<iostream.h>
#include<string.h>

void main(){
        char str[15]="Hello ";
        strcat(str, "World");
        cout<<str<<endl;
}//MAIN
```

Figure 17.27a – String concatenation using strcat( )

```
Hello World
```

Figure 17.27b – Output of Figure 17.27a

A STREAM THAT CONTAINS MANY STRINGS

A single stream can contain many strings in sequence, as the following program demonstrates. The location of the beginning of each string within the stream is saved in an array of pointers, in this case called p.

```cpp
#include<iostream.h>
#include<string.h>
char* p[20];
char strcans[100];
char word[10];
void main(){
        int len,i=0,j=0,n=0;
        cout<<"ENTER 5 WORDS"<<endl;
        while(i<5){
                cout<<"ENTER A WORD :";
                cin>>word;
                p[i]=strcans+n;
                strcpy(strcans+n,word);
                len=strlen(word);
                n=n+len+1;
                i++;}//WHILE
        cout<<"THE LIST IS"<<endl;
        while(j<i){
                cout<<p[j]<<endl;
                j++;}//WHILE
}//MAIN
```

Figure 17.28a – Program with a stream containing five words in sequence and an array of pointers to the beginning of the words

```
ENTER 5 WORDS
ENTER A WORD :alireza
ENTER A WORD :ebrahimi
ENTER A WORD :jason
ENTER A WORD :tolga
ENTER A WORD :edyta
THE LIST IS
alireza
ebrahimi
jason
tolga
edyta
```

Figure 17.28b – Output of Figure 17.28a

FORMAT FUNCTIONS OF IOSTREAM

When we output text to the screen or to a file, we may want to format it into columns of a certain width or format numbers to display properly; to do this we can use functions provided in the **#include<iomanip.h>** directive.

setw(int i) set the output field value to I

setprecision(int i) number of digit to the right of decimal point

setfill(char c) fill character with whatever c is

This example uses the **setprecision**() function to display the fixed floating point number to two decimal places. The **setw**() function sets the width of the column and **setfill**() designates a character that will fill the empty spaces, note that the default justification for numbers is right.

```
#include<iostream.h>
#include<iomanip.h>
void main(){
      float num=25.453;
      cout<<"0123456789"<<endl<<endl;
      cout<<setiosflags(ios::fixed);
      cout<<setw(10)<<setprecision(2)<<setfill('$')<<num;
}//MAIN
```

Figure 17.29a – Using setw( ), setprecision( ), and setfill( )

```
0123456789

$$$$$25.45
```

Figure 17.29b – Output of Figure 17.29a

JUSTIFICATION: FORMAT IOSTREAM

To format text to fit within a set amount of space use **setw( )** to allocate the size of the column. **setiosflags(ios::left)** and **setiosflags(ios::right)** are used to justify the text to the left or to the right. The **resetiosflags( )** function is used to reset the justification set by the **setiosflags( )** function.

```
#include<iostream.h>
#include<iomanip.h>
void main (){
        cout << "0123456789" << endl;
        cout <<setw(10)<< 2222 << endl;
        cout <<setw(10)<< "ABCD" << endl;
        cout <<setiosflags(ios::left)<<setw(10)<<2222<<endl;
        cout <<setw(10)<<"ABCD"<<endl;
        cout <<setw(10)<<resetiosflags(ios::left)<<2222<<endl;
        cout<<setw(10)<<"ABCD"<<endl;
}//MAIN
```

Figure 17.30a – Program to demonstrate text formatting

```
0123456789
      2222
      ABCD
2222
ABCD
      2222
      ABCD
```

Figure 17.30b – Output of Figure 17.30a

INVISIBLE INPUT CHARACTER: PASSWORD PROGRAM USING getch()

This password program uses the **getch**() to allow the user to type their password without having the letters show on the screen. The **getch**( ) function gets the character directly from the keyboard without displaying it on the screen. The following program displays a star in place of each letter typed.

```cpp
#include <conio.h>
#include<iostream.h>
#include<string.h>
int main(){
        char str[7];int limit=0;
        while(limit<=3) {
                cout<<"\nPlease Enter your password (6 char) :"<<endl;
                for(int i=0;i<6;i++){str[i] = getch(); cout<<'*';cout.flush();}//FOR
                str[i]='\0';
                if(strcmp(str,"secret")==0){
                        cout<<"\nYour Password is ACCEPTED"<<endl;
                        return 1;}//IF
                else{cout<<"\nYour Password is incorrect. Please try again."<<endl;
                        limit++;}//ELSE
        }//WHILE
        cout<<"\nSorry, you've used all your chances."<<endl;
        return 0;
}//MAIN
```

Figure 17.31a – Program using getch( ) to mask input

```
Please Enter your password (6 char) :
******
Your Password is incorrect. Please try again.
Please Enter your password (6 char) :
******
Your Password is incorrect. Please try again.
Please Enter your password (6 char) :
******
Your Password is ACCEPTED
```

Figure 17.31b – Output of Figure 17.31a

FILE ENCRYPTION

Security of a document is a major concern in information handling. Encryption is an easy way to secure a document and many algorithms have been designed to tackle this problem. A file is a stream of characters; and the encrypted result as well is a file of characters that has to be brought back to its original form. By simply changing an ASCII value to its next value or replacing a character with the next character or using an associate character array are some of the solutions to this interesting problem. The following program creates an encrypted file using an associated array; it then uses the associate array to decrypt the file and display the result.

```
#include<fstream.h>
#include<stdio.h>

void main(){
        char c;
        char key[]={'M','O','Q','S','T','L','N','P','U','X','Z','F','A','G','B',
                                'H','C','V','D','E','I','R','Y','J','W','K'};
        ifstream fin1("data1.txt",ios::in);
        ofstream fout("data2.txt",ios::app);
        while(fin1>>c)
                fout<<key[c%65];
        fout.close();
        ifstream fin2("data2.txt",ios::in);
        while(fin2>>c)
                cout<<key[c%65];
}//MAIN
```

Figure 17.32a – Example of simple file encryption and decryption

HELLO

PTFFB

Figure 17.32b - data1.txt   *Figure 17.32c - data2.txt*

HELLO

Figure 17.32d – Output of Figure 17.32a

If you lost the decryption key to a file and want to bring it back to its original form, how would you decrypt it? A solution is to count the frequency of each letter and look at the table of the most frequently used letters. Then sort the letters according to their frequency and substitute the most frequently used letters in language with the most frequently used letters in the encrypted file. For example, in English, the letter E is the most frequently used letter in the alphabet so try to substitute the most frequent letter in the encrypted file with E, and so on.

ARITHMETIC OPERATIONS BEYOND THEIR MEMORY LIMIT

Adding or multiplying two numbers can result in overflow due to the size of memory assigned by the compiler to each data type. Storing each number in a string, then applying an arithmetic operation and storing the result in another string can resolve this problem. For example, each corresponding character element is converted to its numerical value starting from the right the numbers are added, and the sum and carry are saved. The answer is stored to a third string, character-by-character, and displayed. This way there is no limit on the size of the numbers that can be entered.

```cpp
#include<iostream>
#include<string>
using namespace std;
void main(){
        string snum1, snum2, sum;
        int len1, len2, d1, d2;
        int d3=0;
        int carry=0;
        cout<<"Enter a number to add: ";        cin>>snum1;
        cout<<"Enter another number: ";         cin>>snum2;
        len1 = snum1.length();
        len2 = snum2.length();
        if(len1>=len2) sum.resize(len1+1);
        else sum.resize(len2+1);
        int sumlen=sum.length();
        while(len1>0 && len2>0){        d1 = snum1[--len1]-48;
                                        d2 = snum2[--len2]-48;
                                        d3 = d1 + d2 + carry;
                                        if(d3>=10) {carry=1; d3=d3-10;}
                                        else carry=0;
                                        d3 = d3 + 48;
                                        sum[--sumlen]=d3;}//WHILE
        while(len1>0){ d1 = snum1[--len1]-48;
                        d3= d1 + carry;
                        if(d3>=10) {carry=1; d3=d3-10;}
                        else carry=0;
                        d3 = d3 + 48;
                        sum[--sumlen]=d3;}//WHILE
        while(len2>0){ d2 = snum2[--len2]-48;
                        d3 = d2 +carry;
                        if(d3>=10) {carry=1; d3=d3-10;}
                        else carry=0;
                        d3 = d3 + 48;
                        sum[--sumlen]=d3;}//WHILE
        if(carry!=0) sum[--sumlen]='1';
        else sum[--sumlen]='0';
        cout<<"The sum is: "<<sum<<endl;        }//MAIN
```

Figure 17.33a – Program to add two large numbers using strings

```
Enter a number to add: 1234567890123456789
Enter another number:  9876543210987654321
The sum is: 11111111101111111110
```

Figure 17.33b – Output of Figure 17.33a

NAMESPACE

In the original header file which has the suffix of .h, all the names used in the header files were global; in addition, the user is able to define their own header files, for ex. #include "search.h". A problem can arise with having everything global if names used in the user-defined header files collide with names used in the system header files. To resolve this problem, namespace was introduced and added to the standardization of C++. For beginners this idea is complex but in the long run it is beneficial. The idea of namespaces is that names are defined within a scope (namespace) to avoid name conflicts. By including namespace, two identical names can be used in the same program.

STRING CLASS FROM STANDARD TEMPLATE LIBRARY (STL)

STL is a large library consisting of classes, their data structures, and algorithms. STL in itself is complex and sophisticated and was added to the language during the standardization of C++. One important class of STL is the definition of string as a data type. This allows strings to be treated in the same manner as other data types such as integer or character and allows the use of operators such as = =, =, and +. Recall, a string is created by an array of characters and terminates with a null character. You used functions strcmp( ) , strcpy( ) and   strcat( ) to compare, copy, and concatenate two strings. With the introduction of STL strings, it is possible to manipulate strings by using the comparison operator (= =) to compare strings, the assignment operator (=) to assign one string to another and the addition operator (+) to concatenate strings.

CONSTRUCTING (INITIALIZING) AN STL STRING

There are several ways to initialize an STL string as shown below:

```
string mystr= "A QUICK BROWN FOX JUMPS OVER A LAZY DOG";
string str2 (mystr);
string str3 (mystr, 8,5);
```

In the last example above the first argument is a string, the second argument is the position of the string, and the third argument is the number of characters to use.

ACCESS OF A STRING ELEMENT

Just like an array, string elements start from 0; therefore, mystr[5] gives the sixth location starting from zero. Alternatively, the method mystr.**at**(5) gives the same result, as shown below.

```
#include<iostream>
#include<string>
using namespace std;
void main(){
        string mystr= "A QUICK BROWN FOX JUMPS OVER A LAZY DOG";
        cout<<mystr[5]<<endl;
        cout<<mystr.at(5)<<endl;
}//MAIN
```

Figure 17.34a – Using the at( ) function to access a string element

```
C
C
```

Figure 17.34b – Output of Figure 17.34a

CONVERTING STL STRING TO NULL TERMINATED STRING (C STRING)

The function **c_str**( ) converts an STL string to a null terminated string so that it is compatible with the traditional operations of C-style strings. One reason to convert a class string to C-style string is when associating a file name to a string as in the program that follows.

```
#include<fstream>
#include<iostream>
#include<string>
using namespace std;
void main(){
        string filename;
        cout<<"ENTER FILE NAME: ";
        cin>>filename;
        ifstream fin(filename.c_str(),ios::in);
        if(fin){
                float salary;
                fin>>salary;
                cout<<"SALARY: "<<salary<<endl;}//IF
        else cout<<"FILE DOES NOT EXIST"<<endl;
}//MAIN
```

Figure 17.35a – Program that converts an STL string to a C-style string

```
ENTER FILE NAME: payroll.dat
SALARY: 150000
```

Figure 17.35b – Output of Figure 17.35a

STL STRING CONCATENATION: str1 + str2

The following program demonstrates the use of the + (concatenation) operator in place of a function. An advantage of using STL strings is that it makes the program much easier to understand.

```
#include<iostream>
#include<string>
using namespace std;

string mystr1="Alireza";
string mystr2="Ebrahimi";
string mystr3;

void main(){
        mystr3 = mystr1 + " " + mystr2;
        cout<<"STRING 1 IS   : "<<mystr1<<endl;
        cout<<"STRING 2 IS   : "<<mystr2<<endl;
        cout<<"NEW STRING IS : "<<mystr3<<endl;
}//MAIN
```

Figure 17.36a – Using the + operator for concatenation in STL

```
STRING 1 IS   : Alireza
STRING 2 IS   : Ebrahimi
NEW STRING IS : Alireza Ebrahimi
```

Figure 17.36b – Output of Figure 17.36a

MAKING PARTIAL STRING OR SUB-STRING:
mystr.substr(startpos, numofposition)

The string class function **substr( )** returns a sub-string beginning at a given starting position up to the number of characters specified.

```
#include<iostream>
#include<string>

using namespace std;
void main(){
        int start,nchar;
        string mystr="Alireza Ebrahimi";
        cout<<mystr<<endl;
        cout<<"substr(0,3)"<<endl;
        cout<<mystr.substr(0,3)<<endl;
        cout<<"substr(3,9)"<<endl;
        cout<<mystr.substr(0,20)<<endl;
        cout<<"Enter Your starting point :";
        cin>>start;
        cout<<"Enter how many character to get :";
        cin>>nchar;
        cout<<mystr.substr(start,nchar)<<endl;
}//MAIN
```

Figure 17.37a – Creating a sub-string using the substr( ) function

```
Alireza Ebrahimi
substr(0,3)
Ali
substr(3,9)
Alireza Ebrahimi
Enter Your starting point :10
Enter how many character to get :5
rahim
```

Figure 17.37b – Output of Figure 17.37a

STRING CLASS FUNCTIONS - MAJOR CATEGORIZATION

One important feature of the string class is the use of the assignment operator (e.g. =), the relational operator(e.g == or <), and + operator (append) similar to the way that it is used with other data types such as integer or float. Alternatively, member functions such as **assign**(), **compare**(), and **append**() respectively perform the same operations as above. Preferably, these functions are used when operations are to be performed on part of the string (not entire string). String manipulation involves more than the above operations, and to perform further operations many functions are added to the string class. The main string functions are: **find**(), **insert**(), and **replace**(). The above functions can be categorized into three parts, when the function is applied to the entire string, part of the string (substring), and when it is applied to a character. Finally, there are functions that do not have parameters, they are implied with the string object, such as, **size**(), **length**(), **clear**(), and **empty**(). Note that the order of the parameters differs from one group of string functions to another. For example: in str1.**assign**(str2,x,n), str2 is the first parameter, while in **compare**, **replace**, and **insert**, the str2 is the last parameter, str1.**compare**(x,n,str2). A justification for having the string at the end is that x and n apply to str1 rather than str2 (note that x is the starting position and n is the number of characters).

STRING ATTRIBUTE FUNCTIONS: mystr.**length**( ), mystr.**size**( ), mystr.**capacity**(), mystr.**max_size**( )

These functions return information about the string, such as its length, capacity, and maximum size. Function **max_size**( ) returns the maximum number of elements a string can have in the system. This is similar to the limit of other data types, such as the maximum size of integer, long, and double. Do not confuse **max_size**( ) with **size**( ). **size**( ) gives the number of elements in a particular string. The **capacity**( ) function returns the maximum number of characters the string can hold without the allocation of more memory.

```
#include<iostream>
#include<string>
using namespace std;

void main(){
        string lastname("Ebrahimi");
        cout<<"LENGTH OF NAME: "<<lastname.length()<<endl;
        cout<<"SIZE OF NAME: "<<lastname.size()<<endl;
        cout<<"CAPACITY OF NAME: "<<lastname.capacity()<<endl;
        cout<<"MAX SIZE OF NAME: "<<lastname.max_size()<<endl;
}//MAIN
```

Figure 17.38a – Program to display string attributes using STL functions

```
LENGTH OF NAME: 8
SIZE OF NAME: 8
CAPACITY OF NAME: 31
MAX SIZE OF NAME: 4294967293
```

Figure 17.38b – Output of Figure 17.38a

TO FIND A STRING OR A SUBSTRING IN A STRING: find(str)

To search if a string contains a string or a sub-string (characters), the find member function of string class is used. There are several overloaded (varieties) of the **find( )** function. **find( )** returns the index of where the string match starts to take place. If there is no match, **find( )** will return an integer greater than the size of the string provided by the **size( )** function. This program makes use of the **find( )** function to check for a sub-string.

```cpp
#include <iostream>
#include <string>
using namespace std;
void main(){
        string name;
        getline(cin, name);
        if (name.find ( "Ph.D.",0)<name.size())
                cout<<"Dear Dr. "<<name<<","<<endl;
        else
                cout<<"Dear Mr./Ms. "<<name<<","<<endl;
}//MAIN
```

Figure 17.39a – Using the find( ) function to search for a sub-string

```
Alireza Ebrahimi Ph.D.
Dear Dr. Alireza Ebrahimi Ph.D.,
```

Figure 17.39b – Output of Figure 17.39a

Alternatively, the string class has a member known as **npos** which is normally –1 or the length of the string which can be used instead of function **size( )**.

COMPARE FUNCTION: str1.compare(str1start, str1nch, str2, str2start, str2nch)

The **compare( )** function compares two strings. If the invoking string (first string) is less than the second string the method (function) returns a negative number (<0); if the first is larger then second string it returns positive (>0). If both strings are identical it returns zero. The resulting value (return value) of string class function **compare( )** is similar to the C-style function **strcmp( )**. The general form of string class compare is shown above, where part of first string is compared with part of the second string (sub string). However, several overloaded functions are created by variation of the entire string of one string over part of another string or vice versa. The **compare( )** function has several overloaded forms working with and/ or each sub strings performing a partial comparison from a point of a string to another point. When it is necessary to compare two entire strings, it is more convenient to use (< ,>, = =) rather than the **compare( )** function. The **compare( )** function can be used for a partial search. This program uses the compare function to test the equality of the first three letters of both strings.

```cpp
#include<iostream>
#include<string>
using namespace std;

void main(){
        string str1="Alireza";
        string str2="Ebrahimi";
        if(str1.compare(0,3,str2,0,3)==0)
                cout<<"THE STRINGS ARE EQUAL";
        else
                cout<<"THE STRINGS ARE NOT EQUAL";
}//MAIN
```

Figure 17.40a – Using the compare( ) function to compare two sub-strings

THE STRINGS ARE NOT EQUAL

Figure 17.40b – Output of Figure 17.40a

ASSIGN FUNCTION: str1.assign(str2, start, nch)

The string class **assign( )** function is used to assign an entire string, part of a string, or a sequence of one character (identical). When an entire string needs to be assigned, it is more convenient to use the = assignment operator.

```
#include<iostream>
#include<string>
using namespace std;
void main(){
        string firstname, lastname, fullname;
        firstname.assign("Alireza");
        lastname.assign("Ebrahimi");
        fullname.assign(firstname+" "+lastname);
        cout<<fullname<<endl;
}//MAIN
```

Figure 17.41a – Program using the assign( ) function

```
Alireza Ebrahimi
```

Figure 17.41b – Output of Figure 17.41a

```
#include<iostream>
#include<string>
using namespace std;

void main(){
        string slogan1="DO THE BEST AND LEAVE THE REST";
        string slogan2;
        string slogan3;

        slogan2.assign(slogan1,3,18);
        slogan3.assign(18,'X');
        cout<<slogan2<<endl;
        cout<<slogan3<<endl;
}//MAIN
```

Figure 17.42a – Using the assign( ) function to assign part of one string to another, and to assign a sequence a character

```
THE BEST AND LEAVE
XXXXXXXXXXXXXXXXXX
```

Figure 17.42b – Output of Figure 17.42a

585

APPEND FUNCTION

The string class append function appends one string to the end of another string or adds a character or a sequence of identical characters. This function performs the same operation on strings as the overloaded operators += for concatenation. This program shows how both are used.

```
#include<iostream>
#include<string>
using namespace std;
void main(){
        string name="Alireza";
        name+=" Ebrahimi";
        name.append(" Ph.D.");
        cout<<name;
}//MAIN
```

Figure 17.43a – Using the append( ) function and += for concatenation

```
Alireza Ebrahimi Ph.D.
```

Figure 17.43b – Output of Figure 17.43a

REPLACE FUNCTION: replace(str1pos, str1nc, str2, str2pos, str2nc)

The string class **replace**() function erases part of a string and replaces it with another string. The replacement string can be a string, an array, or a sequence of characters repeated several times. The program below uses **replace**() to erase the word "FOX" and replace it with the string "RABBIT." The first parameter is the beginning position of the substring you want to erase, the second parameter is the number of characters to be erased, and the third parameter is the string that is written starting at **str1pos**.

```
#include<iostream>
#include<string>
using namespace std;
void main(){
        string str1="A QUICK BROWN FOX JUMPS OVER A LAZY DOG"; ;
        string str2="RABBIT";
        str1.replace(14, 3, str2);
        cout<<str1<<endl;
}//MAIN
```

Figure 17.44a – Replacing part of a string with another using the replace( ) function

```
A QUICK BROWN RABBIT JUMPS OVER A LAZY DOG
```

Figure 17.44b – Output of Figure 17.44a

INSERT FUNCTION: mystr.insert(startpos, str2)

At the specified position (startpos) of the invoking string (mystr), insert the second string (str2). The insert function has another form, which inserts part of the string. In this case, the starting position and the number of characters to be inserted must be specified.

```cpp
#include<iostream>
#include<string>
using namespace std;

void main(){
        string str1="A FOX JUMPS OVER A DOG";
        str1.insert(2,"QUICK BROWN ");
        str1.insert(31,"LAZY ");
        cout<<str1;
}//MAIN
```

Figure 17.45a – Demonstrating the insert( ) function

```
A QUICK BROWN FOX JUMPS OVER A LAZY DOG
```

Figure 17.45b – Output of Figure 17.45a

ERASE FUNCTION: mystr.erase(start = 0, numpos = npos)

Starting from the **start** position of the string and removing a **numpos** character from string, this function erases the specified section of the string as shown below.

```cpp
#include<iostream>
#include<string>
using namespace std;

void main(){
        string slogan="Do the best and leave the rest.";
        slogan.erase(12,31);
        cout<<slogan;
}//MAIN
```

Figure 17.46a – Demonstrating the erase( ) function

```
Do the best
```

Figure 17.46b – Output of Figure 17.46a

587

SWAP FUNCTION: swap(str1, str2)

The string class **swap( )** function exchanges the contents of two strings. Instead of saving one string to a temporary string in order to swap, you can simply use the **swap( )** function as shown in the program below.

```
#include<iostream>
#include<string>
using namespace std;
void main(){
        string str1="hello";
        string str2="bye";
        cout<<"BEFORE SWAP: "<<str1<<" "<<str2<<endl;
        str1.swap(str2);
        cout<<"AFTER SWAP  : "<<str1<<" "<<str2<<endl;   }//MAIN
```

Figure 17.47a – Program using the swap( ) function to swap the contents of two strings

```
BEFORE SWAP: hello bye
AFTER SWAP  : bye  hello
```

Figure 17.47b – Output of Figure 17.47a

STRING CLASS INPUT AND OUTPUT

The string class overload >> is used to input from (**cin**>>) and to output to (**cout**<<). The **cin** and **getline( )** and **cout** with string is used in the same way as an array of characters is used in C-style except that the character null is not appended at the end of the string.

```
#include<iostream>
#include<string>
using namespace std;
void main(){
        string id;
        string streetaddress;
        cin>>id;
        getline(cin, streetaddress);
        cout<<"YOUR ID IS: "<<id<<endl;
        cout<<"YOUR ADDRESS IS: "<<streetaddress<<endl;  }//MAIN
```

Figure 17.48a – Demonstrating string class input and output

```
0123456
73-81 61st AVE
YOUR ID IS: 0123456
YOUR ADDRESS IS: 73-81 61st AVE
```

Figure 17.48b – Output of Figure 17.48a

C LANGUAGE INPUT/OUTPUT CHARACTER MANIPULATION

To take a character input the C language uses the **getchar**( ) macro which is written as **getc**(stdin). Similarly, the **putchar**( ) displays its character argument. To input a string in C the function **gets**( ) which is known as get string takes one argument, the string variable in which data is stored. The **puts**( ) function, known as put string also takes one string argument and displays it with an additional new line. For the above function you must include the directive **#include <stdio.h>**.

WRITING AND READING ENTIRE DATA STRUCTURE TO AND FROM A FILE

The following program takes in data items of a data structure, in this case the class employee, and writes the information to a file using the **write**( ) and **read**( ) functions. These functions take two parameters, the first is the pointer to the array of characters to be read or written, and the second is the number of characters. In this program, names and salaries are entered by the user and written to a file. The information is then read from the file and displayed back to the user, and demonstrates how data structures can be handled when working with a file.

```
#include<fstream.h>
class employee{
      public:
      char name[30];
      double salary; };//CLASS
void main(){
      int i;
      employee stateemp[5];
      cout<<"WRITING TO FILE."<<endl;
      for(i=0;i<5;i++){
            cout<<"PLEASE ENTER NAME    : ";
            cin.get(stateemp[i].name,30);
            cout<<"PLEASE ENTER SALARY : ";
            cin>>stateemp[i].salary;cin.get();}//FOR
      ofstream fout("state.dat");
      fout.write((char *) (&stateemp),sizeof(stateemp));
      cout<<"READING FROM FILE."<<endl;
      ifstream fin("state.dat");
      fin.read((char *)(&stateemp),sizeof(stateemp));
      for(i=0;i<5;i++){
            cout<<"NAME : "<<stateemp[i].name<<endl;;
            cout<<"SALARY: "<<stateemp[i].salary<<endl;}//FOR
}//MAIN
```

Figure 17.49a – Program that writes and reads an array of data structures to and from a file

```
WRITING TO FILE.
PLEASE ENTER NAME    : John
PLEASE ENTER SALARY : 10.50
PLEASE ENTER NAME    : Michael
PLEASE ENTER SALARY : 12.00
PLEASE ENTER NAME    : Andrew
PLEASE ENTER SALARY : 11.50
PLEASE ENTER NAME    : Sean
PLEASE ENTER SALARY : 10.00
PLEASE ENTER NAME    : Donna
PLEASE ENTER SALARY : 10.50
READING FROM FILE.
NAME : John
SALARY: 10.5
NAME  : Michael
SALARY: 12
NAME  : Andrew
SALARY: 11.5
NAME  : Sean
SALARY: 10
NAME  : Donna
SALARY: 10.5
```

Figure 17.49b – Output of Figure 17.49a

TOPICS NOT COVERED HERE

String manipulation and pattern matching is an important aspect in today's computing. The function **strcmp( )** is the fundamental pattern matching built-in function, however there are other built-in functions such as **strstr( )** that matches the second string (substring) to first string, **strchr( )** that matches an occurrence of one character to a given string, and **strtok( )** which tokenizes a string by providing a delimiter, such as separating a string into words (token). Do not worry if you do not understand how all of the string manipulations work; an understanding of one string manipulation leads to an understanding of the rest. By this time you should be able to program many different pattern matching problems and easily understand them. However, some pattern matching techniques are done in an efficient manner, which makes it difficult for a beginner programmer to understand. The majority of character functions are discussed here with the exception of some such as **isprint**(c) and **iscntrl**(c). Again, you can write any of the character manipulation functions yourself by simply adding one or two **if** statements. Since these functions are provided and have been used for many years, it is worth it to reuse them; but if you have an agenda and you feel your program is better, go ahead and do it. In this chapter, conversion from string to numbers was discussed; and as an exercise, you can make your own function or use the function **fcvt( )** to convert a floating point number to a string.

Using strings as STL opens a chapter on how other STL components and algorithms work with strings. An iterator can be used to navigate through a string. For example, a string can be initialized through the use of iterator functions such as **begin( )** and **end( )** which return a pointer to the first and last elements of a string. Some of the string class such as mystr.at(index) throws range error exception if the index is out of range. Exception handling will be discussed in the future chapter. Finally, the **#include <string>** directive must be included to use to bring the standard string library; however, the **basic_string** can be used as well.

CLOSING REMARKS AND LOOKING AHEAD

We can conclude that the character is the foundation of other data types such as integer or float. However, each character is represented by a standard numeric code such as ASCII. We have been using the input and output objects (routines) such as **cin**>>hoursworked and **cout**<<hoursworked for a quite while. The **cin** as an object takes the data and reads it into a data type variable. The I/O operations are divided into two categories of formatted and unformatted. The common use of **cin**>> and **cout**<< are known as formatted operations since the type of data is formatted. However, unformatted I/O treats the data as a sequence of characters (bytes) such as **cin.get**(c) and **cin.put**(c). The C++ extraction operator >> is used to extract input from an input stream, mainly keyboard, by **cin** object of **ifstream** as a standard input stream. **cin** object alone converts input characters to the appropriate data type where data is to be assigned using white space as a separator (delimiter). Leading white spaces are skipped. You can see that character variables are a subset of integer variables except that they store the ASCII characters. The ASCII characters can range from 0 to 127 to accommodate the graphic characters and characters that are used by languages other than English. One byte is used to store a character. In the next chapter we will look more closely at programming errors from syntax, run time (semantic), to logical errors and how to combat these situations. Errors and debugging is a costly and time-consuming portion of any programming assignment. In the next chapter, we will look at STL as a can of solutions for many current data structures and algorithms. The next chapter will examine some important features of STL and its contribution to problem solving and understanding of data structures.

SELF-TEST TRUE-FALSE CHAPTER 17 CHARACTER MANIPULATION

__1. Each character is represented by a numeric code known as the ASCII code.

__2. cin without setting cin>>noskipws; ignores the leading white space of input.

__3. for(char c=97; c<=122; c++) cout<<c<<" "; will print out the capital letters of the alphabet.

__4. get( ) can be used to build a string character by character or take in an array of characters.

__5. get(str, 10, '\n') will read up to ten characters of input or until EOF is reached.

__6. getline( ) extracts the new line from the input stream and discards it, while get( ) does not.

__7. The put( ) function can be used to write characters to the screen or to a file.

__8. isupper( ) converts a character to upper case while toupper( ) tests if a character is upper case.

__9. if((c>='a')&&(c<='z')) return(c-('a'-'A')); will make an upper case letter lower case.

__10. if((c>='A')&&(c<='Z')) return 1; else return 0; will return true if character c is upper case.

__11. peek( ) can be used to examine the next character from the input stream without advancing.

__12. C/C++ is useful in writing a lexical analyzer because of its character manipulation abilities.

__13. The character string "123" can be used in the same way as the integer 123.

__14. stricmp(s1, s2) compares two strings regardless of whether they are upper or lower case.

__15. A temporary string is not needed to swap the contents of two character arrays using strcpy( ).

__16. void func(char *s, char *t){while(*s++=*t++);} this function will compare two strings.

__17. The strncmp( ) functions is used for the partial comparison of two strings.

__18. A stream contains many strings; pointers are used to locate the beginning of each string.

__19. getch( ) from stdio.h does not echo the typed character back to the screen.

__20. Simple file encryption can be done by changing ASCII values or by using an associate array.

__21. It is not possible to write a program to handle numbers beyond the computer's memory limit.

__22. Basic operations such as =, ==, and + can be used with STL strings.

__23. The STL replace( ) function will overwrite part of a string with another string.

__24. write( ) and read( ) can be used to write or read a data structure to and from a file.

__25. The putback( ) function puts back the last character read by the get( ) function.

CHAPTER 17 CHARACTER MANIPULATION ASSIGNMENTS

Q17a) What is a character? Why is it important to understand character manipulations? Is it true that numerical data is a set of characters before becomes a number? For example, is 123 (one hundred twenty three) primarily considered to be the set of characters 1, 2, and 3 (one, two, and three)?

Q17b) Write a program to get a character and display it. Try to input several possible cases including white spaces and control characters. Record the problems. Hint: One or more strikes on the keyboard may represent a single character.

Q17c) What can be considered as a white space? Write a program that replaces a white space with a character, &.

Q17d) What is the difference between cin>>x and cin.get(x). List and explain 3 general cases of the get( ) function and differences between each.

Q17e) Run the following program for different data types. Re-run the program after removing the cin.fail( ).

```
#include<iostream>
#include<stdlib.h>
using namespace std;
void main(){
      int empid;
      cout<<"PLEASE ENTER EMPLOYEE'S ID: ";
      do {cin>>empid;
        if(cin.fail())  {
            cout<<"ERROR\n";
            exit(1);}//IF
      else{cout<<"PLEASE ENTER EMPLOYEE'S ID: ";}//ELSE
      }while(1);//DO WHILE
}//MAIN
```

Q17f) Explain the basics of the ASCII code and how it is used in a program. Seven bits are reserved to represent ASCII values. Write a program to display the ASCII characters. How are the extended ASCII characters represented or displayed?

Q17g) The ASCII value for an uppercase letter A is 65 and a lower case letter a is 97. The ASCII for the blank space is 32 and for 0 is 48. Interestingly, the NULL character has an ASCII value of 0. Why do uppercase letters have lower values than lower case letters? What is the difference between an upper case letter and a lower case letter? Write a simple program that converts uppercase A to a lower case a. Write a program that determines whether a character is a letter or a digit, using ASCII values.

Q17h) Write a program to display a set of address labels from a data file that only has three lines, which include: name, street address, and city address. Use fin.get(line1) with ignore('\n'), as well as getline(line1) to experience the differences.

593

Q17i) A data file consists of address labels. Display only the town names and ignore the rest of the address. Use the fin.ignore('\n') function to ignore the first two lines and use fin.get(town, ',') to extract the town name.

Q17j) Write a program that takes an input of characters and determines whether the input is a number or a word. Words start with a letter and numbers start with a digit. Words and numbers are separated by a blank space.

Q17k) Use get( ) and putback( ) to read a number or to read a word. Similarly, rewrite the program to use peek( ) to examine whether to read a number or a word.

Q17l) What is the purpose of the put( ) function? How can it be compared to cout?

Q17m) Write a function called changecase( ) that coverts a lowercase character to its uppercase character and vice versa. Use the following functions:

isupper(c)   toupper(c)   islower(c)   tolower(c)

Q17n) Create a string, character by character, placing NULL at the end to determine the end of the string. Display the string. What would happen if you remove the null character and then try to display the string?

Q17o) Explain the job of each of the following string manipulation functions.

strcat(s1, s2)   strlen(s1, s2)   strcmp(s1, s2)   strncmp(s1, s2)
stricmp(s1, s2)   strcpy(s2,s1)

Q17p) Write a function called chrcmp( ) that compares two characters. The function returns zero if two characters are equals, negative if the first character is less, and positive if the first character is more than the second character. Hint: Use return(c1-c2).

Q17q) How does the strcmp( ) function actually compare two strings? Why does the function return zero when two strings are equal? What happens when the first string is less than the second string?

Q17r) Write a customized string comparison function that, instead of an array of characters, it uses pointers and pointer increments such as *p++.

Q17s) What is the output of the following program?

```
#include<iostream.h>
#include<string.h>
void main( )
{       char s1[20], s2[10];
        s1 = "Old ";     s2 = "Westbury";
        strcat( s1, s2 );   cout << s1 << endl;
}//MAIN
```

Write your own version of string concatenation.

CHAPTER 17: CHARACTER MANIPULATIONS, STRING CLASS, AND IOSTREAM

Q17t) Write a simple program that rounds off a decimal number to 2 digits and tabs the number over without using "\t". You may want to use iomanip with ios::right and setfill('$').
For example,

> 108.35926
> $$$$$$108.36

Q17u) Declare and define a large string called lexan[1000] which holds other strings. The length of the previous string determines the address of the next string, which is stored in an array of pointers. Write a program which stores and displays a series of strings by using the pointers and the lexan[ ]. The above concept can be used for a symbol table.

Q17v) Write a program that asks the user to enter a secret word, e.g. a C++ keyword. The program tries to find the word by a few yes/no trial questions. The user word should not be displayed. Hint use getch( ).

Q17w) Explain the concept of encryption and why it is so important in terms of security. Explain an algorithm for encryption. Write a program that uses a file or an array of characters for ciphering/deciphering.

Q17x) Write a program to multiply two large integer numbers that may exceed the size maximum size for integer by using character manipulation. Display the result.

Q17y) Using STL strings, write a program to perform the following C-style string manipulations:

strcat(s1, s2)   strlen(s1, s2)   strcmp(s1, s2)   strncmp(s1, s2)
stricmp(s1, s2)   strcpy(s2,s1)

Q17z) Explain what the following statements do:

```
employee stateemp[5];
fout.write((char *)(&stateemp), sizeof(stateemp));
fin.read((char*)(&stateemp), sizeof(stateemp));
cout<<stateemp[0].name<<" "<<stateemp[0].salary<<endl;
```

CASE STUDY CHAPTER 17: CHARACTER MANIPULATION

a) Include in the menu an option called "Print Check" that prints a check for each employee by display a net pay amount in words. Include dollars and cents. Use <iomanip> to format your check and cout<<setfill('$') for leading blanks when printing net pay amount.
b) Include a partial search and a smart search using STL string functions such as substr( ), find( ), and compare( ).
c) Provide a user and administrator security system that requires a password. Do not display the character entries for the passwords, instead display the character *.
d) Apply encryption to secure certain information on employees. Use an encryption key.

CHAPTER 18

STANDARD TEMPLATE LIBRARY

WHY STL (STANDARD TEMPLATE LIBRARY)?

There are common data structures and algorithms that are used over and over in programs. C++ provides ready-made solutions for these data structures and algorithms by including them in a library. Therefore, a programmer can simply use them rather than make them. The advantage is that the programmer can use these data structures and algorithms that are defined, standardized, tested, and ready to be used rather than starting from scratch each time. In addition to the original built-in functions of C/C++, in 1994 STL became part of the standard library by adding new classes that work with any data type, promoting reuse rather than reinventing the wheel. Certain data structures and algorithms are used over and over by programmers, so why not automate these data structures and algorithms? Certain components of STL are better suited for different circumstances.

For beginners or even experienced programmers STL can be difficult to grasp. The syntax of STL is a little intimidating. After observing the capabilities of STL, the value of this tool becomes obvious and you want to use it more. Just keep in mind that the goal of STL is to provide you with a collection of generic tools so that you can enhance your programmability. If you have had difficulty building a linked list and operating it manually, using STL you can request an automatic double linked list with the all the necessary functions to operate it. Just remember STL by itself is a vast topic and you need time to become acquainted with it.

THREE COMPONENTS OF STL: CONTAINERS, ALGORITHMS, AND ITERATORS

STL comes with three components that work with each other to solve problems of all different kinds. These three components are known as containers, iterators, and algorithms. As the name suggests, a container represents storage units that hold data elements (data structure). An iterator is like a loop that moves and scans through the container. An iterator that points to the contents of a container can be used to traverse through the elements of that container. Each container has its own algorithms (functions); there are also algorithms that work with all containers. In summary, the algorithms are the programs (functions) that are applied to data structures.

CONTAINER TYPES

Containers can be divided into two parts: sequence containers and associative containers. Sequence containers are: vector, list, and deque (double-ended queue). Associative containers are sets and maps. From sequence containers other containers have been created, such as stacks and queues, which are known as adapters.

STL ITERATORS

The main job of STL iterators is to access the elements of a container. The word iterator reminds one of a loop or iteration; however, iterators are more like pointers than loops. Some see STL iterators as smart pointers. Iterators are an abstraction of pointers. An iterater points to a container and the iterator can be incremented, decremented, and checked for equality (= =, !=) in the same way as a pointer pointing to an element of an array. The content of what an iterator points to can be accessed with * indirection operator (*iter) or (*iter).first for the map and set (or alternatively iter ->first). The functions begin( ) and end( ) return iterators than can be used to access the beginning of the container and the terminating end of the container. Iterators are the bridge between algorithms and containers. Containers may have specified iterators. In addition to traversing the data elements of a container, there are two kinds of iterators that are connected to the input/output streams known as input iterator (**inputIterator**) and output iterator (**outputIterator**). These iterators allow you to copy the contents directly to the output device or access the data from the input device and copy it to the container.

STL ALGORITHMS

STL consists of several standardized generic functions (algorithms) that can be used on any of the containers. Therefore, many container functions can be applied to other containers. For example, the functions **insert( )** and **remove( )** insert and remove elements from a vector, list, or string using the same interface (function call and parameters).   The list of other major algorithms are: **find( )** (to look for a value), **binary_search( )** (search for value in a sorted sequence), **unique( )** (ensures that the sequence is unique, no duplicates), **sort( )** (sorts sequence in ascending order), **replace( )** (replaces the old value with the new value), **for_each( )** (applies a function to every element in the sequence), **max_element( )** (finds the maximum element in the sequence), **min_element( )** (finds minimum element in the sequence), and **count( )** (returns the frequency of a value in the data). There are other algorithms that will be discussed later.

TEN IMPORTANT STL CONTAINERS:

vector: A **vector** contains a sequence of contiguous storage units (linear) and objects are pushed at one end (back end). The elements of a vector can be accessed randomly. A vector is similar to a C-style array, but you do not have to declare the size. The function **size( )** returns the current number of elements in the vector and the function **push_back()** pushes an element into the vector. The general syntax for vector, is *vector <datatype> objectname*, for example: **vector <string> v**
Vector is the best container when you want to push an element at the end of a sequence.

deque: A sequence of noncontiguous storage; elements can be pushed at both the beginning and the end.

list: A sequence of noncontiguous storage where elements can be inserted anywhere in the sequence, at the beginning, middle, or end.

stack: It is a last in first out container which can be built from any of the above containers (vector, list, dequeue). Example, *stack(c)* where **c** can be built from *vector(t)*, *dequeue(t), or list(t)*.

queue: It is a first in first out container and can be created from either list or deque; elements can be inserted at the beginning or end.

priority_queue: It is a first in, first out, sorted container and can be built from either vector or deque.

map: Associated array with keys and values, for each key there is one value. For example: name and telephone number.

multimap: Same as map but now you can have duplicates.

set: Is a set of objects with no duplication allowed.

multiset: Is a set of objects where duplications are allowed.
It is possible to perform what you want to do with more than one kind of container but there is usually one container that is optimal for the application. The first task is to find the right container and the rest will fall into place.

STL NAMING CONVENTIONS

There are more than a hundred names used in STL and remembering all of them is not an easy task except if they are used on a continuous basis. There are names that can be misleading; for example the word **deque** does not mean to remove (dequeue), the opposite of enqueue. In STL deque means *d*ouble *e*nded *que*ue. The names in STL are lowercase and for the most part are spelled out. When there is more than one word, they are separated by an underscore, for example **binary_search( )**.

SEQUENTIAL CONTIGUOUS DYNAMIC ARRAY WITH ONE END: vector

The STL vector is a single-ended sequential container and is one of the most widely used containers. One reason for its popularity is its resemblance to the C-style array. Vectors perform the same functions as arrays and much more. With vectors, you do not need to worry about the size in the declaration or the maximum size. The major operations on a vector are shown in the following program:

```
#include<iostream.h>
#include<vector>
using namespace std;

void main(){
        vector <int> v;  //declaring v as a vector of type int
        int element;
        cin>>element;
        v.push_back(element); //inserting an element into vector, no need to increment the index

        cout<<v[0]<<endl; //through the index an element of vector can be accessed
        cout<<*v.begin()<<endl; //to access first element, and vector base address

        cin>>element;
        v.push_back(element); //push more element into vector

        vector <int>::iterator p; //declaring an interator point to the vector of type int
        p = v.begin();
        while(p != v.end( )){ //end() will point to one-past-the-end
                cout<<*p<<" "; p++; }//display the content of iterator (what p points to)
        }// MAIN
```

Figure 18.1a – Program to show operations on an STL vector container

```
1
1
1
2
1 2
```

Figure 18.1b – Output of Figure 18.1a

vector PROGRAM WITH OPERATIONS: empty( ) AND size( )

In addition to the above vector member functions, the following program demonstrates how you can use the functions **empty( )** and **size( )**. The function **empty( )** returns true if the vector is empty. The function **size( )** returns the number of elements in the vector.

```
#include<iostream>
#include<vector>
using namespace std;

void main(){
        vector <double> employee;
        double salary;

        if(employee.empty()) cout<<"VECTOR IS EMPTY"<<endl;
        cout<<"NUMBER OF ELEMENTS IN THE VECTOR: "<<employee.size()<<endl;
        cout<<"ENTER EMPLOYEES SALARIES, CTRL/D TO STOP: "<<endl;
        while(cin>>salary){
                employee.push_back(salary);}//WHILE
                cout<<"NUMBER OF ELEMENTS IN THE VECTOR: "<<employee.size()<<endl;
        for(int i=0; i<employee.size();i++) cout<<employee[i]<<" "<<endl;
}//MAIN
```

Figure 18.2a – Program using the empty( ) and size( ) functions on a vector

```
VECTOR IS EMPTY
NUMBER OF ELEMENTS IN THE VECTOR: 0
ENTER EMPLOYEES SALARIES, CTRL/D TO STOP:
10.75 7.50 6.75 11.00 7.75
NUMBER OF ELEMENTS IN THE VECTOR: 5
10.75
7.5
6.75
11
7.75
```

Figure 18.2b – Output of Figure 18.2a

VECTORS, ITERATORS, AND ALGORITHMS

The next program takes in five names, sorts them, and displays them in order. The names are stored in a string vector called **v**; the vector is declared as: **vector<string> v**

After getting the name from the user you have to push it back into the vector using: **v.push_back(name);**

To sort the names use the sort function **sort(v.begin(),v.end());** from the algorithm class. In order to print the vector container we have to create an iterator to loop through the vector: **for(vector<string>::iterator p = v.begin(); p != v.end(); p++)**

```
#include<iostream>
#include<vector>
#include<string>
#include<algorithm>
using namespace std;

void main(){
        vector<string> v;
        string name;

        for(int i=0;i<5;i++){
                cout<<"ENTER YOUR NAME: ";
                cin>>name;
                v.push_back(name); }//FOR

        sort(v.begin(),v.end());
        cout<<"THE NAMES ARE:"<<endl;

        for(vector<string>::iterator p = v.begin();p!=v.end();p++){
                cout<<*p<<endl; }//FOR
}//MAIN
```

Figure 18.3a – Sorting a vector of strings using the sort( ) function

```
ENTER YOUR NAME: Michael
ENTER YOUR NAME: Brian
ENTER YOUR NAME: Tina
ENTER YOUR NAME: Alireza
ENTER YOUR NAME: Ebrahimi
THE NAMES ARE:
Alireza
Brian
Ebrahimi
Michael
Tina
```

Figure 18.3b – Output of Figure 18.3a

vector OPERATIONS sort( ), binary_search( ), and unique_copy( ) ALGORITHMS

The following program illustrates vector operations by pushing elements into the vector using **push_back**( ) that is specific to vectors, and **sort**( ) and **binary_search**( ) that are common algorithms.

```cpp
#include<iostream>
#include<vector>
#include<string>
#include<algorithm>
using namespace std;
void main(){
        vector<string> v;
        vector<string>::iterator result;
        string name,searchname;

        for(int i=0;i<5;i++){
        cout<<"ENTER YOUR NAME: ";
        cin>>name;
        v.push_back(name); }//FOR

        sort(v.begin(),v.end());
        cout<<"THE NAMES ARE:"<<endl;

        for(vector<string>::iterator p = v.begin();p!=v.end();p++){
                cout<<*p<<endl; }//FOR

        cout<<"PLEASE ENTER THE NAME YOU ARE LOOKING FOR: ";
        cin>>searchname;
        binary_search(v.begin(),v.end(),searchname);
        if(true){cout<<searchname<<" FOUND"<<endl;}
        else{cout<<"NOT FOUND"<<endl;}
}//MAIN
```

Figure 18.4a – Program using the push_back( ), sort( ), and binary_search( ) functions

```
ENTER YOUR NAME: alireza
ENTER YOUR NAME: ebrahimi
ENTER YOUR NAME: donna
ENTER YOUR NAME: victor
ENTER YOUR NAME: linda
THE NAMES ARE:
alireza
donna
ebrahimi
linda
victor
PLEASE ENTER THE NAME YOU ARE LOOKING FOR: ebrahimi
ebrahimi FOUND
```

Figure 18.4b – Output of Figure 18.4a

603

The following program creates two vectors of string type **v** and **w** and inserts several names into vector **v**. The vector must be sorted before the **unique_copy**( ) function is performed. The **unique_copy**( ) function rewrites the contents of **v** into **w** allowing no duplication, creating a unique copy.

```cpp
#include<iostream>
#include<vector>
#include<string>
#include<algorithm>
using namespace std;

void main(){
        vector<string> v (8);
        vector<string> w (8);
        v.push_back("jason");v.push_back("alireza");v.push_back("tolga");v.push_back("alireza");
        v.push_back("tolga");v.push_back("ebrahimi");v.push_back("mary");v.push_back("ebrahimi");

        sort(v.begin(),v.end());

        cout<<"THE NAMES WITH NO DUPLICATES ARE: "<<endl;

        unique_copy(v.begin(),v.end(),w.begin());

        for(vector<string>::iterator p = w.begin();p!=w.end();p++){
                cout<<*p<<endl; }//FOR
}//MAIN
```

Figure 18.5a – Program to demonstrate the unique_copy( ) function

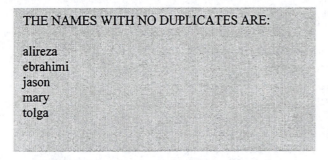

```
THE NAMES WITH NO DUPLICATES ARE:

alireza
ebrahimi
jason
mary
tolga
```

Figure 18.5b – Output of Figure 18.5a

THE BEST AND THE WORST OF vector

The vector container is the best container for pushing elements at the back and removing elements from the back. The vector is randomly accessed. When an element is inserted or removed from anywhere except the last element, the vector will reshuffle itself to preserve its random access. In summary, a vector is a dynamic C-style array that is resized automatically and therefore is optimized for random access.

CONTAINERS COMMON OPERATIONS

The following operations are common to all containers:

assignment operator =	assigns one container into another container.
= = equality, != inequality	checks if two containers are equal or not equal (true/false).
size( )	returns the number of elements in the container.
empty( )	returns true if the container is empty, otherwise false.
clear( )	clears the container by deleting all elements
insert( )	inserts one or a sequence of elements into container
erase( )	erases one or a sequence of elements from container.
begin( )	returns an iterator to the first element of the container.
end( )	returns an iterator to one-past-the-last element of container

<deque> DOUBLE ENDED QUEUE CONTAINER

Deque stands for double-ended queue and is a sequential container that supports random access. Operations can be performed easily at both ends. Like the vector, subscripts (indexing) can be used to read or modify the container's contents. The basic operations of vectors are applicable to the **deque** as well as additional operations such as **push_front( )** and **pop_front( )** that insert and remove from the front of the container. As with vectors, an iterator can be used to scan through the deque using **begin( )** and **end( )**.

HOW TO INCLUDE AND WORK WITH A deque:

In order to include a deque you need to write the header **#include<deque>.** The declaration of the deque object uses this form: **deque <t> objectname**
The identifier **t** can be any data type or class and **objectname** is a valid identifier name and can be initialized many ways (many constructors). The major declarations and operations on deques are shown in the following examples.

> **deque <int> obdq**   declaration of a deque
> **obdq [i]**   accessing the ith element of deque (position **i**).
> Similarly, an element of the deque can be accessed using the function **at( )**.
> **obdq.at(i)**
> **obdq.push_front(5)**   pushes element 5 into the font of the deque.
> **obdq.pop_front( )**   removes the front element of the deque.
> **obdq.front( )**   returns the front element
> **obdq.back( )**   returns the last element

deque OPERATIONS: SAMPLE PROGRAM

The following program implements the deque and performs operations such as:
push_front( ), **push_back( )**, **size( )**, **at( )**, **front( )**, and **back( )**.

```
#include<iostream>
#include<deque>
using namespace std;

void main(){
        deque <int> obdq;
        obdq.push_front(5);
        obdq.push_front(7);
        obdq.push_back(8);
        obdq.push_back(2);
        for(int i=0; i<obdq.size(); i++){
                cout<<obdq[i]<<" ";
                cout<<obdq.at(i)<<endl;}//FOR
        obdq.pop_front(); //7 REMOVED
        cout<<obdq.front()<<endl;
        cout<<obdq.at(2)<<endl;
        obdq.pop_back();
        cout<<obdq.back();
}//MAIN
```

Figure 18.6a – Program showing operations on the deque container

606

```
7 7
5 5
8 8
2 2
5
2
8
```

Figure 18.6b – Output of Figure 18.6a

STL list: INSERT AND REMOVE FROM ANYWHERE WITHIN

The STL **list** is a doubly linked list. It is a sequential container that allows insertion and removal elements efficiently. In addition to the sequential container's operations, the list performs operations such as **sort( )**, **splice( )** and **remove( )**. A list does not support random access; therefore indexes are not used.

SEQUENCE ADAPTER: <stack> , <queue>

There is no doubt about the importance of stacks and queues, however these data structures are not built as their own containers but are adapted from existing sequence containers such as vector, deque, and list. For this reason the stack, queue, and priority_queue are known as *sequence adapters*. These adapters have a restricted interface and are limited to certain intended operations.

STACK AS A CONTAINER ADAPTER

Stack is one of the most important data structures based on the Last-In-First-Out principle (LIFO). The stack is restricted a few operations, such as: **push( )** which inserts an element into the container, **pop( )** which removes an element from the container, and **top( )** that accesses the top element of the stack. Additionally, the function **empty( )** will check if the stack is empty. The **pop( )** function can only be applied only if the stack is not empty. STL stack will support the above operations with the exception that **pop( )** will not return an element but removes that element from the stack. In STL top is not an index. The top element may only be accessed and operated on by the function **top( )**. STL stack is known as a container adapter since it is built from the existing sequence containers such as: vector, deque, and list. The default container for STL stack is deque. A vector seems to be a better choice because it allows data to be accessed from one end rather than both ends. If the vector container is selected to build the stack from the function **full( )** will not be part of the STL stack because it is automatically resized. A maximum size may be set as illustrated in the following examples. **mystack** is a stack container of type **int,** which by default uses deque. **yourstack** uses a vector container of type **int.**

stack<int> mystack;   stack <int vector <int>> yourstack;

The following program declares a stack of integers and demonstrates the operations of a stack such as: **push**( ), **pop**( ), and **top**( ). The function **empty**( ) is used check if the stack is empty.

```
#include <iostream>
#include <string>
#include <stack>
using namespace std;
void main(){
        stack <int> mystack;
        mystack.push(2);
        mystack.push(8);
        mystack.push(3);
        cout<<"THE TOP ELEMENT IS: "<<mystack.top()<<endl;
        mystack.pop();
        cout<<"THE TOP ELEMENT IS: "<<mystack.top()<<endl;
        mystack.push(7);
        while(!mystack.empty()){
                cout<<mystack.top()<<endl;
                mystack.pop();
        }//WHILE
}//MAIN
```

Figure 18.7a – Program with stack operations push( ), pop( ), top( ) and empty( )

```
THE TOP ELEMENT IS: 3
THE TOP ELEMENT IS: 8
7
8
2
```

Figure 18.7b – Output of Figure 18.7a

The next program creates a stack of type string; the contents of an array is dumped into the stack by the **push**( ) function. The function **empty**( ) is used as a loop control variable; the loop pops the entire stack and displays the top of the stack each time.

```
#include <iostream>
#include <stack>
#include <string>

using namespace std;
void main() {
  cout<<"STACK"<<endl;
  stack<string> stk;
  cout<<"PUSH... ";
  string input[ ]={"jason","dawnett","tolga","edyta","alireza","ebrahimi"};
  for(int i=0;i<5;i++){
    stk.push(input[i]);
         cout<<input[i]<<' '; }//FOR
  cout<<endl<<"POP.....";
  while(!stk.empty()){
    cout<<stk.top()<<' ';
    stk.pop(); }//WHILE
  cout<<endl;
}//MAIN
```

Figure 18.8a – This program creates a stack from an array of strings and displays it

```
STACK
PUSH... jason dawnett tolga edyta alireza
POP.....alireza edyta tolga dawnett jason
```

Figure 18.8b – Output of Figure 18.8a

QUEUE CONTAINER ADAPTER

A queue is a well-known data structure based on the first-in-first-out principle (FIFO). A queue performs two major operations: adding an element to the back of the container and removing the first element. Historically, adding an element to the back of the queue is known as enqueue and removing an element from the front of the queue is known as dequeue. However, these terms were not adopted for the general operations on containers and instead the words push and pop, the same words used for a stack, are used for queue. By default a queue uses a deque container to hold the elements. The vector container cannot be used as a queue since the vector does not have **pop_front( )**. Generally speaking, any container that has **push_back( )**, **back( )**, **front( )**, and **pop_front( )** can be used to implement a queue. Using push and pop for both the stack and queue as naming conventions is a little confusing especially for those who learned these data structures without STL. Historically the computer instructors tried to differentiate between the stack and queue by providing abstractions in which naming has played an important role.

STL QUEUE: queue <T> and priority_queue <T>

The following program demonstrates both operation on a queue and a priority queue separately. The **push( )**, **pop( )**, and **empty( )** functions are used. In the queue, the strings are pushed and popped in the same order. In the priority queue, the items are popped according to a priority. The highest priority item is removed first. In this case the string with the highest character (ASCII) value is removed first.

```cpp
#include <iostream>
#include <queue>
#include <string>
using namespace std;
void testqueue() {
        cout<<"QUEUE";
        queue<string> myque;
        myque.push("AAAAA");
        myque.push("BBBBB");
        myque.push("CCCCC");
        cout<<endl<<"DEQUEUE...";
        while(!myque.empty()){
                cout<<myque.front()<<' ';
                myque.pop(); }//WHILE
        cout<<endl<<endl;
        }//TESTQUEUE
void testpriorityqueue(){
        cout<<"PRIORITY QUEUE";
        priority_queue<string> mypque;
        mypque.push("AAAAA");
        mypque.push("BBBBB");
        mypque.push("CCCCC");
        cout<<endl<<"DEQUEUE...";
        while(!mypque.empty()){
                cout<<mypque.top()<<' ';
                mypque.pop(); }//WHILE
        cout<<endl;
        }//TESTPRIORITYQUEUE
int main() {
        testqueue();
        testpriorityqueue();
        return 0;
        }//MAIN
```

Figure 18.9a – Operations on the STL queue and priority queue

```
QUEUE
DEQUEUE...AAAAA BBBBB CCCCC

PRIORITY QUEUE
DEQUEUE...CCCCC BBBBB AAAAA
```

Figure 18.9b – Output of Figure 18.9a

610

ANALYSIS OF SEQUENCE CONTAINERS- INSERTION, DELETION

Sequence containers such as vector, deque, and list, according to their design purpose and the manner in which the operations are performed, can be analyzed. For example, in the vector and queue containers, operations are similar to a C-style array. In a vector insertion and deletion at the end are constant O(1) while insertion and deletion at any other location is linear. In a queue insertion and deletion at both ends are constant O(1) while insertion and deletion at any other location is linear. A list is implemented as a bi-directional (linked) list, so insertion in the middle of the list is constant rather than linear. Note that list is not a random access container and element access is linear O(n).

ASSOCIATIVE CONTAINERS

The associative containers are map, multimap, set, and multiset. An associate container uses a key to access the data rather than sequentially going through the container. The data are stored as pairs of keys and values in a tree data structure, usually a balanced binary tree. A key value is converted to the location where the data is stored internally. In a tree structure the data can be looked up, inserted, and deleted quickly with a speed of log (n). Two examples of maps are a dictionary or a telephone book. Associative containers support the following functions: **find( )**, **count( )**, **upper_bound( )**, and **lower_bound( )**. The **upper_bound( )** function returns an iterator to the last instance of the search key selected. If the search key is not found, the function will return an iterator to the next greater key found. The **lower_bound( )** function returns an iterator to the first occurrence of the key selected or if it is not found will return an iterator to the first key less than the search key.

map ASSOCIATIVE CONTAINER

A map stores the data as pairs of keys/values. A map accesses an element by an index of the same type as the key, as opposed to an array that can only use an integer index. For example, the type of key can be a string, in other words the key serves as an index. The key and the value can be accessed through an iterator, for example **p->first** and **p->second** where **p->first** will access the key, and **p->second** will access the value. The header <map> defines the template class for the map as well as the multimap. Multimap differs from the map container in that it has multiple keys.

WRITING A PROGRAM TO COUNT FREQUENCIES OF WORDS

The following program uses map to keep track of word frequency. The index is a string instead of an integer. The map container looks like an array where the index can be of any type.

```
#include<iostream>
#include<map>
#include<string>
using namespace std;
void main(){
        map <string, int > freq;
        map <string, int >::const_iterator  miter;
        string word;
        while(cin>>word){
                freq[word]=freq[word] + 1; }//WHILE
        for(miter=freq.begin(); miter!=freq.end(); miter++)
                cout<<miter->first<<" " <<miter->second<<endl;
        }//MAIN
```

Figure 18.10a – Program to count the frequency of words

```
Alireza
Ebrahimi
Robert
David
Ebrahimi
Ebrahimi
Alireza
^Z

Alireza 2
David 1
Ebrahimi 3
Robert 1
```

Figure 18.10b – Output of Figure 18.10a

pair < K, V> CLASS from #include <utility>

A pair is a data structure, which consists of two elements, namely first and second. We can create a pair of different types such as string and int. Associative containers are made of pairs. The first member of a pair from a map container consists of the key and the second element consists of the value. The pair class and its operations such as **make_pair (key, value);** are declared in the #include <utility>. The operation **make_pair(key,value);** creates a new pair and therefore can be used in conjunction with associative containers.

For example **m.insert(make_pair("ebrahimi","917-328-1090"));** uses the key string "ebrahimi", inserting the pair into the associate map at the position indicated by the key ebrahimi. The insertion will not take place into the map if the key already exists.

612

```cpp
#include <iostream>
#include <map>
#include <string>
using namespace std;

int main(){
   map<string, string> directory;

   directory["Tolga"] = "631-476-3710";
   directory["Jason"] = "516-695-1158";
   directory["Ebrahimi"] = "516-876-3089";

   string name;char choice = 'y';
   while (choice != 'n'){
                   cout<<"Please Enter Name for Search :";
                   cin>>name;
      if (directory.find(name) != directory.end())
         cout << "The phone number for "
            << name << " is " << directory[name]
            << "\n";
      else
         cout << "Sorry, no listing for "<< name << "\n";
         cout<<"Do you want to search again? (y/n):";
         cin>> choice; }

}//MAIN
```

*Figure 18.11a – This program uses the STL map container to create a
phone directory to find telephone numbers by name*

```
Please Enter Name for Search :Tolga
The phone number for Tolga is 631-476-3710
Do you want to search again? (y/n):y
Please Enter Name for Search :Jason
The phone number for Jason is 516-695-1158
Do you want to search again? (y/n):y
Please Enter Name for Search :Ebrahimi
The phone number for Ebrahimi is 516-876-3089
Do you want to search again? (y/n):y
Please Enter Name for Search :Simmi
Sorry, no listing for Simmi
Do you want to search again? (y/n):n
```

Figure 18.11b – Output of Figure 18.11a

MAP INSERT

The following program demonstrates the map container, using the pair class for inserting a pair into the map. Note, the map will not allow duplication; therefore, only the first entry for each key is retained. It allows you to enter the data but will only display the first occurrence of a duplicate key.

```cpp
#include <iostream>
#include <map>
#include <string>
using namespace std;
void main(){
    map<string, string> directory;
   typedef pair<string,string> mypair;
    string name, phone;char choice = 'y';
    while (choice != 'n'){
                cout<<"Please Enter Name:";
                cin>>name;
                cout<<"Please Enter Phone Number:";
                cin>>phone;
                directory.insert(mypair(name,phone));
                cout<<"Do you want to enter again? (y/n):";
                cin>> choice;
        }//WHILE
        map<string,string>::iterator i;
        cout<<"Map includes :"<<endl;
        for (i=directory.begin();i!=directory.end();i++){
                cout<<i->first<<" "<<i->second<<endl;
        }//FOR
}//MAIN
```

Figure 18.12a – This program allows insertion to the map with no duplication

```
Please Enter Name:Tolga
Please Enter Phone Number:631-476-3710
Do you want to enter again? (y/n):y
Please Enter Name:Tolga
Please Enter Phone Number:516-903-4821
Do you want to enter again? (y/n):y
Please Enter Name:Jason
Please Enter Phone Number:516-695-1158
Do you want to enter again? (y/n):y
Please Enter Name:Jason
Please Enter Phone Number:631-622-4847
Do you want to enter again? (y/n):n
Map includes :
Jason 516-695-1158
Tolga 631-476-3710
```

Figure 18.12b – Output of Figure 18.12a

614

MULTIMAP INSERT

The following program demonstrates the multimap container, using the pair class for inserting a pair into the multimap. The multimap will allow duplication. For example, a name can have more than one telephone number. The multimap allows you to enter duplicate keys and will display each entry.

```
#include <iostream>
#include <map>
#include <string>
using namespace std;
void main(){
    multimap<string, string> directory;
         typedef pair<string,string> mypair;
    string name, phone;char choice = 'y';
    while (choice != 'n'){
                cout<<"Please Enter Name:";
                cin>>name;
                cout<<"Please Enter Phone Number:";
                cin>>phone;
                directory.insert(mypair(name,phone));
                cout<<"Do you want to enter again? (y/n):";
                cin>> choice;      }//WHILE
        multimap<string,string>::iterator i;
        cout<<"Map includes :"<<endl;
        for (i=directory.begin();i!=directory.end();i++){
                cout<<i->first<<i->second<<endl;   }//FOR
}//MAIN
```

Figure 18.13a – Program using the multimap container allowing duplication

```
Please Enter Name:Tolga
Please Enter Phone Number:631-476-3710
Do you want to enter again? (y/n):y
Please Enter Name:Tolga
Please Enter Phone Number:516-903-4821
Do you want to enter again? (y/n):y
Please Enter Name:Jason
Please Enter Phone Number:631-622-4847
Do you want to enter again? (y/n):y
Please Enter Name:Jason
Please Enter Phone Number:516-695-1158
Do you want to enter again? (y/n):n
Map includes :
Jason631-622-4847
Map includes :
Jason516-695-1158
Map includes :
Tolga631-476-3710
Tolga516-903-4821
```

Figure 18.13b – Output of Figure 18.13a

multimap ASSOCIATIVE CONTAINER

A multimap is an associative container where data is stored as a pairs of keys and values like a map but with multimap the key can be associated with more than one value. Multimap is a one-to-many association; for example, Ebrahimi can have several phone numbers. Multimap, like the map provides a fast search (access) of the elements in the container. In the map and multimap the elements are sorted in ascending order by default, which compares using the less (<) operator, unless otherwise specified. The multimap values cannot be accessed by indexes; instead iterators must be used.

set ASSOCIATIVE CONTAINER

The set container, like the map, is an associative container. A key value is associated with each element. A set holds elements and allows set properties as well as a fast search for a key. The main operations for a set container are: union, intersection, difference, symmetric difference, and the function includes( ).

set OPERATIONS

The following set algorithms can be applied on any sorted container in addition to the **set** container. The prototype for each of the functions is shown below:

set_union(bs1,es1,bs2,es2, bs3)

set_union( ) : To merge two ordered sequences and generate a new sequence containing all the elements of both sequences without redundancy.

set_intersection( ) : Creates a set containing all the common elements of the two sets.

set_difference( ) : Creates a set containing elements of the first set that are not contained in the second set.

set_symmetric_difference( ) : Creates a set containing elements that are in the first set but not the second and elements that are in the second set but not in the first, eliminating all common elements of the two individual sets.

includes( ) : It is a membership test. It will test if every member (element) of second set is also a member of the first set (true or false).

The following program demonstrates set operations:

```
#include <algorithm>
#include<iostream>
#include<set>
using namespace std;
void main(){
        int s1[]={1,2,3,4,5,6,7,8,9};
        int s2[]={2,4,6,8};

        cout<<"SET UNION IS: ";
        set_union(s1,s1+4,s2,s2+4, ostream_iterator <int> (cout," "));
        cout<<endl;
        cout<<"SET INTERSECTION IS:";
        set_intersection(s1,s1+4,s2,s2+4,ostream_iterator <int> (cout, " "));
        cout<<endl;
        cout<<"SET DIFFERENCE IS: ";
        set_difference(s1,s1+4,s2,s2+4, ostream_iterator <int> (cout," "));
        cout<<endl;
        cout<<"SET SYMETRIC DIFFERENCE IS: ";
        set_symmetric_difference(s1,s1+4,s2,s2+4, ostream_iterator <int> (cout," "));
        cout<<endl;
        if(includes(s1, s1+4, s2, s2+4)) cout <<"SET2 includes in SET1"<<endl;
        else cout<<"SET2 IS NOT IN SET1"<<endl;
        }//MAIN
```

Figure 18.14a – Program to demonstrate operations on a set

```
SET UNION IS: 1 2 3 4 6 8
SET INTERSECTION IS:2 4
SET DIFFERENCE IS: 1 3
SET SYMETRIC DIFFERENCE IS: 1 3 6 8
SET2 IS NOT IN SET1
```

Figure 18.14b – Output of Figure 18.14a

multiset CONTAINER

A multiset container, like a set container, by default sorts its elements in ascending order. In contrast to a set container, a multiset container allows duplication of its elements. For a multiset container the #include <set> is used.

set OPERATIONS WITH multiset

We have learned that in the set container there is no redundancy, however in the multiset container redundancy is permitted. Now the question is how the set operations are performed on multisets. The union will have the largest numbers of elements while the intersection will have the smallest number of elements.

In the following program two arrays are initialized to hold the elements of two different sets. Notice that both sets contain redundant elements. The set algorithms will regard each set as a multiset and the results of the multiset operations are shown below.

```
#include<iostream>
#include <algorithm>
#include<set>
using namespace std;
void main( ){
        int s1[]={1,1,3,6,9,9};
        int s2[]={2,2,2,4,6,6,8};
        cout<<"SET UNION IS: ";
        set_union(s1,s1+4,s2,s2+4, ostream_iterator <int> (cout," "));
        cout<<endl;
        cout<<"SET INTERSECTION IS:";
        set_intersection(s1,s1+4,s2,s2+4,ostream_iterator < int> (cout, " "));
        cout<<endl;
        cout<<"SET DIFFERENCE IS: ";
        set_difference(s1,s1+4,s2,s2+4, ostream_iterator <int> (cout," "));
        cout<<endl;
        cout<<"SET SYMMETRIC DIFFERENCE IS: ";
        set_symmetric_difference(s1,s1+4,s2,s2+4, ostream_iterator <int> (cout," "));
        cout<<endl;
        }//MAIN
```

Figure 18.15a – Program to demonstrate set operations on a multiset

```
SET UNION IS: 1 1 2 2 2 3 4 6
SET INTERSECTION IS:
SET DIFFERENCE IS: 1 1 3 6
SET SYMMETRIC DIFFERENCE IS: 1 1 2 2 2 3 4 6
```

Figure 18.15b – Output of Figure 18.15a

INTIALIZING ASSOCIATIVE CONTAINERS WITH ASSOCIATED ARRAYS

Associated arrays are arrays that work with each other in parallel. An element in one array is related to the element in the same position in the other array. The associative property has been carried out on the associative containers, such as map and set. In the array the index can only be an integer, but in associate containers the index can be of any type matching the type of the key value, such as a string or even a class. To initialize a container from an existing associate array one can use a loop to go through the array and assign it to each container position such as **mapdirectory[name]=telephone[i];** assuming the map is defined as:

map <string, string> mapdirectory;

A map container can be traversed by its iterator e.g. **mapdirectory.begin( );** and **mapdirectory.end( ).** To access the first and second elements of a map container; use:

      map <string, string, less <string> > miter;

Either of the following routines will display the contents of the first and second element:

      (*miter).first; (*miter).second;

      miter->first; miter->second;

Note that the elements in associative containers are sorted in order (self-ordering) even though they are not initially sorted in the associative containers. Therefore algorithms that change the order of a container may not work with associative containers.

set AND multiset SEARCH OPERATIONS

The set and multiset containers are optimized for fast access of elements in logarithmic time (log N) instead of linear time-O(N). To accommodate the set fast access operation the generic algorithms of STL are overloaded. Therefore it is recommended to use the set operations rather than generic operations of the same nature. The following explains some of the set and multiset operations.

find(element) : returns the position of the element found in the container or **end( )** if not found.

lower_bound(element) : It will find the first element in container that is *equal* to or *greater* than the element in question, and returns its position. The function

lower_bound() will return the first position where the element would be inserted.

upper_bound(element) : It will find the first element in container that is *greater* than the element in question, and returns its position. The function **upper_bound( )** will return the last position where the element would be inserted.

Understanding lower_bound and upper_bound can be very confusing. As an exercise, try the lower_bound and upper_bound with multiset where duplications are allowed.

equal_range(element): Returns both lower_bound and upper_bound as a pair in one operation.

count(element) : Finds the element and returns the number of occurrences (how many) of the element in the container.

The following program demonstrates operations on set such as **insert( )**, **lower_bound( )**, and **upper_bound( )**. Note that indirection * is used to display the contents of the iterators.

```
#include <set>
#include <iostream>
using namespace std;
void main(){
        set <int> myset;
        myset.insert(1); myset.insert(3);myset.insert(5); myset.insert(7); myset.insert(9);
        cout<<"FOUND: "<<*myset.find(5)<<endl;
        cout<<"LOWER BOUND OF 2: "<< *myset.lower_bound(2)<<endl;
        cout<< "UPPER BOUND OF 2: "<<*myset.upper_bound(2)<<endl;
        cout<<"LOWER BOUND OF 7: "<< *myset.lower_bound(7)<<endl;
        cout<< "UPPER BOUND OF 7: "<<*myset.upper_bound(7)<<endl;
        }//MAIN
```

Figure 18.16a – Demonstrating find( ), lower_bound( ), and upper_bound( )

```
FOUND: 5
LOWER BOUND OF 2: 3
UPPER BOUND OF 2: 3
LOWER BOUND OF 7: 7
UPPER BOUND OF 7: 9
```

Figure 18.16b – Output of Figure 18.16a

STL ALGORITHMS

The STL algorithms work on containers performing certain major operations including several generic algorithms using iterators. While the concept of algorithms is vast, the number of generic algorithms (functions) provided in the #include <algorithm> can be divided into three categories: searching, updating, and numeric algorithms.
Interestingly the STL algorithms work with ordinary C++ arrays. Some of these algorithms are, **sort( ) find( )**, **count( )**, **search( )**, and **merge( )**. Other algorithms are **transform( )** and **for_each( )**. There are algorithms that work with predicates (-if) and algorithms that work with function objects and user-defined functions. Note that there are two kinds of algorithms (functions), algorithms that are standalone and work with several containers and algorithms that are member functions of a particular container. Most algorithms either return an iterator or a boolean value (true or false).

SELECTED GENERIC ALGORITHMS

find(bi, ei, val): Finding the value and returns an iterator denoting the first occurrence of the value in the container. The function returns ei (end of iterator), if the value does not exist. Note that conventions **bi** and **ei** stand for the beginning and end iterators, respectively and **val** is the value in question.

binary_search(bi,ei,val): Searching (finding) in a sorted container and returns a bool value, whether the value is in the container or not.

sort(b,e): It will sort the container, however other criteria can be set on how the sort should take place by providing the third parameter (known as comparator object). In addition to the sort, there are other variations of the sort as well as some other related algorithms as listed below:

> **partial_sort( ) and stable_sort( )**
> **sort(v.begin( ), v.end( ), NoCase( ))**
> **reverse(b, e)**
> **equal(b1,e1,b2)**
> **equal_range( )**
> **min_element(b,e)**
> **max_element(b,e)**

TRANSFORM ALGORITHM: PROGRAM

The transform function will apply a transformation, e.g. a function, to each element of container, and put the result in a destination (container). For example, in the following program, using the **transform( )** algorithm converts all vowels to upper case. In the below program, the algorithm is applied to array -**vowel**. The transform function transforms each element of the vowel array –**vowel** according to the **toupper** function. The result of the transformation is stored into another array (container) called **upvowel**. Note that similar algorithms such as **for_each( )**, **generate( )**, and **fill( )** work on the same container.

```
#include<cctype>
#include<algorithm>
#include<iostream>
#include<iterator>
using namespace std;
void main(){
        char vowel[]={'a','e','i','o','u'};
        char upvowel[6];
        transform(vowel,vowel+5,upvowel,toupper);
        for(char* i=upvowel; i<upvowel+5;i++) cout<<*i<<" ";
        }//MAIN
```

Figure 18.17a – Program to demonstrate the transform( ) algorithm

```
A E I O U
```

Figure 18.17b – Output of Figure 18.17a

FILL AND GENERATE FUNCTIONS: PROGRAM

The **fill**( ) function is used to fill a container with a given value. Another version of **fill**( ) is **fill_n**( ) which will fill the first **n** elements of the container with a given value. Note, with **fill_n**( ) you do not need **end**( ) since the number of elements is specified.
The function **generate**( ) will generate a value by a function for every element of the container. The **generate_n**( ) function will generate values from a function, for the first **n** elements of the container.

```cpp
#include<iostream>
#include<algorithm>
#include<vector>
using namespace std;

void main (){
        vector <char> v(10);
        cout<<v[0]<<endl;
        fill(v.begin(),v.end(),'*');
        copy(v.begin(),v.end(),ostream_iterator<char>(cout," "));
        cout<<endl;
        fill_n(v.begin(),5,'+');
        copy(v.begin(),v.end(),ostream_iterator<char>(cout," "));
        cout<<endl;
        generate(v.begin(),v.end(),rand);
        copy(v.begin(),v.end(),ostream_iterator<char>(cout," "));
        cout<<endl;
        generate_n(v.begin(),5,rand);
        copy(v.begin(),v.end(),ostream_iterator<char>(cout," "));
        cout<<endl;
}//MAIN
```

Figure 18.18a – Using the fill and generate functions

```
* * * * * * * * *
+ + + + + * * * * *
) # ⌐ ä ß l ╥ « R É
I ± ± ╖ Θ l ╥ « R É
```

Figure 18.18b – Output of Figure 18.18a

FOR_EACH FUNCTION: PROGRAM

The **for_each( )** function is a non-modifying algorithm that works for the elements of a container in conjunction with a criterion. One can use the **for_each( )** algorithm to apply an operation on the elements of a container and display it.

```cpp
#include <iostream>
#include <vector>
#include <algorithm>
#include <numeric>
using namespace std;
void even_or_odd(int num){
        num=num%2;
        if(num==0)
                cout<<"THE NUMBERS IS EVEN"<<endl;
        else
                cout<<"THE NUMBERS IS ODD"<<endl;
}//EVEN_OR_ODD
void main(){
  vector<int> v(5);
  fill(v.begin(), v.end(),5);
  for_each(v.begin(), v.end(), even_or_odd);
}//MAIN
```

Figure 18.19a – Applying the for_each( ) algorithm to a vector

```
THE NUMBERS IS ODD
THE NUMBERS IS ODD
THE NUMBERS IS ODD
THE NUMBERS IS ODD
THE NUMBERS IS ODD
```

Figure 18.19b – Output of Figure 18.19a

OTHER STL ALGORITHMS: copy, unique_copy, remove

To copy the elements of one container into another the **copy( )** function can be used, and the range of elements to be copied must be indicated. The **copy( )** function can be used to copy elements to the **ostream_iterator** to display the container elements, instead of using a loop with an iterator:

> **copy(v.begin(), v.end(), ostream_iterator<int>(cout, " "))**

Copy can also be used to copy elements of an array to a container. The name of an array is the pointer to the beginning of the array, and the pointer to the end of the array is the array name plus the size of the array.

unique_copy( ) will copy the elements that are unique(no duplicates) into another container. However, criteria can be set for duplicates. For example, making a function to set a criterion, such as to check if the two numbers are in the same range. The following shows two examples of **unique_copy( )**

> **unique_copy(v.begin(), v.end, ostream_iterator<int>(cout," "))**
> **unique_copy(v1.begin(),v1.end(), v2)**

remove(v.begin(), v.end(), value) will remove the value from the container. The following example will incrementally remove the entire container:

> **vector<int>::iterator i=v.begin();**
> **while(i!=v.end()){ remove(v.begin(), v.end(),*i); i++;}//WHILE**

The function **remove_if(v.begin(),v.end(), ComparatorObj)** will remove the element according to the criteria set by the comparator object.

STL ALGORITHM CATEGORIZATION: MUTATING, NON-MUTATING

STL Algorithms can be divided into two major categories depending on whether the container in question can be changed by the algorithm (mutating) or the container remains the same (non-mutating) or non-modifiable.

Non-modifying algorithms simply explore (trace) the container for certain properties. Among non-modifying algorithms are the following:
find( ), find_if( ), find_end( ), adjacent_find( ), search( ), search_n( ), binary_search(), mismatch( ), lower_bound( ), upper_bound( ), equal_range( ), min( ), min_element( ), max( ), max_element( ), includes( ).

MODIFYING ALGORITHMS (MUTATING)

Modifying algorithms change the content of a container such as modifying, rearranging, or deleting an element of the container. This is the list of modifying algorithms: **sort( )**, **copy( )**, **fill( )**, **generate( )**, **transform( )**, **merge( )**, **remove( )**, **replace( )**, **reverse( )**, **set_union( )**, **rotate( )**, **partition( )**, **permutation( )**, **end_element( )**, **random_shuffle( )**, and **swap( )**.

Set operations such as **set_intersection( )**, **set_difference( )**, and **set_symmetric_difference()** are applicable to other STL containers as well as arrays. There are certain algorithms that are followed by the word copy such as **replace_copy( )**, **reverse_copy( )**, and **rotate_copy( )**; these do not change the original container and make copy to a new container. For example, **unique_copy( )** makes a copy only of the unique elements into a new container.

ALGORITHMS WITH PREDICATES

A predicate is a function that returns true or false. Several STL algorithms especially those with **if** such as **find_if** and **count_if** use predicates to apply to algorithms. In other words, if the predicate function is true for the element of container then the algorithm will apply.

TOPICS NOT COVERED HERE

The purpose of this chapter was to give an understanding of STL and how it can be used to solve problems or as an alternative to programming from scratch. Beside the containers we can name other components such as allocators, predicates, and comparison functions that can be looked at in more detail. Defining an STL class can be lengthy however you can use the keyword **"typedef classtype name"** to create a synonym and use the synonym from then on. There is a container called **bitset** that is used to store bit sequences. The **bitset** can be used to store images or low-level machine instructions; **bitset** will provide bitwise operations and algorithms. Every container has its own allocators that provide necessary memory that the user can customize, but it is provided by default.

In STL algorithms, there are a tremendous number of functions and here we cover the major ones, but there are uses for the others. STL is also open to the addition of new algorithms. New extensions may include the direct implementation of hash tables or graph algorithms such as finding the shortest path. Other possible extensions to the STL are function objects and how to create your own function object and the use of binders and negators. Finally, permutations, numeric, and heap algorithms require their own attention.

CLOSING REMARKS AND LOOKING AHEAD

Through the history of programming many libraries have been developed and then used by others repeatedly. The Fortran programming language continues to be used by many mathematicians and scientists because of its rich library of mathematic and scientific routines. STL was added as a C++ enhancement and later was accepted as the ANSI/ISO standard. STL is made of canned solutions, or off-the-shelf facilities, that are tested and ready to use. The syntax of the STL can be intimidating for beginners, but after a little experience, programmers become accustomed to it and see the benefits of using STL. For beginners, one important feature of STL is the addition of the string class to C++, adding another data type on which operations can be applied. The data structures that are part of STL are knows as containers or collections that hold any data type, including user-defined types (classes). These containers each have common operations and features in addition to their own. The three major STL container groups are sequence containers, associative containers, and bitset containers.

The three sequence containers are: vector, deque, and list. The vector and the deque can be viewed as dynamic C-style arrays. Insertion and deletion can be done only at one end of the vector, and at both ends for the deque. The elements of a vector or deque are accessed in the same way as the elements in an array. The list container, another sequential container, can be viewed as a doubly linked list where insertion and deletion can be done easily anywhere in the list. The list has its own sort function, rather than the general sort algorithm for vector and deque. Data structures mainly focus on topics such as stack, queue, and priority queue, which are part of the STL. These data structures are built from the sequence containers. Other containers known as stack, queue, and priority_queue are built from sequence containers and are called container adapters. The other major containers are associative containers such as map, multimap, set, and multiset. Associative containers are mostly used in situations where one needs to look up and key in order to find its value. The associate containers are superior to the other STL containers mentioned here. While generic algorithms work fine, optimal performance is obtained from a container when using its own member functions. For example the **find( )** member function of the associate container outperforms the generic **find( )** function.

In the next chapter we will look at other features added to C++ to handle errors and make the program less fragile when an exceptional situation occurs; this is known as exception handling. We will discuss error handling in more detail since it has been a major problem in writing software.

SELF-TEST TRUE-FALSE CHAPTER 18 STANDARD TEMPLATE LIBRARY

__1. STL consists of defined, standardized, and tested data structures and algorithms.

__2. STL has three components: containers, iterators, and algorithms.

__3. Containers can be divided into two types: sequence and associative containers.

__4. Iterators are used to access the elements of a container and can be used for input and output.

__5. In STL, deque means removing an element from a queue.

__6. In a vector container elements are pushed at one end and the vector can be accessed randomly.

__7. vector <string> v; declares a vector of strings and it can be sorted with sort(v.begin(),v.end());

__8. The functions empty( ) and size( ) can only be used on the vector container.

__9. unique_copy( ) will copy the contents of a vector including duplicate elements.

__10. A deque is a sequential container where operations take place only on one end.

__11. A container element can be accessed with array notation or by using the at( ) function.

__12. In a list, elements can be inserted anywhere in the sequence: beginning, middle, or end.

__13. Sequence adapters are built from sequence containers and put restrictions on their operation.

__14. The stack is a last in first out (LIFO) container that is built from vector, list, or deque.

__15. The stack operation pop( ) inserts an element and push( ) removes an element.

__16. The queue is a first in first out (FIFO) container and can be made from list or deque.

__17. A map is an associative container that stores data as pairs of keys and values with duplication.

__18. set_union( ) generates a sequence containing the elements of both sets without redeundancy.

__19. set_symmetric_difference( ) creates a set containing all the common elements of the two sets.

__20. includes( ) will test if every member of second set is also a member of the first set.

__21. transform( ) can be used to convert all elements of an array to upper case letters.

__22. The for_each( ) function modifies the elements of a container according to some criterion.

__23. generate( ) will generate a value by a function for every element of the container.

__24. The remove( ) function is a non-mutating algorithm.

__25. A predicate is a function that returns either true or false.

CHAPTER 18 STL ASSIGNMENTS

Q18a) What is the standard template library (STL)? What are the advantages of STL?

Q18b) Name and define the three components of STL.

Q18c) Explain the difference between sequence containers and associative containers. With what adapters can the sequence container be used?

Q18d) How are STL iterators like smart pointers? What are the two kinds of iterators that are used for the I/O streams? What are the purposes of the begin( ) and end( ) functions?

Q18e) Name and explain uses for three STL algorithms.

Q18f) How is a vector similar to a C-style array, and how does it differ?   What do the functions set( ) and push_back( ) do? What data structure container would be best implemented using a vector? How would you declare vector v as a vector of integers? Write the code to input a variable and then push it into the vector.

Q18g) Write a small program that gets numbers from the user and then sorts them in ascending order. Use the STL vector container and the algorithms push( ), begin( ),
end( ), and sort( ). Hint: Use the begin( ) and end( ) functions inside the sort function.

Q18h) Explain the difference between a map and a multimap, as well as the difference between a set and a multiset. In what situation would it be better to use a multimap rather than a map? Why? What needs to be kept in mind when creating a multiset?

Q18i) Name and define 4 STL operations or functions that can be used by any STL container.

Q18j) What is the STL deque and what operation is it usually confused with? What are five major operations for the deque?

Q18k) Write a small program to demonstrate one of the sequence adapters.

Q18l) Given the following information:

```
map<string, string> directory;
string name;
directory["Ebrahimi"] = "245-542-2157"
```

What would the following sample code do?
```
if(directory.find(name) != directory.end( )) {
cout << "Number for <<name<<"is"<<directory[name]<<"\n"; }
else  cout<<"Error";
```

Q18m) Write a search program that incorporates the above code. Add in 2 or more directories, change the output, and add a question that asks if the user would like to search the directory, with the choices y/n, which stands for yes or no.

Q18n) Define a set associative container. What do the following set operations do?

> set_union( )
> set_intersection( )
> set_difference( )
> set_symmetric_difference( )
> includes( )

Q18o) Write a complete program that tests all of the operations in question Q18n, using the following data: {0, 2, 4, 6, 8, 10} and {0, 1, 3, 5, 7, 9}.

Q18p) Convert the program you created in Q18o to use a multiset container. Make some of the data in the strings redundant.

Q18q) What are associated arrays and what is the benefit of implementing them with a map container? Assuming that a map is defined as: map<string, string>mapdir, what would the following code achieve?

> mapdir[name]=phone[i]
> mapdir.begin( ) and mapdir.end( )
> map<string, string, less<string>>miter;
> (*miter).first;
> (*miter).second;
> miter->first;
> miter->second;

Q18r) Name and define two operations for a set container. Write the code to test these two operations.

Q18s) Name three types of STL algorithms provided in #include<algorithm>. How do the STL algorithms work? Hint: How is the data stored? What do the conventions bi, ei, and val stand for and how are they used?

Q18t) What is the output of the following program? What algorithm is being used?

```
#include<cctype>
#include<algorithm>
#include<iostream>
#include<iterator>
using namespace std;
void main( ) {
        char letter[] = {'Q', 'R', 'S', 'T'}
        char dwnletter[5];
        transform(vowel, vowel + 4, dwnletter, tolower);
        for(char* i = dwnletter; i < dwnletter + 4; i++)  cout<<*i<< " "; }
```

Q18u) Since the number of elements is specified for a fill_n( ) function, when traversing through the data, what STL function is not needed? Write code to use fill( ) and fill_n( ).

Q18v) Explain the difference between generate( ) and generate_n( ). Demonstrate this difference with a program.

Q18w) What the different ways the STL copy function can be used?

Q18x) What is the difference between a mutating and non-mutating algorithm? Give examples of both.

Q18y) Explain what is meant by a predicate.

CASE STUDY –PAYROLL SYSTEM PHASE 18: STL

The purpose of this phase is to incorporate STL into your payroll system.

a) Use STL strings in place of character arrays.
b) Save employee information into vectors.
c) Save employee information into lists.
d) Use STL algorithms in your program such as search and sort.
e) Use a priority_queue in your payroll system to determine which employees will get bonuses based on employee ranking.

CHAPTER 19

ERRORS, EXCEPTION HANDLING, AND SOFTWARE ENGINEERING

While your program is running, you may encounter a problem that is unexpected. This problem can bring down the whole system. For example, your program may want to access a file that does not exist or, is in another directory. What would happen if your program is computing the average of a series of numbers, but the counter (denominator) is zero or becomes zero, or what happens to your program when it requests more memory than compiler can provide? Obviously these are unexpected situations that rarely happen and if they occur in an unguarded program, they may cause severe consequences. The strategy to handle errors is to provide a systematic way of detecting them and take the necessary actions to fix them and recover the program.

You may have already taken proper measures to combat the errors in your program simply by using an if-statement accompanied by a display message. The introduction of the **assert( )** function from header **#include <cassert>** is more advanced and takes advantage of the system error messages and aborts the program upon an unwanted situation. One might argue that the **assert( )** function will not be able to recover from the bug. Rather than aborting the program, you can take a different action when the bug occurs. A more sophisticated and systematic approach for error handling is known as *exception handling* that was introduced by ANSI-C++ standard and added to C++. It is called an exception since it is unlikely to happen, but when it does happen it may produce unwanted results. Exception handling consists of enclosing the code that may result in an exception in a **try** block and if an exception occurs it is thrown. The statement that handles the exception is inside the **catch** block. After an exception is thrown (raised), normal control flow will suspend and the program will search for a match or a portion of the program that can handle the exception. After the exception is handled the program will either terminate or resume normal execution after the corresponding catch block.
Use of exception handling can separate error reporting from error handling and as a result handling errors becomes systematic and readable.

In conclusion, use of exception handling does not guarantee that errors will not occur. There is no guaranteed solution in preventing errors. One should consider having a fault tolerance system.

CATEGORIES OF BUGS

Programming bugs (errors) can be categorized into three kinds: compile time, run time, and logical errors. Syntax or compile time errors are known as grammatical errors that are detected by the compiler. Examples of syntax errors are misspelling the keywords, omitting the necessary punctuation such as a semicolon, or not balancing the quotation, parenthesis, or statement pairs. Run-time errors are errors that occur during the execution of the program when it attempts to perform an operation that the system cannot perform (illegal). A popular example of a run-time error is when a program tries to divide a number by zero. Logical errors produce the wrong output, which is caused by applying inappropriate algorithms; for example when subtraction is used instead of addition. One analogy of a logical error would be driving east when intending to go west, and the driver will never reach the desired destination if given the wrong directions. Remember, in order for a program to produce output, the program has passed the stage of syntax and run-time error checking. Logical errors are the most difficult to detect and they are often confused with run-time errors. If there is a run-time error, the system will terminate or an exception will take place. Linkage errors might result when linking two separately compiled programs (functions). Duplication of variable names is an example of a linkage error. There are different opinions as to what is considered a logical error and what is not. Errors can be categorized with respect to the compiler as follows: lexical errors, such as errors resulting from misspelling; syntactic errors, such as unbalanced quotations or parentheses; semantic errors, such as applying an arithmetic operator to incompatible variables (data types), and logical errors, such as calling a recursive function without an exit (infinite).

SYNTAX VERSUS SEMANTIC ERRORS

Another form of error that is often detected by a compiler is known as a semantic (meaning) error. Syntax errors violate the language structure rules while semantic errors are syntactically correct but meaningless. An example of a semantic error is to perform arithmetic operations on 2 non-numeric variables, such as multiplication of 2 strings. Another example of a semantic error is performing arithmetic operations on the names of 2 functions (procedures) that do not return useful values. If the compiler does not detect a semantic error, it becomes a run-time error/logical error that is difficult to detect. For instance, associating an **else** to the wrong **if** statement, or applying the wrong precedence of arithmetic operators.

A common semantic error which is not detectable by compiler is using = when = = is the intended meaning. The semantic errors are more about understanding the meaning of the language constructs as opposed to problem solving. Logical errors are referred to as problem solving errors than errors resulting from language construct semantics.

SHOULD COMPILER ERROR MESSAGES BE TRUSTED

A compiler's job is to detect any errors that violate the language structure and report the error to the user. If there are no errors then it converts the program to a low level language (object code) so that it can be executed. Detecting the error and reporting it accurately isn't an easy task for compilers. Beginners put all their trust in the compiler because it is seen an important program that interprets programs. Due to incorrect and confusing error messages, dependence on the compiler's messages diminishes. With experience, error messages can be interpreted and found useful. One may wonder why a compiler cannot report errors accurately given all the technology we have. The following are some explanations: the line number reported may not be accurate due to the fact that the compiler has already proceeded to the next statement. Another reason for inaccuracy in error reporting is that the statement that contains the error has been eliminated, leading to more errors.

RUN-TIME ERROR - FILE DOES NOT EXIST: SIMPLE ERROR CHECKING

The following program demonstrates how error checking can be simply performed by placing an **if** statement with a report message. The program below displays a message if the file does not exist and exits the execution rather than leaving it to the system to crash.

```
#include<fstream>
#include<iostream>
using namespace std;
void main(){
        int id;
        ifstream fin ("pay.dat");
        if (fin==NULL){ cerr<<"CANNOT OPEN THE FILE"<<endl; exit(1); }//IF
        fin>>id;
        cout<<"ID IS: "<<id<<endl;
        }//MAIN
```

Figure 19.1a – Checking if the file exists

```
CANNOT OPEN THE FILE
```

Figure 19.1b – Output of Figure 19.1a

DIVIDE BY ZERO: A SIMPLE ERROR HANDLING PROGRAM

The program below illustrates a simple error check for divide-by-zero. An **if** statement determines if the denominator is zero and based on that a message is displayed and the program is aborted.

```
#include<iostream>
using namespace std;
void main(){
        int m,n;
        cout<<"ENTER TWO NUMBERS TO DIVIDE: ";
        cin>>m>>n;
        if(n==0) {cerr<<"CANNOT DIVIDE BY ZERO"<<endl ;abort();}//IF
        else cout<<"QUOTIENT IS: "<<m/n<<endl;
        }//MAIN
```

Figure 19.2a – Program to check for divide by zero

ENTER TWO NUMBERS TO DIVIDE: 6 0
CANNOT DIVIDE BY ZERO

Figure 19.2b – Output of Figure 19.2a

OTHER RUN TIME ERRORS

In the preceding programs, we demonstrated two run-time errors: when the file does not exist and when the program divides by zero. Other run time errors are:

INSUFFICIENT MEMORY: This error results when a program tries to allocate memory dynamically, and there is not enough available memory such as:

     phw=new int [100000];

INFINITE RECURSION: Behind the scenes of a recursive function is the stack. On each call to the function, values such as parameters and local variables are pushed into the stack and on the return the values are popped from the stack. If the recursive function never terminates, values will be pushed to the stack with every call and at some point the stack will be exhausted (overflowed) and crash will occur.

RUN-TIME ERROR: READING PASSED END OF FILE

A common run time error for novice programmers is when reading input data, especially from a data file, trying to read passed the end of the file. For example, what would happen if there are only 3 input data in the data file and you try to read 5 data in your program? One would expect that only 3 values would be read and the program would request the additional data however this is not the case. The following program was run on Visual C++6.0, GNU C++, and TURBO C++ 3.0. In all cases, the last data in the file repeated for the remainder of the loop, even after the end of file was reached. Imagine if a payroll system had a loop for writing checks and the end of file was reached before the loop ended. In this case the last person in the data file would keep receiving checks until the loop ends. There are several solutions to this problem. The user can check the
cin.eof( ) to break the loop, or check the status of the other input stream member functions such as: **bad( )**, **fail( )**, or **good( )**. Note that these functions return a Boolean value.

```
#include<fstream.h>
#include<iostream.h>
void main(){
        ifstream fin("employees.txt",ios::in);
        char fname[20], lname[20];
        for(int i=0; i<10; i++){
                fin>>fname>>lname;
                cout<<fname<<" "<<lname<<" ";
                cout<<"1,000.00"<<endl;}//FOR
}//MAIN
```

```
Alireza Ebrahimi
Jason Smith
Robert Williams
Jane Doe
```

Figure 19.3a – Run-time error of reading past end of file   *Figure 19.3c – employees.txt*

```
Alireza Ebrahimi 1,000.00
Jason Smith 1,000.00
Robert Williams 1,000.00
Jane Doe 1,000.00
Jane Doe 1,000.00
Jane Doe 1,000.00
Jane Doe 1,000.00
Jane Doe 1,000.00
Jane Doe 1,000.00
Jane Doe 1,000.00
```

Figure 19.3b – Output of Figure 19.3a

C++ DEBUGGER: BREAKPOINTS, WATCHING VARIABLES, SINGLE STEPPING

Most of the C++ compilers (Visual C++, Borland C++, and CodeWarrior) come with an Integrated Development Environment known as IDE, providing an environment with many features including editing, compiling, and a debugging program. With a debugger one can run the program and watch the values or set breakpoints and observe how the values of the variables change as stepping through the code. With the help of a debugger one can detect and correct the bugs. Using a breakpoint in a program will enable one to execute the program up to the breakpoint and see the code line by line and inspect variable values. Every compiler has it's own debugger that might be a little different than others. If one can't use the debugger one can debug a program by inserting **cout** statements to display the contents of the variable. For example one can insert a **cout** statement inside a loop, **if** statement, or a function to inspect the control flow and check the content of a variable. Comments /*   */ can be used to isolate the problem in the program. If a Unix C++ compiler (e.g. g++ , GNU) is used the debugging information can be obtained by typing the command **man**. On Dos/Windows environments main compilers are from: Borland, Microsoft, and CodeWarrior. Among the popular C++ compilers for the Macintosh environment are Symantec C++ and CodeWarrior.

ASSERTION AS A DEBUGGING TOOL

In order for a program to continue, the assertion must be true at the point where the **assert( )** function is placed. For an assertion to be true, the parameter passed to the assert function must be true. If the assertion fails (false), the execution will be aborted and the message generated by the language will be displayed. The assert function can be used as a debugging tool to trace a program at any given point in the program.

The assert routine (macro) takes an expression (argument) that either evaluates to true or false. The directive #include <cassert> must be included to use **assert( )**. If there is no additional need for the assertion in debugging the program, **assert( )** can be disabled by simply having a #define NDEBUG before the assert include header.

Program for assert:

```
#include <cassert>
#include<iostream>
using namespace std;
void main(){
        int n=0;
        int m=5;
        assert (n>0);
        cout<<m/n<<endl;
}//MAIN
```

Figure 19.4a – Program using the assert( ) function

```
Assertion failed: n>0, file C:\Windows\Desktop\cassert.cpp, line 7
```

Figure 19.4b – Output of Figure 19.4a

DIFFERENT STRATEGIES FOR ERROR HANDLING

How are run-time errors handled? There are many ways to handle the errors. The simplest way to handle errors is to use an **if**-statement with a display routine in a program such as **cout** or **cerr**. A program can be traced, by putting several display routines, such as **cout** to investigate the contents of a variable, by displaying it at different stages of a program. By placing a display routine in the program, one can trace the flow of the program. A debugger is another tool used to trace through the program. A new addition to C++, known as exception handling, is the **try** and **catch** block. The **try** and **catch** block can be used in several ways such as catching and displaying the system run-time messages or user-appropriate messages. Some of the run-time messages that can be detected by exception handling are: divide-by-zero, memory access out of range, and file does not exist.

HOW TO THROW AN EXCEPTION

The keyword **try** denotes that there can be situations that may cause an exception. The chance of error is 1% and most likely the statement will be executed without any problem.

When an exception occurs, the execution of a program will stop at the point of the throw. Its control is transferred to the point where the program will take care of the exception (catch). At the point where the **catch** keyword is matched with its type of throw, the exception is resolved. Exception handling can be complicated and the compiler may go through several steps to handle the exception. The compiler searches for the closest catch block in the same function where the throw is thrown. If a match is not found nearby, the compiler will continue to search until a catch handler is found or until it reaches the outermost scope. In this case, the program will terminate by calling the **terminate( )** function. Note that a stack is used to keep track of catch handlers.

TRY STATEMENT

In order to include exception handling in a program, the statements are enclosed in a try block, the key word **try** follow by braces {}.

```
try {
        // a block of statements that might throw an exception
        //statement1 throw e1
        //statement 2 throw e2
        }//TRY
catch (t1){
        // handles the exception that is thrown by e1
        // the code following the catch perform operation that should be handled
        }//T1
catch (t2) {
        // handles the exception that is thrown by e2
        }//T2
```

If every statement in the try block works well, there would not be a problem. As soon as one of the statements causes a problem, the execution is transferred from that point to the appropriate catch clause- the key word **catch** followed by {}. There would be a catch clause of the same type for each throw type. Each throw type will match its catch type. For example, if id is of the type string the catch clause of string will grab it. Similarly, the catch clause of an integer will grab the integer throws. Remember that any statement in the try block can throw an exception.

try, throw, AND catch: A SIMPLE EXCEPTION PROGRAM

The purpose of the following program is to demonstrate how the try, throw, and catch work together. This program does not show the reasoning behind the exception handling. In the program below the type of throw and type of catch is an integer, but other types can be used or a try can have several throws and several catches with different types. However, only a throw type will match a catch type.

```
#include<iostream>
using namespace std;
void main(){
        try {    cout<<"HELLO LET'S THROW AN EXCEPTION";
                throw 1;
                cout<<"\nNEVER BACK  HERE";
                }//TRY
        catch (int e){
                cout<<"\nEXCEPTION VALUE CAUGHT "<<e<<endl;
                }//CATCH
        cout<<"\nTHE END "<<endl;
}//MAIN
```

Figure 19.5a – Example of try, throw, and catch

```
HELLO LET'S THROW AN EXCEPTION
EXCEPTION VALUE CAUGHT 1

THE END
```

Figure 19.5b – Output of Figure 19.5a

THROW AN EXCEPTION

During the program run-time, what has caused the program to crash and how would you recover it before even the crash happens? Exception handling proposes systematic ways to deal with faults that occur during run-time and carries steps to recover the errors. In the try block a value is thrown that must match the type of the catch block (caught exception type).

The following program crashes during run-time as a result of the index of an array that is out of range. Remember that indexes of an array start at zero and end with one less than the size of the array. A common mistake is to use the size of the array to access the array.

```cpp
#include<iostream>
#include<cassert>
using namespace std;

void main(){
        int a[5];
        int max=4;
        int i= -1;
        try{    if(i<0) throw  "OUT OF RANGE: TOO LOW";
                a[i]=8;
                cout<<a[i]<<endl;       }//TRY
        catch(char * str){ cout<<str<<endl;    }//CATCH
        i=5;
        try{    if(i>=5) throw "OUT OF RANGE: TOO HIGH";
                a[i]=3;
                cout<<a[i]<<endl;       }//TRY
        catch(char * str){  cout<<str<<endl;  }//CATCH
        cout<<"BYE";
}//MAIN
```

Figure 19.6a – Checking for array index out of range

```
OUT OF RANGE: TOO LOW
OUT OF RANGE: TOO HIGH
BYE
```

Figure 19.6b – Output of Figure 19.6a

A try WITH MULTIPLE throws

The following program illustrates the use of try-throw-catch to handle an array index that is out of range. Inside the try block, two throws are used with a string type (array of characters) for the same purpose but each has a different condition. Immediately after the try block, the catch block is placed and accepts the exception of type string. The string is passed to the catch block and is displayed. In a program, we can have several try blocks as well as several catches.

```
#include <iostream.h>
#include <exception>
using namespace std;
void main () {
 int tbl[5];
 int i=0;
 while(i<2){
        try{
         int index;
         cout<<"ENTER A NUMBER BETWEEN (-1..5) TO CATCH THE SYSTEM EXCEPTION: ";
         cin>>index;
         if(index<0){
                throw "OUT OF RANGE\n";}
                    if(index>=5){
                throw "OUT OF RANGE\n";}
             cout<<"MY ARRAY IS "<<tbl[index]<<endl;
             }//TRY
        catch(char* str){
                   cout<<str;
             }//CATCH
        i++;
 }//WHILE
}//MAIN
```

Figure 19.7a – Exception handling with multiple throws

```
ENTER A NUMBER BETWEEN (-1..5) TO CATCH THE SYSTEM EXCEPTION: -1
OUT OF RANGE
ENTER A NUMBER BETWEEN (-1..5) TO CATCH THE SYSTEM EXCEPTION: 4
MY ARRAY IS -858993460
```

Figure 19.7b – Output of Figure 19.7a

NESTED EXCEPTION HANDLING WITH FUNCTIONS

Until now you may have wondered what all the fuss about exception handling is if it could be accomplished by a series of **if** statements. However, placing a series of **if** statements in a program would make it messy. By using error-handling techniques, error handling can be centralized in the main program where the functions are called, and an exception can be thrown elsewhere in those functions, or even in further nested functions.

```
#include<iostream.h>

void inverse(int [], int,int);

void main(){
        const MAXSIZE=5;
        int a[]={8,5,3,1,0};
        int index;
        try{
                cout<<"ENTER THE INDEX FOR INVERSE: ";
        cin>>index;
        inverse(a,index,MAXSIZE);
        }//TRY
        catch (char *s){ cout <<"EXCEPTIONAL ERROR: "<<s<<endl; }//CATCH;
        }//MAIN
```

Figure 19.8a – Nested exception handling with functions

```
ENTER THE INDEX FOR INVERSE: 3
THE INVERSE IS: 1

ENTER THE INDEX FOR INVERSE: 10
EXCEPTIONAL ERROR: OUT OF RANGE

ENTER THE INDEX FOR INVERSE: 4
EXCEPTIONAL ERROR: DIVIDE BY ZERO
```

Figure 19.8b – Output of Figure 19.8a

TYPELESS EXCEPTION FOR UNCAUGHT EXCEPTIONS: catch(…)

A catch block can have any type; however, if you want the catch handler to be able to catch any exception then you need to place three periods inside the parentheses after the catch keyword. The **catch**(…) handler can be used to catch any other exception that is not caught by other previous catch handlers. This kind of exception is also known as an uncaught exception or an unexpected exception.

As explained earlier, in a catch block you can take a series of steps such as: displaying a message explaining the cause of error, or performing some recovery such as ignoring the current input and reading the next input data or spelling the file name correctly and trying again. Inside a catch handler, you may want to terminate the program.

```
#include <iostream>
using namespace std;
main (){
        try {

        }//TRY
        catch (...){
                cout<<" illegal operation "<<endl;
        }//CATCH
}//MAIN
```

RE-THROWING AN EXCEPTION: throw WITHOUT A PARAMETER

It is possible to throw an exception again (re-throw) inside a catch block. To re-throw an exception, you need the keyword throw without any parameter (exception). By re-throwing, the outer catch can handle the exception. One reason for re-throw is that several handlers (catch) can be used, and each can take care of one situation. Do not be confused by the wording of re-throw, remember that re-throw does not catch the same handler, but looks outside the catch block for the next catch match.

The purpose of the following program is to elaborate on how throw (re-throw) works, without getting involved in the technicalities of it.

```
#include <iostream>
using namespace std;
void fun(void);
void main(){
        try{ fun(); }//TRY
        catch(char*){ cout<<"BALL GOT CAUGHT"<<endl;}//CATCH
        }//MAIN
void fun(){
        try{ throw "THE BALL";}//TRY
        catch(char*){ cout<<"RETHROW THE BALL"<<endl;
            throw;}//CATCH
        }//FUN
```

Figure 19.9a – Re-throwing an exception

```
RETHROW THE BALL
BALL GOT CAUGHT
```

Figure 19.9b – Output of Figure 19.9a

In the following example, a re-throw will be used for the next memory allocation while executing new.

```
#include<iostream.h>
void main(){
        try{ char *p= new char [10000];
                cin>>p;
                cout<<"GIANT WORD IS: "<<p<<endl;
                char *q= new char [1000000000];
                cin>>q;
                cout<<"NEXT GIANT WORD IS: "<<q<<endl; }//TRY
        catch(...){ cout<<"BAD MEM ALLOCATION"<<endl;
        throw; }//CATCH
        }//MAIN
```

Figure 19.10a – Another example using re-throw

```
Hello
GIANT WORD IS: Hello
Goodbye
NEXT GIANT WORD IS: BAD MEM ALLOCATION
```

Figure 19.10b – Output of Figure 19.10a

STANDARD LIBRARY EXCEPTIONS

The standard library defines certain types of exception objects that can be used to find out what has happened, along with diagnostic messages to describe the error. An example of exception handling could be if we are dealing with a stack data structure and we are pushing values into and popping values from the stack. The question is, what happens if there is no more room in the stack to push a value (overflow) or if there is no value in the stack left to pop (underflow). An exception handler can take care of these situations by throwing an **overflow**( ) or **underflow**( ) exception; the exception is caught and the necessary action is performed. Despite all the exceptions in a situation, in case of an uncaught exception, the functions **terminate**( ) and **unexpected**( ) are used as escape mechanisms.

EXAMPLES OF STANDARD LIBRARY EXCEPTION CLASSES

The standard library defines several exception classes that can be used in exception handling cases.

out_of_range	**range_error**	**runtime_error**	**logic_error**	**length_error**
domain_error	**overflow_error**	**underflow_eror**	**invalid_argument**	

The above names may be confusing at first, but after some practice you will overcome the differences. For example, **out_of_range** is used for array and container subscripts while **range_error** gives a boundary for a data type such as the **char** ASCII value range.

```cpp
#include<iostream>
#include <stdexcept>
using namespace std;
int findavg(int, int);
void main(){
        int a[]={2, 4, 10, 5, 16};
        try { throw out_of_range("OUT OF RANGE ERROR");
                cout<<findavg(a[1],a[5]);
                }//TRY
        catch(const exception& e){
                cout<<"TRY TO ACCESS ARRAY OUT OF BOUND"<<endl;
                cout<<e.what()<<endl;}//CATCH
        }//MAIN
int findavg(int x,int y){ return (x+y)/2; }//AVG
```

Figure 19.11a – Program checking for out of range error

```
TRY TO ACCESS ARRAY OUT OF BOUND
OUT OF RANGE ERROR
```

Figure 19.11b – Output of Figure 19.11a

C++ STANDARD EXCEPTIONS

The C++ standard library comes with a set of exceptions known as standard exceptions that are formed with a hierarchy divided into three categories of **logic_error**, **runtime_error**, and other exceptions. This division could be confusing but try to be patient. In this exception hierarchy the **logic_errors** are the errors that can be caught before the program begins running or by checking the parameters to the functions and the constructors. One example of an exception error belonging to **logic_error** is **out_of_range,** regarding an array or a container. The other categories of exception errors are known as **runtime_error** for the errors that are caught during the running of the program such as **overflow_error** and **underflow_error**. The third category of exception errors is **bad_exception,** such as **bad_alloc** for memory failure. In order to take advantage of these standard exceptions we have to know which function and operator will throw them and under which header they are defined. For example, the **bad_alloc** exception is thrown by **new** and is defined in the header <new>. The following program allows the user to enter the size of memory to be allocated, and if it is too big, a **bad_alloc** exception is thrown without needing the keyword **throw**.

```
#include<iostream>
#include<new>
using namespace std;
void main(){
    double *ptr;
    int size;
    try{
        for(int i=0; i<4; i++){
        cout<<"ENTER THE SIZE OF MEMORY: ";
        cin>>size;
        ptr=new double[size];
        cout<<"MEMORY ALLOCATED"<<endl;}//FOR
        }//TRY
    catch(bad_alloc e){
        cout<<"EXCEPTION ERROR: "<<e.what()<<endl;
        }//CATCH
    }//MAIN
```

Figure 19.12a – Program throwing bad_alloc exception

```
ENTER THE SIZE OF MEMORY: 500
MEMORY ALLOCATED
ENTER THE SIZE OF MEMORY: 50000
MEMORY ALLOCATED
ENTER THE SIZE OF MEMORY: 500000000
EXCEPTION ERROR: bad_alloc
```

Figure 19.12b – Output of Figure 19.12a

EXCEPTION HEADER FILES

Standard C++ defines two header files <exception> and <stdexcept> that define several built-in exception classes. For each of these exception classes there is a constructor through which a string or error message can be passed to the class. The header <exception> contains classes, types, and functions that are used for handling errors.

EXAMPLE OF STANDARD EXCEPTION: IOS_BASE::FAILURE

A standard exception **ios_base::failure** is thrown when the input data does not correspond to its data type. If the data entered is different than integer, the standard exception **ios_base::failure** will be thrown and we have to write the catch block to catch the exception and take an appropriate action, giving the programmer a choice to handle it. In the program below, the programmer decided to display a message.

```
#include<iostream>
using namespace std;
void main(){
        int num;
        try{
                while(cin>>num){
                        cout<<"NUM IS "<<num<<endl;}//WHILE
        }//TRY
        catch(ios_base::failure){
                cout<<"SERIOUS ERROR IN DATA ENTRY"<<endl;}//CATCH
        cout<<"VALID DATA ENTRY"<<endl;
}//MAIN
```

Figure 19.13a – Example using standard exception ios_base::failure

```
434343
NUM IS 434343
hdhdhd
VALID DATA ENTRY
```

Figure 19.13b – Output of Figure 19.13a

EXCEPTION CLASS AND EXCEPTION OBJECT

One important feature of exception handling is the ability to work with any data type including user-defined types such as a class and its instance, an object. An exception object contains the necessary information needed to pass to an exception handler as to what to do. C++ has its own standard exception library containing several classes that a user can use, or a user can build its own exception class. For example, **domain_error** is one of the exceptions when an argument is outside of the set of values for a function. The **domain_error** is defined in the standard library in the header #include <stdexcept>.

AGAIN, WHAT IS PROGRAMMING?

Programming is not just writing codes and being skilled in a particular programming language's constructs. It is a human activity that involves other social responsibilities. One might argue that programming is science, art, psychology, engineering, or philosophy. I am sure we can benefit from the above fields by incorporating them into programming, and even give more weight to one field over another, depending on the situation.

A program (software) is a dynamic entity that is continuously changing, even as the software is ready to be released. You are not writing the program for yourself, you have to know what your client wants and understand their needs. The cost, time (schedule), and people (psychology) are among the important factors that must be considered in programming.

What are the most widely accepted approaches to programming? In Program Integration (composition), a program is built from several pieces (units). These units have to be written, tested, and put together (integrated). Problems may arise as result of integrating one unit to the existing integrated units.

WHERE IS THE PROBLEM? : AVOID THE BIG BANG

Many people have the tendency of writing many lines of code and waiting until the end to test it as to whether it works or not. It is better to test the program as it is written; for a large program, the testing strategy should be taken into consideration ahead of time. Can you imagine having a thousand lines of code and not knowing why your program is not working? Even if your program works and you have the desired output, you cannot conclude that your program is correct without testing it. While testing a program is not an easy job, you should make your program in such a way that it can be easily tested. Again, it is up to you and specifications as to how much you want to test, putting firewalls everywhere as exhaustive testing or being paranoid by testing every test itself, building a fault tolerance system. Testing itself may take away a lot of your energy, and may be costly. As a programmer you should consider the situations that may result in errors and consider what ought to be done in these cases. Try to continually test the program as it progresses, and start as soon as possible. By testing incrementally you can focus on where the errors occur and fix them on the spot, rather than delaying them until you need to see the big picture. At that stage surprises may be encountered that are difficult to trace and repair. One more thought: testing should be propagated throughout the entire development of software, not just the coding, but the whole process. The software development process should be viewed as an iterative incremental, spiral process rather than a kind of waterfall process where one phase finishes and another begins.

SOFTWARE ENGINEERING: LIFE CYCLES

Software is a program but a program may not necessarily be software since it is more than just a bunch of code. Software is a real-world program that requires careful planning in all phases of its development and its maintenance, including documentation. Building software has been equated to the construction of buildings and bridges using engineering standards and tools making a branch of engineering disciplines known as software engineering. The term software engineering was coined at a NATO conference in 1968 in response to the software crisis. Therefore in software engineering you apply systematic, disciplined, and measurable approaches to the development and operation of software, as well as its maintenance. For the birth, life, and death of software, there are events and processes that take place and can be systematically approached; this is known as a life cycle. A life cycle covers requirements, design, implementation, testing, and maintenance. Testing can be divided into: unit testing, integration testing, and system testing. Note that testing should be incorporated in all phases of software life including design review and early stages.

In top-down design you break the program into manageable units (functions) as much as you can and then deal with the details at a later time. The bottom-up approach starts with the most inner part of a unit, mainly a crucial unit, and builds from there until the whole system is built. When there is a question regarding the feasibility of a design, bottom-up is a good approach, otherwise top-down is a common design approach.

Each module (e.g. function) should have elements that are closely related to one another (high cohesion). Each module should be less dependent on one another (low coupling).

In the object-oriented approach, software is built from a set of classes by promoting code reuse through derivation, overloading by offering additional meanings, use of templates for generic programming, and establishing exception handling for a systematic way to detect and respond to errors.

SOFTWARE REQUIREMENTS

Requirement analysis is the process of finding and understanding what the customer wants and how the program will satisfy these requirements. One example of requirements would be what the main program's menu should look like and how the program interacts with the user. The gathering of requirements may come by interviewing the customer, known as C-requirements, and passing the C-requirements to the developer (programmer), known as D-requirements. It is important that the requirements are

648

understood by all parties involved in software development, otherwise the product will be different than originally intended. A verification step at this stage should ensure the correctness of the requirements.

UML (UNIFIED MODELING LANGUAGE): A VISUAL MODELING

UML is a visual and practical approach for developing a system (software or hardware). UML stands for Unified Modeling Language and consists of a collection of standard graphic notations (elements) used in designing object-oriented systems. A standard is an important way of communication to all parties involved in modeling a system such as users, analysts, developers, testers, managers, and others. In a modeling you want to be able to take the user's needs and map it to the requirements and eventually generate the code. Similarly, in a modeling process, you should be able to trace the system backwards from the code to the requirements and the user's needs. In the past, several approaches were used to standardize system Modeling and Design but none were satisfactory. Finally, unifying three methods from three pioneers, Grady Booch, Jim Rumbaugh, and Ivar Jackobson set a standard for object-oriented analysis and design which was adopted in Fall 1997 by OMG (Object Management Group).

UML USE CASES AND ACTORS

In order to document and gather the requirements for building software (or hardware), UML uses a standard technique called *use case*, where each use case identifies and summarizes the user's intents and the responsibilities of the system, meaning a use case collects scenarios.

An **actor** is usually a user participating in the use case scenario that can have different personalities. In other words, anything having behavior is an actor. Note that an actor can be a user interacting with program, an operating system, or server. An actor is shown by a stick figure, a use case by an oval diagram, and communication (link) between an actor and use case is drawn as a line. A use case diagram consists of an overview of several use cases, actors (initiating actor, benefiting actor), and their communications.

UML DIAGRAMS

UML comes with a variety of diagram types to represent a collection of classes in the form of blocks connected differently depending on their relationship such as inheritance and aggregation structures. A major part of UML is to understand the notation of UML diagrams, how to produce them, and how these diagrams are related to each other. The following is a list of different diagrams used by UML:
Case Diagram, Class Diagram, Object Diagram, State Diagram, Sequence Diagram, Collaboration Diagram, Activity Diagram, Component Diagram, and Deployment Diagram.

A class diagram consists of classes and their relationship and each class icon is divided into three parts such as class name, attribute (data), and operations. Access modifiers such as +, -, and # correspond to public, private, and protected.

Employee
+Name #Salary -Age
+displaysalary +setsalary

UML AND RATIONAL ROSE

Traditionally, to build software, the requirement is written and programmers write the code. Somehow the design as an important step is hidden, without any standard, difficult for others to follow. Now, with emergence of the object-oriented paradigm, there is a demand that before coding a program, you must represent the objects, hierarchical relations, and other interactions between the objects using a modeling language, now mainly UML.

Rational Rose provides an environment that enables you to design use cases and their diagrams, interaction among the objects and class diagrams, component diagrams to map to implementation components, and finally a deployment diagram.
Note that since UML is not a programming language, you cannot write a program in UML. However, with the Rational Rose and other CASE tools, you can generate codes for C++, Java, and Visual Basic. You can also reverse engineer a Visual C++ program into existing components of Rose. You should not interpret code generation wrong, since we still need programmers.

As an exercise, using UML, describe and draw the use cases and class diagrams for a payroll system. For further information, you can look for UML tutorials and diagram examples on the Internet.

FLOWCHARTING

There was a time when flowcharts, as pictorial representations, were required before even writing a program. Computer time was expensive and PCs were not in homes yet. Programmers found themselves bounded to the charts. For many years the flow chart was one of the road maps of programming. To draw a flowchart, at first the problem is transferred to a logical blueprint using blocks with specific shapes indicating the nature of the operations. For example, the diamond-shape block represents a decision with one entry and two exits (true exit, false exit) and is used for testing (conditions). A rectangle is used for an operation or a sequence of operations. A rectangle with two vertical lines is used for a sub-program. A parallelogram is for input and output. An ellipse indicates the beginning and end of a flowchart. A pointed arrow is used for the direction of control flow. In case of a larger flowchart (more than one page), circles are used as connectors in such away that a circle with a number in one flowchart will match the connecting circle in another chart. One drawback to flowcharts was that programmers often neglected to adjust the chart when the program was changed, making the flowchart incorrect. One scenario that contributed to this problem is the situation where programmers changed the strategy of a program, even using trial and error tactics, and, on sudden success while the programmers celebrated the working program, a change to flow chart was forgotten. Many programmers drew the flowchart after the program was written or even used flowchart generators that defeated the original purpose of flow charts. As an exercise, draw a flowchart for finding the roots of a quadratic equation and then write the program and if you are happy with it, draw a flow chart for your payroll program.

TOPICS NOT COVERED HERE

Since there are several statements in a program, including input/output or computation, an exception in one statement may cause a side effect on another. While you want the main program to catch and report all exceptions, you should avoid throwing certain exceptions from copy constructors and destructors. A function can propagate a certain type of exception during its execution. Throwing and catching an exception by a function can have an impact on the function itself as well as other related functions, therefore it is possible throw an exception specification to specify the type of exception a function has as part of the function declaration. For example, according the following specification: **fun(char c) throw (e1, e2);** the function will only throw e1 and e2 as its exception. Any other exception throw by function will result in a call to **unexcepted( )**, which calls **terminate( )**, which in turn calls **abort( )**.

Exception handling is a powerful feature of C++, along with templates; however, designing and implementing an exception-safe code with templates can be difficult. In exception handling, the functions **abort( )** and **exit( )** are used to terminate the program. These functions are C oriented rather than C++ and therefore lack the housekeeping to clean up and release the resources that are no longer in use. Some exception handling techniques are compiler dependent and, for that reason, you may want to check your compiler's manual; in case it does not support certain exception handling features, you can write your own exception handling.

The include <errno.h> and its new version <cerror> contain the variable **errno** that can be set by an operation and then tested against other values provided by the header such as constants **ERANGE** and **EDOM** for **range_error** (number being too large) and **domain_error** (unaccepted function argument), respectively.

```
if (errno==EDOM) cerr<<"ERROR IN DOMAIN – bad argument ";
if (errno==ERANGE) cerr<<"TOO LARGE NUMBER";
```

The topics of software development and software engineering by themselves are gigantic and here we have only touched a bit of them. Obviously it is better to prevent errors rather than fixing them. Fixing an error may result in changing all parts of a program which requires time and cost. It is necessary to write a program in a structured, well-defined manner. Try to reuse what is already tested.

An exception is not only bound to built-in data types such as integer or double, a programmer can built its own customized generic exception class that reports the exception errors by including a proper message and the location of the error.

Exception safety is a major concern when dealing with STL containers. So that the program behaves predictably when an exception is thrown, catch the exception and take the proper action such as destroying the constructed object and re-throwing the exception when needed. In other words, the thrown exception should leave the container in a predictable state so the container would not lose track of allocated storage and the container can be destroyed properly. Exception handling in STL containers can be a very extensive subject that you may want to explore at your own time, answering question such as what would happen to a container when an exception is thrown during an operation, would the contents of a container restore to the same state as it had before, or would its contents become unpredictable, and finally would the list container be better than vector?

While exception handling is a good tool for error handling, you should not think that it will detect and handle all the errors including the deliberate entries, and do not use exception handling for purposes other than errors or treat it as another control structure such as **if** and **return**.

CLOSING REMARKS AND LOOKING AHEAD

Like the phrase "human to err", writing program and the process of software development is error-prone. One way to prevent an error is to start at the early stages of software development life cycles such as specification, design, and implementation so that at any of these stages, through testing and feedback, the errors can be recovered and fixed. In fact, in software development because of an error, the software may have to be redesigned or re-implemented and/or even go through several iterations of development (iterative design).

The theme of this chapter is to understand errors and try to handle a category of errors. A traditional way of handling errors is to place an **if** statement with an error message and exit the program or check the return value of a function for an error code such as –1, or NULL. Keeping track of each error code can be error-prone itself; making this traditional method an inefficient way to handle errors since in case of a failure, there would be no error code. Exception handling by using try-throw-catch is a technique that addresses the weaknesses of traditional error handling. The use of exception handling in a program makes error handling systematic and manageable. In fact, exception handling plays an essential role in languages other than C++ including the .NET framework. In Java you will not find a real program without exception handling.

Note that standard exception was added to C++ at a later time; therefore you should make sure that your compiler supports it An exception class is used as the argument to a throw statement to communicate with the exception handler.

How do we write a program that does not contain a bug? Should we go offensive or defensive? Like defensive driving, how we are preventing an accident? Taking all protective measures to the fullest extent. What would be the overhead in time and space? In the next chapter, the end of this book, I will give a final concluding remark in addition to a mixed bag (potpourri), including features, subjects, and topics that that did not fit into categories discussed in the previous chapters.

SELF-TEST TRUE-FALSE CHAPTER 19 ERRORS, EXCEPTION HANDLING, AND SOFTWARE ENGINEERING

__1. Use of exception handling does not guarantee that errors will not occur.

__2. Programming bugs can be categorized into three kinds: compile time, run time, and logical errors.

__3. Semantic errors violate the language structure rules and generate error messages.

__4. ifstream fin("data.txt"); if(fin==NULL) cout<<"NO FILE";   will check if the file exists.

__5. Insufficient memory is a run time error that occurs when the dynamic allocation of memory fails.

__6. An IDE provides features such as editing, compiling, and debugging.

__7. An assert( ) function must be false in order for a program to continue.

__8. An if statement can be used to catch some run-time errors.

__9. The keyword try denotes that there can be situations that may cause an exception.

__10. A program can be terminated by calling the terminate( ) function.

__11. If there is more than one throw, each having a different data type, there must be a catch for each type.

__12. catch(…) can be used to catch any other exception not caught by previous catch handlers.

__13. Re-throwing inside of a catch block is not allowed.

__14. In the case of an uncaught exception, unexpected( ) can be used as an escape mechanism.

__15. The out_of_range exception is used for array and container subscripts.

__16. range_error gives a boundary for a data type such as the char ASCII value range.

__17. C++ standard library divides exceptions into three categories: logic_error, runtime_error, and others.

__18. A bad_alloc exception is thrown when trying to allocate more memory than is available.

__19. ios_base::failure is thrown when the input data does not correspond to its data type.

__20. domain_error is an exception for when an argument is outside of the set of values for a function.

__21. Software is a program but a program may not necessarily be software since its more than just code.

__22. It is better to write an entire program and test it at the end, rather than testing at each phase.

__23. UML is a visual and practical approach for developing a system.

__24. UML comes with variety of diagram types such as case diagram, class diagram, object diagram etc.

__25. UML is a programming language that you can write many different programs.

CHAPTER 19 ERRORS, EXCEPTION HANDLING, AND SOFTWARE ENGINEERING ASSIGNMENTS

Q19a) Explain how the function assert( ) from the header file <cassert> is used. How does the error handling method of try and catch work?

Q19b) What are the three kinds of programming bugs? Explain each of them. What is the difference between syntax and semantic errors? Can we trust compiler error messages? Explain.

Q19c) Write a simple C++ program that checks if an input file exists or not. Write a program that divides two numbers and checks if the denominator is zero.

Q19d) Explain the following three run time errors: insufficient memory, infinite recursion, and reading passed end of file.

Q19e) Run the following program for different data types. Re-run the program after removing the line "throw 1;" (5th line).

```
#include <iostream>
using namespace std;
void main(){
try { cout<<"HELLO LET'S THROW AN EXEPTION";
    throw 1;
    cout<<"\nNEVER BACK HERE";
    }//TRY
catch (int e){
    cout<<"\nEXEPTION VALUE CAUGHT"<<e<<endl;
    }//CATCH
    cout<<"\nTHE END" << endl;
}//MAIN
```

Q19f) Define the functionality of the following standard library exception classes: out_of_range, range_error, runtime_error, logic_error, length_error, domain_error, overflow_error, underflow_error, and invalid_argument.

Q19g) What is the output of the following program? Input: Ebrahimi
```
#include <iostream>
using namespace std;
void main(){
        int num;
   try {                while(cin>>num){
                        cout<<"NUM IS "<< num << endl;}//WHILE
        }//TRY
        catch(ios_base::failure){
                cout<<"SERIOUS ERROR IN DATA ENTRY" << endl;}//CATCH
        cout <<"VALID DATA ENTRY" << endl;                }//MAIN
```

Q19h) Explain why a programmer should test his/her program often and not wait until the program is completed to test.

Q19i) What are the topics that are covered in the life cycles of software engineering? What is software requirement analysis? Give an example of a requirement analysis.

Q19j) What is UML? Explain use case and actor. What is rational rose? Name 5 diagrams used by UML.

CASE STUDY CHAPTER 19: ERRORS, EXCEPTION HANDLING AND SOFTWARE ENGINEERING

a) Extend your program to check if the input files exist or not. Your program should include error handling to detect if it attempts to open a file that does not exist. If the input file does not exist, your program should display an error message.
b) Include error checking and validation in your system for input, computation, and output. For example, a name should not contain any numbers, all numbers must be digits and positive, and the maximum hours one can work should be limited to 112 hours per week.
c) Modify the payroll program so that the program will not crash when the use enters an incorrect data type (e.g. Entering a number instead of a character).
d) In your payroll program, use standard library exception classes and standard exception classes to prevent errors in your program.
e) Describe your project from the point of view of the software life cycles.

CHAPTER 20

POTPOURRI (MIXED BAG)

While wrapping up this book, I found there were many concepts and topics that should have been introduced in earlier chapters but did not fit into a single chapter. These topics are introduced here as a mixed bag with a variety of flavors. Also, I want to congratulate you for getting this far and covering the many chapters. Obviously you have obtained a unique and worthwhile experience. You should be proud and put into use what you have learned. In my own experience, I have found that repetition is the key to my own learning, whether learning a programming language or a natural language like Spanish or even Chinese.

BIT-WISE OPERATIONS

One power of C/C++ is the ability to perform low-level operations that are done by machine languages. These operations are performed on bits. Recall, numbers and addresses are represented in binary form internally. In many applications, especially hardware, it is desirable to work with these bits. The language of C/C++ is known as a language that works closely with hardware. Because of the importance of bit-wise operations, C/C++ chooses to use one key strike for bit-wise operators (**&, |**) and two strikes for the logical operators (**&&, ||**). The following symbols are used for the C/C++ bit-wise operations.

|	bit-wise or operator
&	bit-wise and operator
^	bit-wise exclusive or operator
<<	shift left operator
>>	shift right operator
~	bit complement (unary operator)

BIT-WISE OPERATIONS: EXAMPLES

The general form of the bit-wise *or* operation is *variable1 | variable2* where each variable of type integer is converted to binary (bits). The bit-wise *or* operation of two bits is zero if both corresponding bits are zero (0), otherwise the resulting bit is one (1).

The general form of the bit-wise *and* (**&**) is *variable1 & variable2*, where each variable of type integer is converted to binary. The bit-wise *and* operation of two bits is one if the two corresponding bits have values of 1, otherwise the resulting bit is zero.

The general form of the bit-wise *exclusive or* (^) operation is *variable1 ^ variable2*, where both variables and resulting variable are of type integer and are converted to binary. The *exclusive or* of two bits is zero if the two bits are the same, otherwise it is one. The *exclusive or* is different from the bit-wise *or* in that the *exclusive or* of two bits with values 1 results to zero.

The **&** operator is often used to mask off certain bits, e.g. *value & 1111111*. The result sets all of the bits of the value to zero except the first 8 bits (low-order).

In the following program, the binary representation for 3 is 011 and 5 is 101. The resulting bit-wise *or* is 111 which is 7, the resulting bit-wise *and* is 001 which is 1, and the resulting *exclusive or* is 110 which is 6.

```
#include <iostream.h>
void main(){
        int x,y,z;
        x=3; y=5;
        z=x | y;
        cout<<" BITWISE | OF TWO  VALUES IS:"<<z<<endl;
        z=x & y;
        cout<<" BITWISE & OF TWO  VALUES IS:"<<z<<endl;
        z=x ^ y;
        cout<<" BITWISE ^ OF TWO  VALUES IS:"<<z<<endl;
        }//MAIN
```

Figure 20.1a - Program to demonstrate the bit-wise operators

```
BITWISE | OF TWO  VALUES IS:7
BITWISE & OF TWO  VALUES IS:1
BITWISE ^ OF TWO  VALUES IS:6
```

Figure 20.1b - Output of Figure 20.1a

BIT-WISE SHIFTS: SHIFT LEFT <<, SHIFT RIGHT >>

The general form of the *shift left* operator is *variable << n*, where *n* is the number bits to be left shifted. As the bits are shifted left, a zero bit fills the shifted position (zero left padding). After each left shift, a 0 is added next to the *least-significant bit* of the binary number, which makes the number twice as large (multiply by 2). Similarly, the general form of right shift is *variable >> n*, where *n* is the number of bits to be right shifted. As the bits are right shifted, the shifted position (*high-order bit*) is filled with zero (zero right padding). After each right shift, the binary number looses the right bit, which is the same as dividing the number by 2. As an exercise try to shift left a negative number, including −1, or use the rotate operation to perform a circular shift by moving the lost bit to the other side. In the following program the value of 4 is left shifted by 2, resulting in a value of 8 and the value of 4 is right shifted by 2, resulting in a value of 2.

Additionally note that the left shift and right shift operators are overloaded in C++ for input and output, and are known as extraction and insertion (**cin>>** , **cout <<**).

658

```
#include<iostream.h>
void main(){
        int x =4;
        x= x << 2;
        cout<<" VALUE OF X AFTER LEFT SHIFT:"<<x<<endl;
        x = x >> 1;
        cout<<" VALUE OF X AFTER LEFT SHIFT:"<<x<<endl;
        }//MAIN
```

Figure 20.2a - Program using bit-wise shift left

```
VALUE OF X AFTER LEFT SHIFT:16
VALUE OF X AFTER LEFT SHIFT:8
```

Figure 20.2b - Output of Figure 20.2a

COMPLEMENT OPERATOR ~

The form of the complement operator is *~variable,* where a binary bit is converted to its opposite is also known as 1's complement using the unary operator ~ (tild). For example, the complement of 1 is 0 and the complement of 0 is 1. A variable of type integer is converted to its binary form and complement is applied to it.

```
#include<iostream.h>
void main(){
int x=1, y=~x;
cout<<"      "<<hex<<x<<endl;
cout<<hex<<y<<endl;
cout<<hex<<x+y<<endl;}//MAIN
```

Figure 20.3a – Program to demonstrate the complement operator

```
      1
fffffffe
ffffffff
```

Figure 20.3b – Output of Figure 20.3a

SWAP FUNCTION USING EXCLUSIVE OR

If you are wondering what you can do with the bit-wise operators, here is an example that uses *exclusive or* to swap two values without introducing a temp variable so the program uses less memory. There are other tricks that can be done using the bit-wise operations to do certain things in an unordinary way. For example: performing multiplication by using shift left, division by using shift right, and subtraction by addition of the 2's complement. As an exercise, encrypt/decrypt a file using an *exclusive or (^)*. You may want to *exclusive or* each character with a selected ASCII character.

```
#include<iostream.h>
void swap(int &x, int &y){
       y=x^y;
       x=x^y;
       y=x^y;}//SWAP


void main(){
       int x=5, y=6;
       cout<<"BEFORE: "<<x<<"  "<<y<<endl;
       swap(x,y);
       cout<<"AFTER:   "<<x<<"  "<<y<<endl;}//MAIN
```

Figure 20.4a – Program using exclusive or to swap two values

```
BEFORE: 5  6
AFTER:  6  5
```

Figure 20.4b – Output of Figure 20.4a

COMMAND LINE ARGUMENTS

Until now you may have wondered why in C/C++ in the **main( )** we use open and close parentheses without anything inside the parentheses. Now is time to give the reason for it. One rationale for using parentheses is that the main program is a function and therefore, it can have parameters (arguments). For example, **void main( )** is a function that does not take any parameters (argument-less) and returns nothing. However, a main program can have general parameters such as **int main(int argc, char* argv[ ])**. This main function has two special arguments, one known as argument counter (**argc**) which counts the number of arguments, and argument vectors (**argv[ ]**) which is an array of pointers to each argument. Automatically, these arguments are set and as a programmer you can use them to your advantage.

HOW THE MAIN PROGRAM IS CALLED

The main program is called from the operating system environment using a command prompt (DOS or UNIX prompt). The executable file name of the main program can be used to pass the parameters. For example, **copy** fileA fileB **to** fileC. The copy command calls an executable file known as copy.exe (generated from copy.cpp) with five arguments (argc is 5 including the file name). argv[0] is pointing to copy, argv[1] points to fileA, argv[2] points to fileB, argv[3] points to the word to, and argv[4] points to fileC. It is the programmer's job to handle these arguments (words) and treat them as intended, whether they are a file or other information. You can understand how a system programmer has built the system commands by understanding the command line arguments. In fact you can make them friendlier and customize them to suit your own taste.

SYSTEM PROGRAMMING

One job of a system programmer is to build the commands that become the interface between the user (operating system) and the computer while carrying out the request of the user and utilizing the computer's resources. For example, in **UNIX** the command **cp fileA fileB** copies the contents of fileA to fileB. Similarly, in DOS, the prompt **copy fileA fileB** does the same job. A system programmer can even make the above commands friendlier by inserting the word "to" between the source file and the destination file: **copy fileA to fileB**. If you understand the command line arguments, then you can build your own commands and customize them. You can make your own command-line calculator (e.g. add 2 + 3) or you can create generic searches (e.g. **search tel Ebrahimi**). The following program demonstrates a sample command line program for a copy command:

```
#include<fstream.h>
void main(int argc, char* argv[]){
    if(argc<4)
        cout<<"TOO FEW PARAMETERS";
    else{
    ifstream fin(argv[1],ios::in);
    ofstream fout(argv[3],ios::out);
    char c;
    while(fin>>c){
    fout<<c;}//WHILE
    fout.close();
    fin.close(); }//ELSE
}//MAIN
```

Figure 20.5a – Program demonstrating command-line arguments

```
copy fileA to fileB
```

Figure 20.5b – Output of Figure 20.5a

```
ABCDEF
```
```
ABCDEF
```

Figure 20.5c - fileA   *Figure 20.5d - fileB*

This program copies the contents of one file, character by character, to another file. The above program is named copy.cpp. To create the copy command, you must compile the program with the line g++ -o copy copy.cpp; this sends the executable code to the copy command. To run this copy program, at the prompt type: copy fileA to fileB.

RUN TIME TYPE ID (RTTI)

In C++, the run time type information feature is supported by the **typeid** operator, which determines the type of a variable during run time. To use this feature you must include the header **#include <typeinfo>**.

With the use of the **typeid** operator, two objects can be compared to determine if they are of the same type or not. One reason to use typeid is to figure out the type of object during run time and cast (convert) it if necessary.

```cpp
#include<typeinfo>
#include <iostream>
using namespace std;
void main(){
        double pi=3.14159;
        cout<<"TYPE OF VARIABLE IS: "<<typeid(pi).name()<<endl;
        if(typeid(pi).name() == typeid(double).name())
                cout<<"THEY ARE SAME TYPE"<<endl;
        }//MAIN
```

Figure 20.6a – Program using the typeid operator

```
TYPE OF VARIABLE IS: double
THEY ARE SAME TYPE
```

Figure 20.6b – Output of Figure 20.6a

TYPE CONVERSION: CASTING, DYNAMIC CASTING, REINTERPRET

A type can be converted legally, implicitly or explicitly, to another type. A type can be converted implicitly through assignment, one type to another, as long as the smaller type is assigned to the larger type to avoid loss of precision. A type can be converted explicitly by the use of an operator, known as a cast operator. The general form is *(type) variable*. For example, the function **sqrt(x)** takes double as its argument, therefore for an integer value, it is necessary to convert the **int** type to **double** by casting it with the following: **sqrt((double) x)**. Note that the value of the variable is passed as a **double**, but the value of variable x does not change.

662

Other than the C-style type casting, there are four more casting techniques in C++. In addition to casting the basic data types, the pointer type and user-defined types (classes) can be cast. The four different castings have a similar form: **static_cast** *<newtype>* (*expression*) and are explained below.

reinterpret_cast: is mainly used for casting with a pointer, such as casting one pointer type to another pointer type or a pointer type to a non-pointer (e.g. int) type or vice versa.
static_cast: is like C-style casting e.g. converting double to int.
const_cast: is for constant casting and takes away the **const** casting.
dynamic_cast: inspects the variable (object) type at run time and returns a valid pointer if the object is of the expected type or a null pointer if the object is not of the expected type. The **dynamic _cast** is mainly used in situations where the correctness of the type conversion cannot be determined during compile time.

```cpp
#include <iostream>
using namespace std;
void main(){
        int myint;
        double mydoub = 876.54;
        myint=(int)mydoub;
        cout<<"C-STYLE CASTING:"<<myint<<endl;
        myint=static_cast <int> (mydoub);
        cout<<"STATIC CASTING:"<<myint<<endl;
        }//MAIN
```

Figure 20.7a – Program to illustrate C-Style and Static Casting

```
C-STYLE CASTING:876
STATIC CASTING:876
```

Figure 20.7b – Output of Figure 20.7a

MULTIPLE FILE PROGRAM AND SEPARATE COMPILATION

A big program can be broken into separate units: functions, modules, or even header file(s). Each of these units can be written in separate files, which can be compiled separately and linked together at a later time. There are many advantages to multiple-file programs and separate compilation; some advantages are: localizing error handling at an early stage, teamwork, reusability, and better organization. In a Linux environment, the command will compile the taxrate and overtime units:
    g++ –c taxrate.cpp overtimepay.cpp
Similarly, the following command links a set of independent files that are compiled separately:
    g++ -o taxrate.o overtimepay.o main.cpp

HEADER FILES: MAKING YOUR OWN INCLUDE

As a program becomes larger, it is recommended to divide the program into modules and parts and keep them in separate files, rather than having them all in one file. However, these files may need to access some common variables as well as functions (prototypes) and can be saved under a name with the extension **.h** that can be used as a header file. One advantage is, rather than repeating the same information, we can simply include the file on top with the only difference that instead of angle brackets we use double quotations. Another advantage of header files is that any change or update in the header file is visible to others.

For example, for a sort program that reads data and prints the unsorted and sorted data, we can use the following common code that is saved under a file called **sort.h**.

```
#define MAXSIZE  10
#include <iostream>
#include <fstream>
#include <ctype>
using namespace std;
double lst[MAXSIZE];
void printlist(double lst[]);
```

The following sort main program resides in a source file named sort.cpp and uses two header files; the header file sort.h and process.h are created for the function's definitions.

```
#include "sort.h"
#include "process.h"
main(){
}///MAIN SORT.CPP
```

The following functions for the sort program are kept in another header file known as **process.h**. Remember that this header file uses the previously created header file as shown below.

```
#include "sort.h"
void readdatat(){     }
void printdata(){     }
int findlocmin(){     }
```

A const FUNCTION

A function can be declared as a constant (const) by providing the keyword **const** after the argument list (after parentheses) in the function declaration as well as in the function definition.

A constant function does not modify its implicit arguments. Note that the implicit arguments are those that are accessible by **this** pointer. An example of a const member function is the const accessor function because its job is simply to access the member data of a class and not to modify it. Defining a function as const prevents the object (variable) from accidental or deliberate change.

```cpp
#include<iostream.h>
class employee{
        double salary;
public:
        double getsalary() const{
                return salary;}
        void setsalary(double amount){
                salary=amount;}
        void printsalary() const{
                cout<<"SALARY: "<<salary<<endl;}
};//EMPLOYEE
void main(){
        employee ebrahimi;
        ebrahimi.setsalary(1000.00);
        ebrahimi.printsalary();
        double bonus=500.00;
        cout<<"SALARY WITH BONUS: ";
        cout<<ebrahimi.getsalary()+bonus;
}//MAIN
```

Figure 20.8a – Program utilizing a const function

```
SALARY: 1000
SALARY WITH BONUS: 1500
```

Figure 20.8b – Output of Figure 20.8a

In this program, the function declaration and definition are in the same place. The format for the function declaration of a constant function is as follows:
double getsalary( ) const;.
In this program, both **getsalary( )** and **printsalary( )** are constant functions and hence, they do not modify the object. If you try to change **salary** in either one of these member functions, the compiler gives an error message. For example, adding the line:
salary=salary+500; to the **getsalary( )** function would cause the compiler to give the following error message:
"l-value specifies const object".

ENUMERATION DATA TYPE: enum

The word **enum** stands for enumeration; this is another integral data type, like boolean. The data type enum can have more than two values, in contrast to bool which has only two values, false and true (0 and 1). For example, a weekday enum data type can have five values: mon, tue, wed, thur, and fri. Similarly, a weekend enum type can have two values: sat and sun. By using the enumerated word instead of an integer constant, the program becomes more readable. By setting an enumerator to a value, the rest of the enumerators will increase by 1. You can engage the enumerator in an equality test, assignment, or use it as a loop control variable. By default the enumerator value starts at zero.

> **enum wdays {mon=1, tue, wed, thur, fri, sat, sun};**
> **wdays weekdays, weekend;**
> **enum colors {red, green, blue};**

Caution: the names used in enumeration must be C++ legal names and not a literal or number, although the names can hold these values.

> **enum monthofyear {Jan=1,Feb,Mar, Apr, May, Jun, July, Aug, Sep, Oct, Nov, Dec};**
> **monthofyear month;**

ENUMERATION EXAMPLE: NUMBER OF DAYS PASSED SO FAR IN YEAR

The following program computes the number of days passed in the year by providing the month and the day. The program uses two enumeration data types: one to determine the name of the month and one to find the number of days in each month. Two functions return enumeration types. Note that the starting value of the enumeration list is 0 and it is incremented by 1 each time. However, another initialization can be specified and the increment remains at one. Also note that enumeration values are constant and cannot be changed so they cannot be incremented and therefore cannot be used in a loop to go through a range. For example, you cannot use the enumerated type **month**++. However, some implementations, such as Borland Turbo C++ will run the above with warning. One solution for the loop is to cast the increment to its enumerated type.

> **month=monthofyear(month+1); //or**
> **month= (monthofyear) month+1;**

Despite the limited capabilities of enumeration as a defined type, use of enumeration contributes to program readability; but some have reservations that it makes the program larger with redundant effort. For your own exercise, try to expand this program to consider the leap years and include a function that takes an enumeration type as a parameter.

```
#include<iostream.h>
enum months {Jan=1, Feb, Mar, Apr, May, Jun, Jul, Aug, Sep, Oct, Nov, Dec, ERROR=0};
enum daysinmonth {daysinJan=31, daysinFeb=28, daysinMar=31, daysinApr=30,        daysinMay=31,
daysinJun=30, daysinJul=31, daysinAug=31, daysinSep=30, daysinOct=31, daysinNov=30, daysinDec=31,
DAYSERROR=0};
        months getmonth(int monthnumber){
                switch(monthnumber){
                case 1: return Jan; case 2: return Feb; case 3: return Mar;
                case 4: return Apr; case 5: return May; case 6: return Jun;
                case 7: return Jul; case 8: return Aug; case 9: return Sep;
                case 10: return Oct; case 11: return Nov; case 12: return Dec;
                default: return ERROR;}//SWITCH
                }//GETMONTH
        daysinmonth getdays(int monthofyear){
        switch(monthofyear){
                case 1: return daysinJan; case 2: return daysinFeb;
                case 3: return daysinMar; case 4: return daysinApr;
                case 5: return daysinMay; case 6: return daysinJun;
                case 7: return daysinJul; case 8: return daysinAug;
                case 9: return daysinSep; case 10: return daysinOct;
                case 11: return daysinNov; case 12: return daysinDec;
                default: return DAYSERROR;   }//SWITCH
                }//GETDAYS
void main(){
        months calendar; //enum TYPE
        daysinmonth daysofcurrentmonth; //enum TYPE
        int monthofyear, dayofmonth, dayspast=0;
        cout<<"ENTER AN INTEGER FOR THE MONTH: ";
        cin>>monthofyear;
        cout<<"ENTER AN INTEGER FOR THE DAY: ";
        cin>>dayofmonth;
        calendar=getmonth(monthofyear);
        daysofcurrentmonth=getdays(monthofyear);
        do{    switch(calendar){
                case Jan: case Mar: case May:
                case Jul: case Aug:       case Oct:
                case Dec: dayspast+=31; break;
                case Feb: dayspast+=28; break;
                case Apr: case Jun: case Sep:
                case Nov: dayspast+=30;break;     }//SWITCH
                monthofyear--;
                calendar=getmonth(monthofyear); }while(calendar>=Jan);
                dayspast=dayspast-daysofcurrentmonth+dayofmonth;
                cout<<"NUMBER OF DAYS PAST IN YEAR SO FAR: "<<dayspast;   }  //MAIN
```

Figure 20.9a – Example of enumeration

```
ENTER AN INTEGER FOR THE MONTH: 4
ENTER AN INTEGER FOR THE DAY: 16
NUMBER OF DAYS PAST IN YEAR SO FAR: 106
```

Figure 20.9b – Output of Figure 20.a

PROGRAM NAMING CONVENTIONS AND STYLES: IDENTIFIERS

The names that are used in a program such as keywords and user-defined words are known as identifiers. C/C++ is case sensitive, which means that a lower case name is not the same as an upper case name. C/C++ is designed in favor of lower case letters with the representation of keywords and libraries in lower case letters. Besides the reserved words, it is up to you to choose any combination of styles or any convention that you like. But be consistent and not misleading by choosing improper names. Try to choose names that are related to their purpose and do not choose names that can be easily confused with each other. Try to use short names for indices. The following illustrates some naming conventions that you can use in your program. For example, the beginning of a word is capitalized, as in Counter or HourlyRate. The beginning of a first word may be lower case but the beginning of the following word is upper case as in hourlyRate. Underscores may be used between words, as in hourly_rate. Many programmers personalize words by adding the prefix my to words such as in mystack and mysalary. For example, the word delete is a reserved word and cannot be used, so you may want to use mydelete instead. To distinguish a class name from its object name, the prefix *the* is added before the class name in the object name. For example, with a class named stack, the object name *thestack* is used. For an array's index or a loop control variable, a single letter such as i, j, k, m, or n is used. Historically, (in Fortran) these names represented integer values by default (I through N). As a result of some of the language naming restrictions, programmers adjust their programs accordingly; for example, by spelling count as *kount*. Interestingly, the language Basic started with one letter identifiers or one letter with one digit identifiers. Many languages limit identifiers to 4 to 6 characters, which caused a lot of problems because some compilers ignored additional characters and that also caused a new problem. Now character limit does not play a role, in fact C/C++ can have identifiers 31 characters long. Do you have an opinion? The assembly language uses mnemonic symbols such as **ST** for store. Blank spaces are not permitted in identifiers. Do you think it would be better to have blanks within an identifier? What would be the pros and cons of having identifiers with embedded blank spaces?
Try to not use the letter l (el) as a name since it looks like numeric 1.

PROGRAMMING CONVENTIONS USED IN THIS BOOK

I tried the following conventions with my novice programmers and I found better results compared to other conventions. However, you may build a convention that is even better than this. I taught programmers to stick with the convention in the beginning unless they have a reason not to. In programs I mainly use lower case letters, without even using an underscore to separate words, to avoid confusion. I left out comments on purpose so the learner can focus on the code and get to know it and not loose track, rather than hiding the code inside comments. The end of each block whether an if, loop, function, or main is commented with the word itself in capital letters (e.g. //**MAIN**). Display messages are in upper case (e.g. **cout<<"HELLO"**). In this book I stayed away from lengthy programs, and tried to fit them onto two or a maximum of three pages. I believe it is hard for learners to follow a large program when having to page back and forth.

NAMESPACE

C++ is a growing language and the latest extension of the Standard Template Library (STL) makes C++ larger than ever. In a program, it is possible that you are using names for classes, variables, or functions that are the same. To solve the problem of name clashes, a new extension to the language known as the namespace feature, was created. C++ has placed almost all the standard library names under a namespace called **std** and allows others to create their own namespaces. You can create your own namespaces as well or use names from other namespaces. For beginner programmers, the concept of namespace is troublesome and the reason behind it is not understood. It is one of those "wait until later" subjects. For example, in one library, the identifier *find* means one thing and in another library it may mean something else. A namespace is an additional feature that was added to C++ that is used to create a scope (space) for names. By having a namespace, an identifier has its own boundary. Therefore, the same name can be used in two different namespaces without any problem or confusion for the compiler or the programmer. In fact, those who worked with older compilers and are now working with new compilers realize two major changes right away; a header directive without .h, and the statement:

    using namespace std;

The above statement tells your program that you are using the standard namespace where most routines come from and makes **std** the default namespace of your program. An alternative to this statement is to mention the namespace for only names that are used in the program such as:

    std::cin;   **std::cout;**   **std::endl;**

Some beginner programmers feel that including namespace in a program is a redundant action and the benefits of namespaces will not be realized until later. They prefer to use the old style headers without using namespaces. Let us put it this way, the use of namespace becomes necessary especially when you are using STL and strings. Note that building a string from the library <string.h> is different than building a string from the library <string > class.

MAKING YOUR OWN namespace

Creating a namespace is similar to making a class, however, several classes and functions can become members of a namespace. The general form of a namespace is shown below. Caution: do not place a semicolon after the closing brace of the namespace block; it is not needed as in a class.

```
namespace mynames {
        //class
        //template
        //function
        //variable declaration
}//NAMESPACE
```

By adding a directive, all those names in the namespace are available for use.
Every statement that uses a namespace component must specify the namespace such as:

```
mynamespace::vector;
```

Note that the name vector is used both in STL and the above namespace but there is no name collision. Additionally, namespaces can be nested so that we can create packages or similar namespaces.

The following program creates two namespaces called **oldproject** and **newproject**. Note that the two namespaces are able to use the same name for values and functions.

```
namespace oldproject {
class payroll {
        double basesalary;
public:
payroll (){basesalary=100000.00;}
findsalary(){return basesalary; };
 }; //CLASS PAYROLL
}//NAMESPACE

namespace newproject {
class payroll {
        double basesalary;
public:
payroll (){basesalary=100000.00;}
findsalary(){return basesalary; };
}; //CLASS PAYROLL
}//NAMESPACE
#include<iostream>
using namespace std;
void main(){
oldproject::payroll ebrahimi;
newproject::payroll johndoe;
if (ebrahimi.findsalary()== johndoe.findsalary() )
     cout<<"SAME SALARY"<<endl;
}//MAIN
```

Figure 20.10a – Program demonstrating how to create and use namespaces

SAME SALARY

Figure 20.10b – Output of Figure 20.10a

Alternatively, the main program can use one of the namespaces without specifying the prefix each time:

```
main(){
        using namespace newproject;
        if (findsalary()==oldproject::findsalary())
                cout<<"NO PROMOTION HAS HAPPENED "
}//MAIN
```

typedef

The keyword **typedef** stands for type definition and is used to create a synonym (alias) for an existing type. In fact, **typedef** is more like giving a nickname (shorthand) to a long and complicated type such as a type containing pointers, structures, and classes. After creating the type, you can use the synonym name given. The general form of **typedef** is to use the keyword **typedef** followed by the existing type and **newname**, where the existing type is a C/C++ defined type and **newname** is a given nickname.

       typedef existingtype newname;

The following illustrates using the **typedef** keyword by adding a new name **ULI** for an existing type. The use of **typedef** enhances program readability.

```
        typedef unsigned long int ULI
        ULI  x;
```

A side note: the use of **typedef** was more common in C, especially when defining a struct with a tag name. The use of classes in C++ made **typedef** less popular. The following shows how **typedef** is used to simplify a self-referential structure double linked list (dynamic).

```
        typedef  struct nodetag *dlistptr;
        typedef struct nodetag {
                char info[20];
                dlistptr  next;
                dlistptr  prvious; } dlistnode;
```

Without the use of typedef the double linked list would be represented accordingly.

```
        struct nodetag {
                char info[20];
                struct nodetag *next;
                struct nodetag *previous; };

        struct nodetag *dlistnode;
```

In a C-style struct, the tag name is used to declare a variable. In C++, the use of struct tag names is obsolete.

One last note: with the keyword **typedef**, do not confuse its syntax and semantics with the directive **#define**.

PREPROCESSOR DIRECTIVES

A preprocessor is part of a C/C++ program that processes before the compiler takes charge, as the name preprocessor suggests. There are approximately ten directives of which the #include and #define are the most popular. Other directives such as #ifndef, #else, and #undef are mainly used to compile a program in some conditional way. However, with the preprocessor, there are some tokens (names) that hold some information such as _DATE, _TIME for date and time of compilation respectively.

#define AS LITERAL (CONSTANT) SUBSTITUTION

The **#define** directive is a macro with the following general form:

> **#define macroname substitution**

#define is used to substitute a name with its character sequence. Many constant values are given a name with #define. For example, #define PI 3.14159 means that in a problem, whenever PI is encountered, PI will be substituted with the value of 3.14159. Before the keyword const was introduced in C/C++, #define was used instead. In fact, many symbolic names such as EOF and NULL are defined by #define.

> **#define EOF   -1**
> **#define NULL   '\0'**

There is no need to end the #define with a semicolon (;), the #define directive will end when a new line (enter key) is pressed. When there is a need for continuation on the line, a backslash (\) is used.

```
#define CHORUS  "Twinkle Twinkle Little Star, How I\
 Wonder What You Are."
#include <iostream.h>
void main() {
cout<<"SING "<<CHORUS<<endl;
cout<<CHORUS<<endl;
}//MAIN
```

Figure 20.11a – Program using the #define directive

```
SING Twinkle Twinkle Little Star, How I Wonder What You Are.
Twinkle Twinkle Little Star, How I Wonder What You Are.
```

Figure 20.11b – Output of Figure 20.11a

672

MACRO AS A FUNCTION

With the use of #define, you will be able to define macros which are like functions, but it is done by substitutions rather than function calls. One advantage of a macro over a function is that you do not have the function overhead, such as pushing the variable onto a stack or keeping track of addresses (return address). For a small number of tasks, a macro is recommended. In assembly language, macros play a larger role. Macros are used in C; but, due to the purpose of type checking, macros are not recommended for use in C++.

For example, in the following program, a macro determines the maximum of two numbers using the directive #define. As an exercise, write a macro called SQUARE (x) to compute the square of x; then write a function to do the same. The extra parentheses are used to guarantee no mix up in substitution.

```
#define FINDMAX(x, y)   ( ( x > y ) ? x : y )
#include <iostream.h>
void main() {
int x = 5;
int y = 8;
cout << "THE MAXIMUM IS " << FINDMAX (x, y) <<endl;
}//MAIN
```

Figure 20.12a – Program demonstrating the use of a macro

```
THE MAXIMUM IS 8
```

Figure 20.12b – Output of Figure 20.12a

CONDITIONAL DIRECTIVE

A conditional directive is used to prevent multiple copies and processing of the same header file. The general form for a *conditional directive* is shown below.

#ifndef MYFILE_H
#define MYFILE_H
#endif

The above code tests if **myfile.h** is defined (included) previously; if not, it will be included. In other words, when #ifndef is true, the code after it is included and processed; otherwise, the code between **#ifndef** and **#endif** is ignored.

#include <time.h> TIME AND DATE

The header **<time.h>** contains functions and types that are used to manipulate and determine the time and date. Time and date are important topics that should be integrated into every large program to keep track of events such as scheduling, appointments, time driven reports, time duration, execution time, analysis, and simulation. In fact, many computer viruses are *time* driven; therefore knowledge of *time* will help you understand how these viruses function and to some extent how to try to combat them.

In header <time.h> there are three different ways time is stored, each with a different purpose and format, as described below:

time_t: a calendar time including time and date.

struct tm t: a time and date is a structure which is broken into several members such as tm_sec, tm_min, tm_hour, tm_year, etc..

clock_t: a time value used for elapsed time (duration) which is measured in clock ticks. The function clock_t clock( ) returns the time since execution. In order to get the time in seconds you must use clock( ) / CLOCKS_PER_SEC.

time_t and **clock_t:** are arithmetic types while **struct tm** holds each component of time and date known as *calendar time*.

We are going to divide the time functions into two divisions of time manipulation and time conversions.

As an example, the function **time(NULL)** is used in the function **srand(time(NULL))** to seed a random number generator so that whenever the function **rand( )** runs, the same series of numbers is not generated.

struct tm TIME COMPONENTS

The members of **struct tm** hold components of time and calendar date, each of which are of type integer. The time members are: **tm_sec** includes seconds (0, 61?), **tm_min** includes minutes (0, 59), and **tm_hour** includes hours (0, 23). The date members are: **tm_mday** includes the month's day (1, 31), **tm_mon** includes months (0, 11), and **tm_year** includes years (since 1900). Other day components are: **tm_wday** includes days since Sunday (0, 6) and **tm_yday** includes days since January 1 (0, 365). In addition, **tm_isdst** includes a Daylight Saving Time flag component (0 no effect, >0 in effect, -1 not applied).

TIME IT TAKES TO RESPOND

The following program computes the amount of time from when the user is prompted to enter the name until the name is entered. The two variables **begin** and **end** are declared as type **time_t** and their addresses are passed to the function **time(&varname)** so that the number of computed seconds is stored and brought back. Note that **time( )** can be used to compute elapsed time for algorithm analysis. As an exercise, extend this program to limit the response time such as waiting for only 10 seconds.

```
#include<iostream.h>
#include<time.h>
void main(){
        char name[20];
        time_t begin, end;
        time(&begin);
        cout<<"NUMBER OF SECONDS ELAPSED SINCE JAN 1, 1970! "<<begin<<endl;
        cout<<"HELLO, WHAT IS YOUR NAME? "<<endl;
        cin>>name;
        time(&end);
        cout<<end<<endl;
        cout<<"TIME ELAPSED FOR "<<name<<"'S RESPONSE: "<<end-begin<<" SECONDS"<<endl;
        }//MAIN
```

Figure 20.13a – Program showing uses for time.h

```
NUMBER OF SECONDS ELAPSED SINCE JAN 1, 1970! 1024338710
HELLO, WHAT IS YOUR NAME?
Ebrahimi
1024338719
TIME ELAPSED FOR Ebrahimi'S RESPONSE: 9 SECONDS
```

Figure 20.13b – Output of Figure 20.13a

STRING TIME VERSUS STRUCTURE TIME

The function **time( )** brings the number of seconds that have elapsed since midnight January 1, 1970 (Unix Epoch Milestone). Conversion functions are used to format the time differently. For example, the function **ctime**(&varname) will return a string representing the full date and time. Similarly, the function **localtime**(&varname) returns a structure of type **tm** where each member holds the appropriate time and date information such as **tm_sec, tm_min, tm_hour, tm_year**, etc..). Additionally, the function **asctime**(structime) converts the structure time to the same form as **ctime( )**. Note that **tm_year** gives the number of years since 1900 (starting calendar time, January 1 is Sunday). The year 1900 is added to get the current year.

```
#include<iostream.h>
#include<time.h>
void main(){
        time_t timenow;
        time(&timenow);
        cout<<ctime(&timenow)<<endl;//CONVERT TIME

        struct tm *timestruct;
        timestruct=localtime(&timenow);
        cout<<timestruct->tm_wday<<" "<<timestruct->tm_mon<<" "<<timestruct->tm_mday<<" ";
        cout<<timestruct->tm_hour<<":"<<timestruct->tm_min<<":"<<timestruct->tm_sec<<" ";
        cout<<timestruct->tm_year+1900<<endl<<endl;

        cout<<asctime(timestruct);
        }//MAIN
```

Figure 20.14a – Program using time( ), ctime( ), localtime( ), and asctime( )

```
Mon Jun 17 17:55:56 2002

1 5 17 17:55:56 2002

Mon Jun 17 17:55:56 2002
```

Figure 20.14b – Output of Figure 20.14a

VARIABLE STORAGE SPECIFIER: auto, static, register, and extern

A storage class specifies where a variable (object) should be stored and determines its visibility and its duration. There are four major storage specifiers that are used for storage class: **auto**, **extern**, **static,** and **register**. Do not confuse the word storage class (categorization) with the object-oriented class. An **auto** (automatic) variable is a local variable in a program (or function) that comes into existence when the program is executed or when a function is called, and ceases to exist when the program is finished or the function is returned. An **auto** variable does not retain its value as it comes into existence once again. Automatically, a variable is of type **auto** storage upon its declaration. However, you can explicitly define a variable an **auto** by prefixing the declaration with the keyword **auto** as shown here: **auto int x;**

```
#include <iostream>
using namespace std;
void testauto( ); //PROTOTYPE
void main(){
        auto int x=5;
        cout<<x<<endl;
        testauto();
}//MAIN
void testauto(){
        int y=6;
        y++;
        cout<<y<<endl;
}//TESTAUTO
```

Figure 20.15a – Program to test the keyword auto

```
5
7
```

Figure 20.15b – Output of Figure 20.15a

An external variable is a variable that is defined outside of a main program (or any function). Other functions can access an external variable by prefixing the keyword **extern** in a variable declaration. External variables are globally accessible, and hence, can be used instead of parameter passing and return values when communicating with functions. I have found that beginner programmers prefer to use external variables to make the program work and then convert the program to use parameters. Note that external variables have their own side effects.

```
#include <iostream>
using namespace std;
void testextern( ); //PROTOTYPE
 int x=5;  //x IS EXTERNAL

 void main(){
        cout<<x<<endl;
        testextern();
}//MAIN
void testextern(){
        extern int x; //OPTIONAL
        x++;
        cout<<x<<endl;
}//TESTEXTERN
```

Figure 20.16a – Program using an external variable

```
5
6
```

Figure 20.16b – Output of Figure 20.16a

Let me conclude this topic by stating that, we often talk about variable declaration but forget to mention the place (memory) where the variable is created or assigned storage. Declaration and definition of a variable are different, in declaration no storage is allocated.

A **static** variable is a kind of variable that retains its value upon the existence of the variable. Therefore, static local variables, in contrast to auto variables, retain their values from one function call to another. One should not confuse a static variable with a static member variable of a class, and the concept of static memory allocation versus dynamic allocation. A static variable can act as a limited external variable by defining it outside the functions (visible to several functions) or it can act as an extended local variable by defining it inside the function (retaining its value).

```cpp
#include <iostream>
using namespace std;
void teststatic( ); //PROTOTYPE
void main(){
        static int x=5;
        cout<<x<<endl;
        teststatic();
}//MAIN
void teststatic(){
        static int y=6;
        y++;
        cout<<y<<endl;
}//TESTSTATIC
```

Figure 20.17a – Program using a static variable

```
5
7
```

Figure 20.17b – Output of Figure 20.17a

register VARIABLES:

A variable can be declared as a register by prefixing the keyword register to its usual declaration. A register variable uses the computer's register instead of regular memory. It is a good idea to declare the most frequent variables as register. The usage of a register's variable makes the program faster and smaller, since a register resides within the CPU, but it is up to a compiler to grant the request.

```
#include <iostream>
using namespace std;
void testregister( ); //PROTOTYPE
void main(){
        register int x=5;
        cout<<x<<endl;
        testregister();
}//MAIN
```

Figure 20.18a – Program using a register variable

```
5
7
```

Figure 20.18b – Output of Figure 20.18a

mutable DATA MEMBERS VERSUS const

The keyword **mutable** allows a const member function to modify a data member. For example, by declaring a data member mutable, a const member function can change that member data. Note that a constant member function cannot change the invoking object data member. An alternative to mutable would be to cast away the const by using **const_cast < >**.

```
class muty {
mutable int m;
public:
update (int x) const { m= x+1; }//UPDATE
getm( )const {return m;}//GETX
};  //CLASS MUTY

#include <iostream>
using namespace std;
void main(){
        muty  objm;
        objm.update(5);
        cout<<objm.getm()<<endl;
}//MAIN
```

Figure 20.19a – Program demonstrating use of a mutable data menber

```
6
```

Figure 20.19b – Output of Figure 20.19a

CLASS HIERARCHICAL RELATIONSHIP: Has-A VERSUS Is-A

A relationship between two classes can be categorized as a Has-A or Is-A Relationship. A relationship is categorized as Has-A when a class contains (composes) one or more classes. Has-A relationship is known as composition or nested class (structure). An example to explain the Has-A relationship is if there are two classes, and one is tree and one is leaf; in this case the tree has a leaf. To describe the Is-A relationship, an apple tree is a tree (apple tree class is derived from tree class). There are other kinds of relationships such as Uses-A and others that we are not concerned with at the moment. In this program, the class date is composed in the class employee (Has-A). For simplicity, the data members of the date class are public so the main program can access them easily. As an exercise, modify the program to include constructors and set the data members to private; you can also create a separate file and an include directive. Note that **hiringdate** is an object of the class **date**.

```cpp
#include<iostream.h>
class date{
public: int year;
        int month;
        int day; };//DATE
class employee {
private: double salary;
public: date hiringdate;
        double getsalary(){return salary;}
        void setsalary(double amount){salary=amount;}};//EMPLOYEE
void main(){
        employee ebr;
        ebr.hiringdate.year=1983;
        ebr.hiringdate.month=1;
        ebr.hiringdate.day=23;
        ebr.setsalary(99999.99);
        cout<<"SALARY: "<<ebr.getsalary()<<endl;
        cout<<"HIRING DATE: "<<ebr.hiringdate.month<<"/"<<ebr.hiringdate.day;
        cout<<"/"<<ebr.hiringdate.year<<endl;
        }//MAIN
```

Figure 20.20a – Program illustrating the Has-A relationship

```
SALARY: 100000
HIRING DATE: 1/23/1983
```

Figure 20.20b – Output of Figure 20.20a

IS-A RELATIONSHIP: PROGRAM

IS-A relationship is when a class is derived from another class. The following program demonstrates an Is-A relationship between two classes; **person** is the base class that consists of general information and the class **employee** is a derived class (specialized) that inherits from the **person** class. As an exercise, modify the program to change the data members to protected, and possibly to explore multiple inheritance instead of single inheritance. An example of multiple inheritance is if a student employee is derived from the class student and the class employee.

```cpp
#include<iostream>
#include<string>
using namespace std;
class person{
public: string firstname;
        string lastname;};//PERSON
class date{
public: int year;
        int month;
        int day; };//DATE
class employee: public person{
private: double salary;
public: date hiringdate;
        double getsalary(){return salary;}
        void setsalary(double amount){salary=amount;}};//EMPLOYEE
void main(){
        employee ebr;
        ebr.firstname="Alireza";
        ebr.lastname="Ebrahimi";
        ebr.hiringdate.year=1983;
        ebr.hiringdate.month=1;
        ebr.hiringdate.day=23;
        ebr.setsalary(99999.99);
        cout<<ebr.firstname<<" "<<ebr.lastname<<endl;
        cout<<"SALARY: "<<ebr.getsalary()<<endl;
        cout<<"HIRING DATE: "<<ebr.hiringdate.month<<"/"<<ebr.hiringdate.day;
        cout<<"/"<<ebr.hiringdate.year<<endl;
        }//MAIN
```

Figure 20.21a – Program illustrating the Is-A relationship

```
Alireza Ebrahimi
SALARY: 100000
HIRING DATE: 1/23/1983
```

Figure 20.21b – Output of Figure 20.21a

FRIEND FUNCTION

A friend function can access the member functions of a class without being a member of the class. Access to a class member is granted to a friend function as if it were a member function. You may wonder why we need a friend. One option to not having friend functions is to make the members public so that a function can access them, but making the data members public omits the idea of information hiding (abstraction). Note that the goal of OO is to separate the implementation from the interface as much as possible. If you have too many friend functions that are accessing your class's private members, you may want to redesign your class.

The use of the keyword **friend** in the function prototype before the function name makes the function a friend of the class, and there is no need to mention the keyword in the function definition.

A FRIEND FUNCTION: PROGRAM

The following program illustrates the use of a **friend** function **addbonus( )** in the class **employee**. The function **addbonus( )** is not a member of the employee class, but has the same access rights as a member.

```
#include<iostream.h>
class employee{
        friend void addbonus(employee &, double);
public:
        employee(double amt){salary=amt;}
        double getsalary() const{return salary;}
private:
        double salary;
        }; //EMPLOYEE
void addbonus(employee &emp, double bonus){
        emp.salary =emp.salary + bonus;}
void main(){
        employee ebrahimi(99999.00);
        cout<<"ORIGINAL SALARY: "<<ebrahimi.getsalary()<<endl;
        addbonus(ebrahimi,1000.00) ;
        cout<<"NEW SALARY: "<<ebrahimi.getsalary()<<endl;
}//MAIN
```

Figure 20.22a – Program with a friend function

```
ORIGINAL SALARY: 99999
NEW SALARY: 100999
```

Figure 20.22b – Output of Figure 20.22a

FRIEND FUNCTION: USED FOR OVERLOADING OPERATORS

One usage of a friend function is to use it with the overloading insertion (<<) operator. An operator overloading function must be a friend function since the object is passed to the function instead of being an invoking object. The way that operator overloading works is that the function carries two parameters, one is a reference to the stream and one is a reference to the object. This allows you to customize a print function. For example, all the members of an object can be printed at once instead of one by one.

```cpp
#include<iostream.h>
#include<string.h>
class person{
public: char firstname[20];
        char lastname[20];};//PERSON
class date{
public: int year;
        int month;
        int day; };//DATE
class employee: public person{
private: double salary;
public: date hiringdate;
        double getsalary(){return salary;}
        void setsalary(double amount){salary=amount;}
        friend ostream &operator<<( ostream & output, const employee &emp);
        };//EMPLOYEE
ostream &operator<<( ostream & output, const employee &emp){
        output<<emp.firstname<<" "<<emp.lastname<<endl;
        output<<"SALARY: "<<emp.salary<<endl;
        output<<"HIRING DATE: "<<emp.hiringdate.month;
        output<<"/"<<emp.hiringdate.day;
        output<<"/"<<emp.hiringdate.year<<endl;
        return output; }//<<
void main(){
        employee ebr;
        strcpy(ebr.firstname,"Alireza");
        strcpy(ebr.lastname,"Ebrahimi");
        ebr.hiringdate.year=1983;
        ebr.hiringdate.month=1;
        ebr.hiringdate.day=23;
        ebr.setsalary(99999.99);
        cout<<ebr;                  }//MAIN
```

Figure 20.23a – Program with a friend function to overload the << operator

```
Alireza Ebrahimi
SALARY: 100000
HIRING DATE: 1/23/1983
```

Figure 20.23b – Output of Figure 20.23a

ARRAY OF OBJECTS

An array of objects works the same way as an array of simple variables such as an array of integers or an array of characters. The difference is that the type is a user-defined (class). The general form of an array of objects and its usages are shown below.

person employee[100]; //array of hundred objects of type person
employee[0]; and Employee[5]; //refer to the first and sixth objects of the array
employee[2].salary; //refers to the salary of the 3rd employee, assuming salary is public
employee[i].display(); //displays the ith employee information

The following program demonstrates the use of an array of objects in a payroll program with an array of five employee objects. Each employee object has its own **hoursworked**, **hourlyrate**, **salary**, and **employeename** as well as the functions: **setname( )**, **getname( )**, **sethoursworked( )**, **computesalary( )**, and **getsalary( )**. The constructor will set the hourlyrate to 20.00 if it is not provided.

```cpp
#include<iostream>
#include<string>
using namespace std;
class employee{
private: int hoursworked;
         double hourlyrate;
         double salary;
public: string employeename;
        employee(){hourlyrate=20.00;}
        void setname(string);
        string getname();
        void sethoursworked(double);
        void computesalary();
        double getsalary();        };//EMPLOYEE
void employee::sethoursworked(double hours){ hoursworked=hours;}
void employee::computesalary(){ salary=hourlyrate*hoursworked;}
double employee::getsalary(){ return salary;}
void main(){
        employee emp[5];
        int hours, i;
        for(i=0; i<5; i++){ cout<<"ENTER NAME: ";
                    cin>>emp[i].employeename;
                    cout<<"ENTER HOURS WORKED: ";
                    cin>>hours;
                    emp[i].sethoursworked(hours);
                    emp[i].computesalary();    }//FOR
        for(i=0; i<5; i++){ cout<<emp[i].employeename;
                    cout<<": "<<emp[i].getsalary()<<endl;  }//FOR
}//MAIN
```

Figure 20.24a – Program with an array of employee objects

```
ENTER NAME: Ebrahimi
ENTER HOURS WORKED: 55
ENTER NAME: Husain
ENTER HOURS WORKED: 44
ENTER NAME: Zainab
ENTER HOURS WORKED: 42
ENTER NAME: Zahra
ENTER HOURS WORKED: 38
ENTER NAME: Mehdi
ENTER HOURS WORKED: 40
Ebrahimi: 1100
Husain: 880
Zainab: 840
Zahra: 760
Mehdi: 800
```

Figure 20.24b – Output of Figure 20.24a

POINTER TO OBJECT VERSUS this POINTER

Like pointers to simple data types, a pointer to an object works in the same way as pointers to simple data types. We can use a pointer to a class object in the same way as a pointer to an integer or to a character. But, do not confuse a pointer to an object that is explained here with the **this** pointer that refers to a specific calling or returning object. Each object contains a **const** pointer to itself known as **this** pointer. Each member function carries **this** pointer implicitly when it is invoked. In other words, when a member function is called, there should be a way for *this function* to refer to other members of the object. This is done implicitly without involving **this** pointer because it is understood, but it could be done explicitly as **this->x** where x is the member data. The pointer **this** is used explicitly in situations where member functions need to return the address of the current object, or when a member function has several parameters of the same class type (other objects). Note that static member functions do not carry implicitly **this** pointer, hence, you need to use it explicitly to access the static members.

POINTER TO OBJECT OF CLASS

The following program builds a list of employees using a single linked list with two classes, each with a pointer to a class. For example, the **node** class has a pointer pointing to itself, and the **employeelist** class has a pointer to a node. For simplicity, we are building a new node and inserting it at the front of the list, readjusting the list upon completion, and then the entire list is displayed.

This program can be expanded to convert the payroll program to use a linked list instead of a static array to save memory. As employees are added, they are inserted to the list, and as they leave, they are deleted dynamically. As an exercise, expand the program to include other functions such as remove( ) and computesalary( ).

```cpp
#include<iostream.h>
class node{
public: double salary;
        node *next;};//NODE
class employeelist{
private:
        node *firstnode;
public:
        employeelist(){ firstnode=NULL;}
        void additem(double);
        void display();        }; //EMPLOYEELIST
void employeelist::additem(double amount){
        node *p=new node;
        p->salary=amount;
        p->next=firstnode;
        firstnode=p;        }//ADDITEM
void employeelist::display(){
        node *p;
        p=firstnode;
        while(p!=NULL){
                cout<<p->salary<<endl;
                p=p->next;}//WHILE
}//DISPLAY
void main(){
        employeelist emplist;
        double empsalary;
        for(int i=0; i<3; i++){
        cout<<"ENTER EMPLOYEE SALARY: ";
        cin>>empsalary;
        emplist.additem(empsalary);}//FOR
        emplist.display();  }//MAIN
```

Figure 20.25a – Program using pointers to objects of a class

```
ENTER EMPLOYEE SALARY:
90000
ENTER EMPLOYEE SALARY:
29000
ENTER EMPLOYEE SALARY:
55000
55000
29000
90000
```

Figure 20.25b – Output of Figure 20.25a

this POINTER PROGRAM: WORKING WITH TWO OBJECTS

A common usage of **this** pointer is when values are returned from member functions and overloaded operators such as = and = =. The following program finds the highest paid employee. The program defines an array of employees (class), and at this time we are only dealing with **id** and **salary**. The function **findhighemp( )** will compare the invoking object with the object that holds the highest salary. The function returns **this** pointer if the invoking object is higher, otherwise it returns the object that holds the higher salary. At the end of the loop the highest paid employee is found and the function **displayemp( )** displays the information. As an exercise, sort the objects according to the salary paid and display the information of each employee.

```
#include<iostream.h>
class employee{
public:  long int id;
         double salary;
const employee & findhighemp(const employee & emp) const;
void displayemp( )const ;    };
const employee& employee:: findhighemp(const employee &highemp)const {
if (salary>highemp.salary) return *this;
else return highemp; }//FINDHIGHEMP
void employee::displayemp( ) const {
        cout<<"EMPLOYEE ID IS:"<<id<<endl;
        cout<<"EMPLOYEE SALARY IS "<<salary<<endl; }//DISPLAYEMP
void main(){
        employee emp[3];
        int i;
        for(i=0;i<3;i++){
        cout<<"ENTER ID: "; cin>>emp[i].id;
        cout<<"ENTER SALARY: "; cin>>emp[i].salary;}//FOR
        employee highemp;
        highemp=emp[0];
        for(i=1;i<3;i++)  highemp=emp[i].findhighemp(highemp); //HIGHEST PAY
        cout<<"HIGHEST PAY EMPLOYEE:"<<endl;
        highemp.displayemp( );             }//MAIN
```

Figure 20.26a – Program using this pointer

```
ENTER ID: 1111
ENTER SALARY: 50000
ENTER ID: 1122
ENTER SALARY: 89000
ENTER ID: 1233
ENTER SALARY: 37000
HIGHEST PAY EMPLOYEE:
EMPLOYEE ID IS:1122
EMPLOYEE SALARY IS 89000
```

Figure 20.26b – Output of Figure 20.26a

ARRAY, A POINTER TO ARRAY, AND AN ARRAY OF POINTERS

An array is used to store a series (contiguous) of the same (homogeneous) data type under a common name. Retrieval and storage of data is done randomly through the index (subscript). You may have seen a variety of arrays. Arrays and pointers are closely related to each other, and any operations done using array subscripts can be done using pointers. C/C++ is somewhat pointer oriented and is proud of this despite criticism from newer languages such as Java and C# that try to distance themselves from pointers, mainly due to the consequences of careless usage. After assembly language lost its popularity, C/C++ became the most popular language to manipulate pointers and memory.

How would you allocate 500 contiguous memory locations? The 500 memory locations can be allocated entirely by the compiler, during run time, or one by one. The following illustrates how to allocate 500 locations in different ways.

The most common array is an array of a data type such as integers or any other data type including user data types (class). Storage of this data type is assigned during compilation time.

For example, **int months[12]** is an array of 12 integers and **employee emp[500]** is an array of 500 employees.
Note that the array name is the address of the first element of the array, **emp** is the same as **&emp[0]** and, similarly, **emp[i]** is the same as ***(emp+i)**.

POINTER TO AN ARRAY: ALLOCATE ARRAY DYNAMICALLY

Storage is allocated dynamically (during run time) and a pointer is assigned to the first address of the array. An array can be accessed through indirection or through an index. For example, **int * p=new int [500];** is a pointer to an array and will allocate an array of 500 integers. The difference between the former allocation and **int p[500];** is that in the former the memory is allocated dynamically and with **int p[500];** the memory is allocated statically. There are advantages and disadvantages to dynamic and static allocation, depending on the situation.
Note that the storage for the pointer is allocated during compile time and the storage for the array is allocated during run time.

AN ARRAY OF POINTERS: ALLOCATE THE MEMORY ONE BY ONE

An array is designated for pointers of some known data type. Storage for pointers is done during compile time and storage for its actual data type is allocated during run time one by one. An example of an array of pointers is ***p[500];** where there are 500 pointers and **p[0]=new int;** allocates memory.
The memory is allocated as you need it and de-allocated when you are finished with it.

```
#include<iostream.h>

void main(){
        int employeeid[5];
        double *hoursworked=new double[5];
        double *hourlyrate[5];
        double grosspay[5];
        for(int i=0; i<5; i++){
                cout<<"ENTER ID: ";
                cin>>employeeid[i];
                cout<<"ENTER HOURS WORKED: ";
                cin>>hoursworked[i]; //*(hoursworked+i)
                cout<<"ENTER HOURLY RATE: ";
                hourlyrate[i]=new double;
                cin>>*hourlyrate[i];
                grosspay[i]=hoursworked[i]*(*hourlyrate[i]);
                delete hourlyrate[i];
                }//FOR
        delete [] hoursworked;
        for(int n=0; n<5; n++){
                cout<<employeeid[n]<<" "<<grosspay[n]<<endl;}//FOR
}//MAIN
```

Figure 20.27a – Program using an array of pointers

```
ENTER ID: 111
ENTER HOURS WORKED: 48
ENTER HOURLY RATE: 9
ENTER ID: 112
ENTER HOURS WORKED: 44
ENTER HOURLY RATE: 10
ENTER ID: 123
ENTER HOURS WORKED: 55
ENTER HOURLY RATE: 7
ENTER ID: 133
ENTER HOURS WORKED: 56
ENTER HOURLY RATE: 6
ENTER ID: 134
ENTER HOURS WORKED: 50
ENTER HOURLY RATE: 5
111 432
112 440
123 385
133 336
134 250
```

Figure 20.27b – Output of Figure 20.27a

C AND C++ DIFFERENCES: DYNAMIC MEMORY ALLOCATION

C language uses the **malloc( )** function to allocate memory dynamically and the function **free( )** to de-allocate (free) memory. C++ uses the operator **new** to allocate memory and **delete** to de-allocate (delete) the allocated memory. The C **malloc( )** function requires the number of bytes to be allocated as a parameter. In the case where the number of bytes cannot be figured out by the programmer, the **sizeof** operator is used to figure out the size of a given data type. The general form of **malloc( )** is:

> **void *malloc(sizeof(datatype))**

The **malloc( )** function returns the beginning address of the allocated memory, however, it is a pointer of the type **void**. The reason for that is so that it can be converted to the type of variable that the programmer requests. In addition, in earlier version of C you must **cast** the return value of **malloc( )** before the assignment. The following examples demonstrate the use of **malloc( )** in C and **new** in C++.

> **int *myptr = (int *)malloc(sizeof(int);**
> **int *myptr = new int;**

You can see that C++ does some of the housekeeping for the user when using **new**. With the inclusion of exception handling, the **new** operator throws an exception when there is a problem in memory allocation (**bad_alloc**).

This is a C program using the **malloc( )**, **sizeof( )**, and **free( )** functions.

```
#include <stdio.h>
#include<stdlib.h>
void main(){
        float *ptr;
        ptr = (float *)malloc(sizeof (float));
        printf("HERE IS THE INPUT: ");
        scanf("%f",ptr);
        printf("HERE IS THE OUTPUT: ");
        printf("%f\n",*ptr);
        free(ptr);
        printf("%f ",*ptr);//MEMORY NOT AVAILABLE
}//MAIN
```

Figure 20.28a – Program demonstrating malloc( ), sizeof( ), and free( )

```
HERE IS THE INPUT: 5.00
HERE IS THE OUTPUT: 5.000000
-1998397155538108400.000000
```

Figure 20.28b – Output of Figure 20.28a

690

The following C++ program uses the **new** and **delete** operators.

```
#include<iostream.h>
#include<stdlib.h>
void main(){
        float *ptr;
        ptr = new float;
        cout<<"HERE IS THE INPUT: ";
        cin>>*ptr;
        cout<<"HERE IS THE OUTPUT: ";
        cout<<*ptr<<endl;
        delete ptr;
        cout<<*ptr<<endl;//MEMORY NOT AVAILABLE
}//MAIN
```

Figure 20.29a – Program demonstrating new and delete

```
HERE IS THE INPUT: 1.5
HERE IS THE OUTPUT: 1.5
-1.9984e+018
```

Figure 20.29b – Output of Figure 20.29a

C/C++ DIFFERENCES – FILE HANDLING

In C, to access an external file, a file variable must be declared, the file has to be opened, and the file has to be accessed through an I/O routine and, finally, the file has to be closed. The form of declaring a C file pointer is: **FILE *infile, *outfile;**

Note, the FILE type is written in capitals and is defined in **stdio.h**; **infile** and **outfile** are file pointers. To open a file, the function **fopen( )** associates an external filename with an access mode and returns a pointer which is assigned to the file pointer. The program uses the file pointer to access the file. The C I/O routines to handle files have a prefix of the letter **f**, such as **fprintf( )**, **fputs( )**, **fscanf( )**, and **fgets( )**. Note that the place of a file pointer is the first argument in **fscanf( )** while it is the last in **fgets( )**. Opening a file using **fopen( )** is shown below:

> **infile=fopen("dat.in", "r");**

The following program opens a file and, if the file does not exist, it displays an error message. The content is written to the screen (**stdout**) as well as to an external file. To test the file copy, the copied file is opened in read mode and is displayed on the screen.

```
#include<stdio.h>
void main(){
        FILE *infile, *outfile;
        int num;
        if((infile=fopen("dat.in", "r"))==NULL)
                        fprintf(stderr, "CANNOT OPEN %s\n", "dat.in");
        if((outfile=fopen("dat.out", "w"))==NULL)
                        fprintf(stderr, "CANNOT OPEN %s\n", "dat.out");
        while(fscanf(infile, "%d", &num)!=EOF){
                fprintf(outfile, "%d\n", num);
                fprintf(stdout, "%d\n", num);
                }//WHILE
        fclose(infile);fclose(outfile);
        if((infile=fopen("dat.out", "r"))==NULL)
                fprintf(stderr, "CANNOT OPEN %s\n", "dat.out");
        printf("\nDISPLAY THE COPIED FILE\n");
        while(fscanf(infile, "%d", &num)!=EOF){
                        fprintf(stdout, "%d\n", num);}//WHILE
        fclose(infile);
}//MAIN
```

Figure 20.30a – Program showing file handling in C

```
1
2
3
4
5

DISPLAY THE COPIED FILE
1
2
3
4
5
```

Figure 20.30b – Output of Figure 20.30a

STATIC DATA MÉMBER

A static data member is a variable that shares all instances (objects) of the class. In other words there is only one copy of the static data member for all of the objects. A static data member starts with the keyword **static**. One usage of a static data member is to count the number of processing objects. A restriction on a static member function is that it cannot access its members by **this** pointer.

STATIC MEMBER FUNCTION

A static member function does not have a **this** pointer and can only access the static member data. You can use a static member function without creating any object of its class. A static member function can work with a static member data to access and modify it. A static member function starts with the key word static. For example, a counter which is a static member data can be accessed by the static member function **findcounter**( ). The following program increments the counter as an object is created and decrements the counter as an object is deleted.

```cpp
class employee {
public:
employee () { counter++; }
~employee () {counter--;}
static int findcounter () { return counter;}//FINDCOUNTER
private:
static int counter;          }; // CLASS

int employee::counter=0;
#include <iostream>
using namespace std;
void main(){
employee *emp1=new employee();
cout<<"COUNTER IS:"<<employee::findcounter()<<endl;
employee *emp2=new employee();
cout<<"COUNTER IS:"<<employee::findcounter()<<endl;
delete emp1;
cout<<"COUNTER IS:"<<employee::findcounter()<<endl;
}//MAIN
```

Figure 20.31a – Program with a static member function

```
COUNTER IS:1
COUNTER IS:2
COUNTER IS:1
```

Figure 20.31b – Output of Figure 20.31a

10 COMMANDS OF HTML:html, a, img, table, form, input, select, li, textarea, mailto

HTML stands for Hyper-Text Markup Language and it consists of numerous tags that are used to format a web page. Although it is called a language, the fact is that it is a marking (tagging) of the text that has an effect when the file is viewed in a browser, where the impact of those tags is shown. An HTML file consists of several tags inserted into a text. The HTML tags are activated when viewed with the browser. The HTML tags are enclosed in < > (angled brackets) indicating the start of the tag; a tag preceded by a / (slash) indicates the end of the effect of the tag. Although there are more than a hundred HTML tags, I recommend that you learn the ten most important HTML tags that are needed to make a web page. The simplest way to create a web page is to start with <HTML> and type whatever you want on the page and end it here </HTML>. Make sure you save the file with the extension **.html**.

Commands can be categorized as text (bold <B>, italics <I>, font <FONT SIZE=+2>), color (<BODY BGCOLOR = red >), anchor references to other pages (<A HREF="www.nba.com">) and self-referencing anchors that search on your page (<A NAME=List> <A HREF="#List">), images (<IMG SRC="ebrahimi.jpg"), form to get information from users (<FORM METHOD="post" ACTION="mailto:ebrahimi@juno.com">), input <INPUT TYPE="text" NAME="name" SIZE="15">, select (<SELECT> <OPTION>), table (<TABLE><TR><TD>), and list (<UL><LI>). While the colors are defined by their names such as green, blue, and pink, they are also represented by #FFFFFF, where FF represents red, green, and blue which ranges from 00, 01 … to FF, this way you can blend your own colors. There are many other useful HTML commands such as: mailto which is used to write an e-mail to a specified address, bgsound which is used to add sound to your page, and radio buttons and check boxes that are types of input that allow the user to select from several options. The following is an example of a simple web page using the basic HTML commands.

```
<HTML>
<TITLE>Dr. Ebrahimi's Webpage</TITLE>
<BODY BGCOLOR="FF0055">
<FONT SIZE="+3">Welcome to Dr. Ebrahimi's Webpage</FONT><BR><BR>
<CENTER><IMG SRC="ebrahimi.jpg"><BR><BR>
<A HREF="http://ebrahimi.cjb.net">Click here</A><BR><BR>
<A HREF="#List">Programming Languages</A><BR><BR>
<TABLE BORDER=1>
<TR>
<TD>Apple</TD>
<TD>Banana</TD>
</TR>
<TR>
<TD>Lettuce</TD>
<TD>Tomato</TD>
</TR>
</TABLE></CENTER><BR>

What is your favorite fruit?
<SELECT NAME="Fruit">
<OPTION>Apple
<OPTION>Banana
<OPTION>Cherry
<OPTION>Watermelon
</SELECT><BR>

<FORM METHOD="POST" ACTION="mailto:ebrahimi@juno.com">
Name: <INPUT TYPE="text" NAME="name" SIZE="15"><BR>
E-mail: <TEXTAREA NAME="email" ROWS=5 COLS=35></TEXTAREA>
<INPUT TYPE="submit" VALUE="send"></FORM>

<A NAME=List></A>
<LI>C++</LI>
<LI>Java</LI>
<LI>Perl</LI>
<LI>JavaScript</LI>
<LI>HTML</LI>
</BODY>
</HTML>
```

Figure 20.32 – Simple web page created with HTML

JAVASCRIPT

JavaScript is a language that is embedded in HTML and is executed in a browser (Internet Explorer or Netscape). Almost every web page now utilizes JavaScript. While the name is JavaScript and people think it is related to Java, it is a distinct language by itself. Dealing with the Internet (Internet programming) is a common purpose of Java and JavaScript, and both are event-driven. The way JavaScript handles input (ex. an input value has to be parsed to its numerical value) is similar to Java. JavaScript can take advantage of HTML to make the page more presentable by using loops and if statements to manipulate many fonts, colors, etc. The syntax of JavaScript is very similar to that of C++ and JavaScript's keywords are mostly from C/C++; out of 22 keywords, 17 are used in C++, 4 keywords are used in Pascal such as var, function, with, and in, and there are some other keywords such as null and typeof. The words write and writeln (write line) to display are also used in Pascal. JavaScript is an event-driven language that, upon certain events such as clicking the mouse or pressing a key, an action takes place.

```
<HTML>
<SCRIPT LANGUAGE="JavaScript">
document.write("Hello World");
</SCRIPT>
</HTML>
```

Figure 20.33a – JavaScript code to say Hello World

```
Hello World
```

Figure 20.33b – Output of Figure 20.33a

The following program is a simple translator that translates english words into spanish using parallel arrays. The user enters a search key and the program performs a linear search for the english word in the english array; when the word is found, the corresponding spanish word is displayed. If the word is not found, an error message is displayed.

```
<HTML><H1>Javascript search</H1>
<SCRIPT LANGUAGE="javascript">
var english=["water","house","book","university","car","computer"];
var spanish=["aqua","casa","libro","universidad","caro","computador"];
var result = 0;
var searchword = prompt("Enter english word to translate: ");
for(i=0;i<english.length;i++){
if(english[i]==searchword){
   document.writeln("Spanish word: "+spanish[i]);
   result = 1;   }//IF
   }//FOR
if(result==0)
   document.writeln("Sorry, NO MATCH for: " + searchword);
</SCRIPT> </HTML>
```

Figure 20.34a – JavaScript translator program

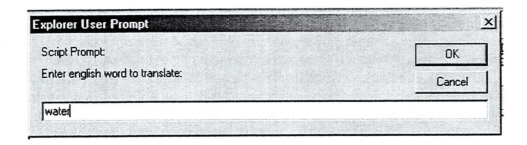

Javascript search

Spanish word: aqua

Figure 20.34b – Output of JavaScript program

WHAT IS CGI (COMMON GATEWAY INTERFACE)

CGI stands for Common Gateway Interface and is a simple protocol (standard) to establish a communication (interaction) between your Web page (located anywhere) via a browser and your program that resides on a Web server. The CGI program (e.g. C++, or Perl) processes data submitted by a form and performs requested tasks such as searching. After submitting a form, the browser uses HTTP to make a request for the URL of a CGI program. The Web server receives the request and executes the CGI program with the data that is passed. The output of the CGI program is usually in the form of a web page which is sent back through the Web server to the requesting browser. An example of CGI usage is a database program that runs on the Internet and lets individuals manipulate the database through the web.

Note that a CGI program is executable and resides in a special directory under the direct control of a Webmaster, commonly known as */cgi-bin,* so that the Web server is directed to execute the CGI program rather than just display it to the browser.

WRITING A CGI IN C++

A CGI takes information from forms on a Web page, processes it, and sends a page back to the user. A CGI program written in C++ is nothing more than just another C++ program that accepts a string as its input and breaks down the input string into tokens (words) and identifies and processes the input based on the requested task. CGI is language independent and the languages **Perl** and **Python** or even a script language such as Unix shell can be used to write a CGI program. One caution, do not try to use Java to write a CGI; instead, use Java Servlets. The language Perl, because of its sophisticated pattern matching (regular expressions), has been the language of choice for writing CGI

697

programs. However, you can stick to C/C++ and write a CGI, rather than using other languages.

In summary, in order to write a simple CGI program in C++, use the input routines of C++ **cin** or **getline( )** to take the data as if it were on a standard input (**stdin**) with the understanding of how the inputs are separated from each other (e.g. by **&** or by **;**). After that, a CGI program is another C++ program and when all processing is done, at the end, the CGI program has to communicate to the web page or create a new one. The CGI communicates back to the web page through the standard output (**stdout**) such as **cout** with embedded HTML tags inside the quotations. Note that the CGI program takes input from the HTML form and encodes it (URL encoding) by making a single string, since URL does not allow spaces. Instead of spaces, separators (delimiters) such as **&** (ampersand) and = (equal sign) are used. In the following example, the string with two input data such as the first name and last name are separated with & is sent to the CGI and the program has to strip the **f=** and save the values correspondingly. For simplicity, we are using one letter for the name of the field.

> **f=John&f=Doe**

C++ CGI PROGRAM

The following HTML file consists of a form with one input data and we want to send the input and get a response by echoing the input back. At first, an HTML file is created and, in the form tag, the action is specified by indicating the name of the executable CGI program (e.g. **ebrahimi.cgi**) which resides in the */cgi-bin* directory. The method of sending the data to the CGI program is **POST** where the data is sent via the program's standard input in contrast to the other method **GET** where the data is sent through a program variable name known as *environment variable*. For the sake of simplicity, the field's name is chosen as one character (e.g. **f**) which with the = sign makes two characters (e.g. **f =**). One job of the CGI is to strip off these two characters and save the rest (e.g. value). The following CGI program takes the encoded URL, strips the first two characters, and saves the rest of the string into another string (e.g. str2), which is echoed back to the user.

Note that the **"Content-type: text/html\n\n"** in
> **cout<<"Content-type: text/html\n\n";**

will inform the server that the CGI program is about to send data to the user in the form of an HTML page. Make sure to include the newline (**\n**).

If you need to convert the above C++ program to C language for the reason of speed, you only need to change **cin** to **scanf("%s",)** and **cout** to **printf("%s",)** and make sure to include **#include <stdio.h>**.

```
<html>
<form action=cgi-bin/ebrahimi.cgi method="post">
<input type=text name=f size=10>
<input type=submit value=submit>
</form>
</html>
```

Figure 20.35a – HTML form to take in user input

```
#include <iostream.h>
void main(){
  char str[100];
  char str2[100];
  cin>>str;

  int i=2;
  int n=0;
  for(i=2; str[i]!=0 ;i++)
  {
   str2[n]=str[i];
   n++;
  }//REMOVE FIRST TWO CHARACTERS FROM POST
  str2[n++]=0;//SET THE END OF THE STRING TO NULL

  cout<<"Content-type: text/html\n\n";
  cout<<str2;
}//MAIN
```

Figure 20.35b – CGI program to take in a string and display it

COMPILING A CGI PROGRAM

The following compiles a CGI program under Linux (***GNU* c++** compiler known as **g++**). However, the executable code is redirected to a file with the extension **.cgi**. The command **chmod** (change mode) makes the executable code accessible to the public (read, no write, execute), but you can have all access permissions (read, write, execute).

> **g++ -o ebrahimi.cgi ebrahimi.cpp**

> **chmod 755 ebrahimi.cgi**

Other operating systems may work differently than a Unix-like OS, but the concept would be the same. Note that one reason to place the CGI program in a specific directory like */cgi-bin* is for security reasons and to make it easier for the system administrator to manage.

A C++ CGI PROGRAM WITH TWO INPUT DATA

The following C++ CGI program uses two input with the hope that you will understand how to write a multiple input program using the same strategy. The strategy is that every data has a field name followed by =, its value, and a separator (&) before the next field's name. The program has to skip two characters to get to the value of the first input and, after that, three characters must be skipped between values. For example: **f=John&f=Doe** Note that the below program is just for you to understand the concept and you may want to generalize it so it can work with any input and any size field name.

```
<html>
<form action=cgi-bin/ebrahimi.cgi method="post">
First Name: <input type=text name=f size=10><br>
Last Name: <input type=text name=f size=10><br>
<input type=submit value=submit>
</form>
</html>
```

First Name: John
Last Name: Doe
submit

Figure 20.36a – HTML form to take in two inputs

```
#include <iostream.h>
void main() {
  char str[100];
  char fname[100];
  char lname[100];
  cin>>str;
  int i=2;
  int n=0;
  for(i=2;str[i]!='&';i++){
   fname[n]=str[i];
   n++;}
  fname[n++]=0;
  n=0;
  for(i+=3;str[i]!=0;i++) {
   lname[n]=str[i];
   n++;}
  lname[n++]=0;
  cout<<"Content-type: text/html\n\n";
  cout<<"<HTML><B>Your Name: </B>";
  cout<<fname<<" "<<lname;
  cout<<"</HTML>";
}//MAIN
```

Figure 20.36b – CGI program to take in two strings and display them

Your Name: John Doe

Figure 20.36c – Output as HTML page

C++ CGI DATABASE

The following program demonstrates how you simply can make a web application where users can interact with your program from anywhere using C++ with CGI capabilities. To make the program short, other database functions such as display, update, and deletion are omitted. The program creates a simple database with simple file handling without using other databases such as Access or SQL tools. The program follows a similar strategy of extracting the variables from the input (URL encoding). The variables need to be separated (i+=3), this extraction could be put into a function. For the sake of simplicity, each function is a separate form in HTML; you may want to try to put it into a single form. For each function, there is a separate CGI program in the cgi-bin directory. As an exercise, you can write those functions and optimize the code and even include object-oriented design.

```
                       empdatabase.html
<HTML>
<BODY BGCOLOR=ffdeaa>
<CENTER><BR><B>Employee Database</B></CENTER><BR>
<HR WIDTH=65%>
<CENTER>Please select from the following choices:<BR><BR>
<FORM ACTION="insertrecord.html">
        <INPUT TYPE="submit" VALUE="1. Insert a Record        "></FORM>
<FORM ACTION="cgi-bin/displayall.cgi">
        <INPUT TYPE="submit" VALUE="2. Display all Records "></FORM>
<FORM ACTION="search.html">
        <INPUT TYPE="submit" VALUE="3. Search Database       "></FORM>
<FORM ACTION="cgi-bin/update.cgi">
        <INPUT TYPE="submit" VALUE="4. Update Record         "></FORM>
<FORM ACTION="cgi-bin/delete.cgi">
    <INPUT TYPE="submit" VALUE="5. Delete a Record      "></FORM>
</CENTER></BODY>
</HTML>
```

Figure 20.37a – HTML for the database menu

Employee Database

Please select from the following choices:

1. Insert a Record

2. Display all Records

3. Search Database

4. Update Record

5. Delete a Record

insertrecord.html
```
<HTML>
<BODY BGCOLOR=ffdeaa>
<CENTER>
<BR><B>Insert Record to Employee Database</B><BR><BR>
<HR WIDTH=65%><BR>
<FORM ACTION="cgi-bin/insertrec.cgi" METHOD="post">
<B>First Name: <INPUT TYPE=text NAME=f SIZE=15><BR><BR>
Last Name: <INPUT TYPE=text NAME=f SIZE=15><BR><BR>
Salary per hour: <INPUT TYPE=text NAME=f SIZE=5 value=0.00><BR><BR>
Hours worked: <INPUT TYPE=text NAME=f SIZE=5><BR><BR>
<INPUT TYPE=submit VALUE="Submit Record"></FORM>
</CENTER></BODY>
</HTML>
```

Figure 20.37b – HTML for inserting a record

Insert Record to Employee Database

First Name: Alireza

Last Name: Ebrahimi

Salary per hour: 56.00

Hours worked: 52

Submit Record

```
       insertrec.cpp
#include <fstream.h>
#include <string.h>
struct employee{ char fname[30], lname[30];
             double salary, hoursworked, netpay;};
void main(){
       char str[150], fnamef[20], lnamef[20], salaryf[10], hoursworkedf[10];
       cin>>str;
       int i=2, n=0;
       for(i;str[i]!='&';i++){ fnamef[n]=str[i];  n++; }//FOR
       fnamef[n++]=0; n=0;
       for(i+=3;str[i]!='&';i++){
             lnamef[n]=str[i];
             n++; }//FOR
       lnamef[n++]=0;  n=0;
       for(i+=3;str[i]!='&';i++){ salaryf[n]=str[i];  n++; }//FOR
       salaryf[n++]=0;  n=0;
       for(i+=3;str[i]!=0;i++){ hoursworkedf[n]=str[i];  n++; }//FOR
       hoursworkedf[n++]=0;
       ofstream record("employee.txt",ios::app);
       record<<fnamef<<" "<<lnamef<<" "<<salaryf<<" "<<hoursworkedf<<endl;
       record.close();
       cout<<"Content-type: text/html\n\n";
       i=0;  employee emp[100];
       ifstream record2( "employee.txt", ios::in);
       cout<<"<BODY BGCOLOR=ffdeaa>";
       cout<<"<BR><CENTER><B>Employee Database: Display All Records</B><BR>";
       cout<<"<BR><HR WIDTH=65%><BR>";
       cout<<"<TABLE BORDER=5><TR><TD><B>First Name</B></TD>";
    cout<<"<TD><B>Last Name</B></TD>";
    cout<<"<TD><B>Salary</B></TD>";
    cout<<"<TD><B>HrsWorked</B></TD>";
    cout<<"<TD><B>Net Pay:</B></TD>";
    cout<<"</TR>";
while(record2>>emp[i].fname>>emp[i].lname>>emp[i].salary>>emp[i].hoursworked){
       emp[i].netpay=emp[i].salary*emp[i].hoursworked;
       cout<<"<TR><TD>"<<emp[i].fname<<"</TD><TD>";
       cout<<emp[i].lname<<"</TD><TD>"<<emp[i].salary<<"</TD><TD>";
       cout<<emp[i].hoursworked<<"</TD><TD>"<<emp[i].netpay<<"</TD></TR>";
       }//WHILE
cout<<"</TABLE><br><br>";
cout<<"</CENTER></BODY>";
record2.close();
}//MAIN
```

Figure 20.37c – CGI program to insert a record into the database and display all

Employee Database: Display All Records

First Name	Last Name	Salary	HrsWorked	Net Pay:
Alireza	Ebrahimi	100	20	2000
John	Doe	20	40	800
Julia	Smith	25	50	1250

```
       search.html
<HTML>
<BODY BGCOLOR=ffdeaa>
<CENTER>
<BR><B>Search Employee Database</B><BR><BR>
<HR WIDTH=65%><BR>
<FORM ACTION="cgi-bin/search.cgi" METHOD="post">
<B>Enter Employee's Last Name: </B>
<INPUT TYPE=text name="f" SIZE=15>
<INPUT TYPE=submit VALUE="Search"></FORM>
</CENTER>
</BODY>
</HTML>
```

Figure 20.37d – HTML to take in search name

Search Employee Database

Enter Employee's Last Name: Ebrahimi [Search]

```
search.cpp
#include <fstream.h>
#include <string.h>
struct employee{
        char fname[30], lname[30];
        double salary, hoursworked, netpay; };
void main(){
        char buff[100], buff2[100];
        cin>>buff;
        cout<<"Content-type: text/html\n\n";
        int i=2;
        while(buff[i]!=0){
                buff2[i-2]=buff[i];
                i++;}//WHILE
        buff2[i-2]=0;
        cout<<"<BODY BGCOLOR=ffdeaa>";
        cout<<"<CENTER><BR><B>Search results</B><BR><HR WIDTH=65%><br><br>";
        employee emp[100];
        ifstream record("employee.txt", ios::in);
        i=0;
        int k=-1;
        while(record>>emp[i].fname>>emp[i].lname>>emp[i].salary>>emp[i].hoursworked)
        {i++;}
        for(int j=0;j<i;j++){
                if(strcmp(buff2,emp[j].lname)==0)
                        k=j; }//FOR
        if(k!=-1){
        emp[k].netpay=emp[k].salary*emp[k].hoursworked;
        cout<<"<TABLE BORDER=5>";
            cout<<"<TR><TD>First Name:</TD><TD>"<<emp[k].fname<<"</TD></TR>";
        cout<<"<TR><TD>Last Name:</TD><TD>"<<emp[k].lname<<"</TD</TR>";
        cout<<"<TR><TD>Salary:</TD><TD>"<<emp[k].salary<<"</TD></TR>";
        cout<<"<TR><TD>Hrs Worked:</TD><TD>"<<emp[k].hoursworked<<"</TD></TR>";
        cout<<"<TR><TD>Net Pay:</TD><TD>"<<emp[k].netpay<<"</TD></TR></TABLE>";}
            else {cout<<"Record not found"<<"<br>";}

cout<<"</CENTER></BODY></HTML>";
}//MAIN
```

Figure 20.37e – CGI program to search for a record and display it

Search results

First Name:	Alireza
Last Name:	Ebrahimi
Salary:	56
Hrs Worked:	52
Net Pay:	2912

A C++ SIMPLE DATABASE TO CONVERT TO OBJECT

The following program is a simple database with insertion, display, modify (update), deletion, and report functions for employee records. The program saves the employee records to a file and computes gross pay. The database has a delete file function with a password. This program uses an array of structs and each employee has its own first and last name, hourly rate, hours worked, and gross pay. At start of the program, the load function is called that uploads the records from the file to an array; similarly, when the program is exited, the store function downloads the array to the file. As an exercise, you may want to redesign the program using an object-oriented paradigm by defining a class called Dbase that has all the operations on the database and consists of the objects of all employees (e.g. 100 employees).

```cpp
#include<fstream>
#include<string>
#include<iostream>
#include<iomanip>
using namespace std;
struct employee{   string fname, lname;
                   double hourlyrate, hoursworked, netpay; }; //employee
employee e[100];
int n=0;
void load(){
        ifstream fin("employee.txt",ios::in);
        while(fin>>e[n].fname>>e[n].lname>>e[n].hourlyrate>>e[n].hoursworked){
        e[n].netpay=e[n].hourlyrate*e[n].hoursworked;
        n++;}//WHILE
        }//LOAD
void store(){
        ofstream fout("employee.txt",ios::out);
        for(int i=0; i<n; i++){
        if(e[i].fname!=" ")
        fout<<e[i].fname<<" "<<e[i].lname<<" "<<e[i].hourlyrate<<" "<<e[i].hoursworked<<endl;
            }//FOR
        }//STORE

void insert(){
        cout<<"Enter employee's first name: ";       cin>>e[n].fname;
        cout<<"Enter employee's last name: ";        cin>>e[n].lname;
        cout<<"Enter employee's salary per hour: "; cin>>e[n].hourlyrate;
        if(cin.fail())
                {cout<<"Error\n"; exit(1);}
        cout<<"Enter employee's hours worked: ";
        cin>>e[n].hoursworked;
        e[n].netpay=e[n].hourlyrate*e[n].hoursworked;
        n++;     }//INSERTS THE RECORD TO ARRAY

void display(){
        cout<<setiosflags(ios::left)<<setw(15)<<"First Name"<<setw(15)<<"Last Name";
        cout<<setw(10)<<"Hourly Rate"<<setw(10)<<"HrsWorked"<<setw(10)<<"Net Pay";
        cout<<endl<<endl;
        cout<<setiosflags(ios::fixed|ios::showpoint|ios::left);
        for(int i=0;i<n;i++){
        if(e[i].fname!=" "){
        cout<<setiosflags(ios::left)<<setw(15)<<e[i].fname<<setw(15)<<e[i].lname;
        cout<<setprecision(2)<<setiosflags(ios::left)<<setw(10)<<e[i].hourlyrate;
        cout<<setw(10)<<e[i].hoursworked<<setw(10)<<e[i].netpay;
        cout<<resetiosflags(ios::left)<<endl;}//IF
        }//FOR
}//THIS FUNCTION DISPLAYS ALL RECORDS IN ARRAY

int search(string s){
        for(int i=0;i<n;i++)if(s==e[i].lname)return i;//FOR
        return -1;
        }//SEARCH BY NAME,-1 NOT FOUND
```

707

```cpp
void update(){
        string searchn;
        cout<<"Enter the Last Name of the Employee to be modified: ";        cin>>searchn;
        int i=search(searchn);
        if(i==-1) cout<<"EMPLOYEE NOT LISTED"<<endl;
        else{
        cout<<endl<<"Please enter the updated information."<<endl;
        cout<<"Enter employee's first name: ";        cin>>e[i].fname;
        cout<<"Enter employee's last name: ";        cin>>e[i].lname;
        cout<<"Enter employee's rate per hour: ";        cin>>e[i].hourlyrate;
        cout<<"Enter employee's hours worked: ";   cin>>e[i].hoursworked;
        e[i].netpay=(e[i].hourlyrate*e[i].hoursworked);}
        }//UPDATE

void deleterec(){
 string searchn;
 cout<<"Enter the Last Name of the Employee to delete: ";  cin>>searchn;
 int k=-1;
 for(int j=0; j<n;j++){
  if(searchn==e[j].lname)
    k=j;}
 if(k!=-1)
 { cout<<" Name: "<<e[k].fname<<" "<<e[k].lname<<endl;
  cout<<" Salary: "<<e[k].hourlyrate<<endl;
  cout<<" Hrs Worked: "<<e[k].hoursworked<<endl;
  cout<<" Net Pay: "<<e[k].netpay<<endl<<endl;}

 char ans;
 cout<<endl<<"Do you want to delete this record? (Y/N): ";
 cin>>ans;
 if(ans=='Y'||ans=='y'){
        e[k].fname=" ";}//IF
 else cout<<"EMPLOYEE NOT FOUND";    }//DELETE

void report(){
 int i=0;
 double totalhrs=0.00, totalpay=0.00;
 for(i=0;i<n;i++){
 totalhrs+=e[i].hoursworked;
 totalpay+=e[i].netpay; }//FOR
 cout<<"Total number of employees: " <<n<<endl<<endl;
 cout<<"Total hours worked by all employees: "<<totalhrs<<endl<<endl;
 cout<<"Total pay of all employees: "<<totalpay<<endl<<endl;  }//REPORT
```

```cpp
void deletefile(){
int pword;
cout<<"Enter your administrative password: ";  cin>>pword;
if(pword==5438){
ofstream record("employee.txt", ios::out);
record<<endl;
load();
record.close();}
else cout<<"Wrong password entered."<<endl; }//DELETE FILE

void backupfile(){
  system("copy employee.txt backup.txt");
  cout<<endl<<"Back-up file has been made."<<endl;
}//BACKUPFILE  use cp command for UNIX

void main(){
        load();
        char choice;
        while (choice!='e'&&choice!='E'){
        cout<<endl<<"Payroll Database"<<endl;
        cout<<"1. Insert Employee Record and Compute Net Pay"<<endl;
        cout<<"2. Display All Records"<<endl;
        cout<<"3. Search Database"<<endl;
        cout<<"4. Update Record"<<endl;
        cout<<"5. Delete Record"<<endl;
        cout<<"6. Generate Report"<<endl;
        cout<<"7. Delete Database File"<<endl;
        cout<<"8. Back-up Database File"<<endl;
        cout<<endl<<" Type e to exit"<<endl<<endl;
        cout<<"Enter the number of your choice:";
        cin>>choice;        cout<<endl;
        switch (choice){
        case '1': insert(); break;
        case '2': display(); break;
        case '3': char s[100]; int index;
                cout<<"Enter the last name of the person you want: ";
                cin>>s;
                index=search(s);
                if(index!=-1) {
                cout<<"Name: "<<e[index].fname<<" "<<e[index].lname<<endl;
                cout<<"Hourly Rate: "<<e[index].hourlyrate<<endl;
                cout<<"Hrs Worked: "<<e[index].hoursworked<<endl;
                cout<<"Net Pay: "<<e[index].netpay<<endl<<endl;}//IF
                else cout<<"EMPLOYEE NOT FOUND"<<endl;
                break;
        case '4': update(); break;
        case '5': deleterec(); break;
        case '6': report(); break;
        case '7': deletefile(); break;
        case '8': backupfile(); break;
        case 'e': store(); break; //EXIT
        default: cout<<"Invalid Choice"<<endl; break; }//SWITCH
        }//WHILE
}//MAIN
```

Figure 20.38a – A simple C++ database

Payroll Database
1. Insert Employee Record and Compute Net Pay
2. Display All Records
3. Search Database
4. Update Record
5. Delete Record
6. Generate Report
7. Delete Database File
8. Back-up Database File

 Type e to exit

Enter the number of your choice:1

Enter employee's first name: Alireza
Enter employee's last name: Ebrahimi
Enter employee's salary per hour: 55.00
Enter employee's hours worked: 50

Payroll Database
1. Insert Employee Record and Compute Net Pay
2. Display All Records
3. Search Database
4. Update Record
5. Delete Record
6. Generate Report
7. Delete Database File
8. Back-up Database File

 Type e to exit

Enter the number of your choice:2

First Name	Last Name	Hourly Rate	HrsWorked	Net Pay
John	Taylor	50.00	48.00	2400.00
Jean	Doe	50.00	42.00	2100.00
Alireza	Ebrahimi	55.00	50.00	2750.00

Payroll Database
1. Insert Employee Record and Compute Net Pay
2. Display All Records
3. Search Database
4. Update Record
5. Delete Record
6. Generate Report
7. Delete Database File
8. Back-up Database File

 Type e to exit

Enter the number of your choice:e

Figure 20.38b – Output of Figure 20.38a

JAVA DATABASE EQUIVALENT TO THE C++ DATABASE

The following **Java** database program demonstrates how your knowledge of C++ will help you to write Java applications. You will realize that the control structures are the same (while, if/else, for); however, there are differences in java file handling and user input. File handling in java is a little more complicated due to the class nature of the file. Input from the keyboard has to be parsed into the desired format. There are two stages of compiling Java programs: compilation and interpretation. The compilation of the **.java** file creates a **.class** bytecode file that can be interpreted in virtually any platform (Virtual Machine). One of the benefits of Java is its portability and its ability to create applets that can be run on browsers. Java does not have pointers and applets cannot directly access files due to security restrictions. To read input or values, StreamTokenizer is used to read either a string (sval) or a number (nval) as instance variables. The Cin class is used for input from the keyboard and once it is compiled, the class can be used in other applications as long as it is in the same directory.

```
import java.io.*;
public class Database {
    private static final int MAX = 100;
    private Cin cin = new Cin();
    private String name[] = new String[MAX];
    private double hourlyrate[] = new double[MAX];
    private double hoursworked[] = new double[MAX];
    private double grosspay[] = new double[MAX];
    private String searchName;
    private String fileName;
    private int n = 0;
    public void load() throws IOException{
        try{  Reader fi = new BufferedReader(
            new InputStreamReader(
                        new FileInputStream("employee.dat")));
          StreamTokenizer fin = new StreamTokenizer(fi);
          int tokenType;
          tokenType = fin.nextToken();
          while((tokenType != StreamTokenizer.TT_EOF)){
              name[n] = fin.sval;
              fin.nextToken();
              hourlyrate[n] = fin.nval;
              fin.nextToken();
              hoursworked[n] = fin.nval;
              grosspay[n] = hoursworked[n] * hourlyrate[n];
              tokenType = fin.nextToken();
              n++; }//WHILE
        }//TRY
        catch(IOException ex){ System.out.println(ex); }//CATCH
    }//LOAD
    public void insert(){
        System.out.print("Enter the employee name: ");
        name[n] = cin.readString();
        System.out.print("What is employee hourly rate? ");
        hourlyrate[n] = cin.readDouble();
        System.out.print("How many hours did the employee work? ");
        hoursworked[n] = cin.readDouble();
        grosspay[n] = hoursworked[n] * hourlyrate[n];
        n++; }//INSERT
    public void display(){
        for ( int i = 0; i < n; i++ ){
                if(name[i]!=""){
          System.out.println( name[i] + " " + grosspay[i] );}//IF
            }//FOR
          }//DISPLAY
```

```java
public boolean search(){
      System.out.print("Enter the search name: ");
   String searchName = cin.readString();
   for(int i = 0; i < n; i++){
     if ( searchName.equalsIgnoreCase(name[i])){
        System.out.println("Found: "+name[i]);
        System.out.println("Grosspay: "+grosspay[i]);
        return true; }//IF
   }//FOR
   System.out.println("Name not found");
   return true;
      }//SEARCH
public boolean modify(){
   System.out.print("Enter the search name: ");
   String searchName = cin.readString();
   for(int i = 0; i < n; i++){
     if ( searchName.equalsIgnoreCase(name[i])){
        System.out.print("What is employee hourly rate? ");
        hourlyrate[i] = cin.readDouble();
        System.out.print("How many hours did the employee work?");
        hoursworked[i] = cin.readDouble();
        grosspay[i] = hoursworked[i] * hourlyrate[i];
        return true; }//IF
   }//FOR
   System.out.println("Name not found");
   return false;
}//MODIFY
public boolean remove(){
   System.out.print("Enter the search name: ");
   String searchName = cin.readString();
   for(int i = 0; i < n; i++){
     if ( searchName.equalsIgnoreCase(name[i])){
        name[i] = "";
        return true; }//IF
   }//FOR
   System.out.println("Name not found");
   return false;
}//REMOVE
public void quit() throws IOException{
  this.store();
  System.out.println("Thank you");
  System.exit(0);
}//QUIT
public void store() throws IOException{
  try{
    FileOutputStream out = new FileOutputStream("employee.dat");
    PrintStream ps = new PrintStream(out);
    for(int i = 0; i < n; i++){
         if ( name[i] != "" )
       ps.println( name[i] + "\t" + hourlyrate[i] +
                    "\t" + hoursworked[i] );
    }//FOR
    out.close(); }//TRY
  catch( IOException ex ){
    System.out.println(ex); }//CATCH
}//STORE
```

```
public static void main( String args[] ) throws IOException{
  Database db = new Database();
  Cin read = new Cin();
  db.load();
  int choice = 0;
  do{System.out.println("\t1-Insert");
    System.out.println("\t2-Display");
    System.out.println("\t3-Search");
    System.out.println("\t4-Modify");
    System.out.println("\t5-Remove");
    System.out.println("\t6-Quit");
    choice = read.readInt();
    if( choice == 1 ) db.insert();
    else if( choice == 2 ) db.display();
    else if( choice == 3 ) db.search();
    else if( choice == 4 ) db.modify();
    else if ( choice == 5 ) db.remove();
    else if ( choice == 6 ) db.quit();
    else System.out.println("Enter correct number");
  } while(true);
}//MAIN
}//DATABASE
```

Figure 20.39a – A simple Java database

```
import java.io.*;
import java.util.*;
public class Cin {
  static InputStreamReader instream = new InputStreamReader( System.in );
  static BufferedReader buffreader = new BufferedReader( instream );
  StringTokenizer token;
  StringTokenizer getToken() throws IOException {
    String str = buffreader.readLine();
    return new StringTokenizer(str); }
  public int readInt(){
    try{      token = getToken();
              return Integer.parseInt(token.nextToken());
          }catch(IOException ex){
      System.err.println("IO EXCEPTION in - readInt");
      return 0;  }  }//READINT
  public double readDouble() {
    try {      token = getToken();
              return new Double(token.nextToken()).doubleValue();
          }catch (IOException ex) {
      System.err.println("IO Exception - readDouble");
      return 0.0; } }//READDOUBLE
  public String readString() {
    try {      return buffreader.readLine();
        } catch (IOException ioe) {
      System.err.println("IO Exception in EasyIn.readString");
      return ""; } }//READSTRING
}//CIN
```

Figure 20.39b – Java Cin class for input

```
        1-Insert
        2-Display
        3-Search
        4-Modify
        5-Remove
        6-Quit
4
Enter the search name: Alireza
What is employee hourly rate? 56.00
How many hours did the employee work?50
        1-Insert
        2-Display
        3-Search
        4-Modify
        5-Remove
        6-Quit
2
Alireza 2800.0
Husain 2025.0
Zainab 2500.0
Zahra 3500.0
Mehdi 3200.0
        1-Insert
        2-Display
        3-Search
        4-Modify
        5-Remove
        6-Quit
6
Thank you
```

Figure 20.39c – Output for Figure 20.39a

TOPICS NOT COVERED HERE

Programming is not a satisfying subject. Programmers are like painters or composers who usually are not completely happy with the masterpieces they create. A programmer looks for better ways to optimize from more friendliness to different interfaces. Like many other fields, programming can be a never-ending story and to this end, I compare the field of programming to the field of medicine with its many specialized sub-fields. A program is the body and a programmer is a physician. For the beginner, the recognition of the symptoms of diseases is a way to learn, not a reason to get frustrated and withdrawn. I found that beginners often feel frustrated when they encounter errors and easily withdraw and conclude that they cannot handle it or that they are not suitable for becoming a programmer or even understanding programming. Beginners have to be reminded that it is okay to be frustrated and that it takes time to overcome any difficulties they may have. Beginners should be encouraged to be patient and learn from their errors, even from their friend's errors.

The following subjects on optimizing and improving your algorithms and program problem solving skills are major topics in undergraduate as well as graduate study.

Data Structure and Algorithm Analysis is a way to analyze algorithms and explore different ways to solve a problem and store and utilize data. Complexity analysis is done by the amount of time and space the program requires. STL has built-in canned solutions for some of the data structures and algorithms that can be reused in programs.

Object-Oriented Programming is the study of object-oriented languages such as Simula, Smalltalk, C++, Ada, Java, and Visual Basic and explores the object-oriented design. OOP is a deep topic, historically starting in the 1960's with Simula and then getting more acquainted with Smalltalk, C++, Ada, and C#. A new trend in software engineering is the use of object-oriented modeling and design, which incorporates UML in the software process such as software life cycles.

I did not cover the differences between C++ and C# (C sharp), but I recommend that you explore Microsoft C# (C sharp) and see how it tries to put together the best of both C++ and Java into one language.

Dynamic Web Pages deals with creating a dynamic web program such as a database for a club to keep track of events and statistics.

If you like entertainment, you can make your own **game programming** and learn how games are created using graphic user interfaces, it is an interesting and lucrative field. Virtual reality is a good tool for creating walk-through situations. You will be surprised to find that many games are written by beginner programmers and with this book you have the essential knowledge needed to build these games. **Simulation** is also an important field that uses computer models to imitate real world situations such as traffic through a telephone system or computer network. Some simulation requires sophisticated statistical analysis. In fact, Simula 67, the first object-oriented language, was created for simulation. Similarly, C++ was designed as a result of simulation.

Visualization and Plan Programming (VPCL) A plan consists of related pieces of code representing a specific action. A plan can be as short as a single statement, such as an incrementer plan, or a series of scattered lines of code used for declaration, initialization, and incrementation to accumulate the number of objects, identified as a counter plan. Another example of a plan is the entire group of codes that form a program function used to sort data, known as the sort plan. Plans should not be mistaken for functions. A function might be a plan but a plan is not always a function since the codes of a plan may be scattered throughout the program. Also, plans are independent of programming languages and can be coded into any programming language. VPCL (Visual Plan Construct Language) is a plan programming language that I designed as part of my dissertation based on findings of novice programmer errors as a result of programming and language construct misconceptions. VPCL consists of a plan library with three phases of learning and programming development. These phases range from elementary (plan observation), intermediate (plan integration), to an advanced level (plan creation), where plans are rehearsed, integrated, and finally developed. In phase 2, VPCL indicates to the user whether or not the plan integration for the given problem is correct. To expand upon this, reasoning can be incorporated into phase 3 of VPCL in the development of new plans. This can be accomplished by observing the user's selections of existing plans from the plan library, or creating new ones. In this manner, VPCL can collect clues to determine the user's intent. An interface engine can be developed to implement this kind of reasoning. Based on the clues and gathered information, VPCL can aid and suggest proper courses of action.

Finally, we can divide programming into two major parts: application programming and system programming. **System programming** is the building of systems such as operating systems (Unix and Windows), and compilers (C++). In operating systems, system programming is used to build system commands as well as to manage memory and other resources such as CPU (processes) scheduling and their interaction. In compiler writing, system programmers write different phases of compilers such as lexical analyzers, parsers, and code generators. System programming requires high programming skill; for example, *Ken Thompson* (*UNIX* first design and **B** language), *Dennis Ritchie* (designer of **C** language) and *Bjarne Stroustrup* (designer of **C++**) are system programmers.

CLOSING REMARKS AND LOOKING AHEAD

It is time to wrap up this journey by saying that you have gone through quite a long road with this book and some parts may have been rough and bumpy. I have a few thoughts to share with you. You may compare what you know to a drop in an ocean, but let me congratulate you for joining the minority group of less than even 1% of society that knows programming or what it takes to become a programmer. I have not met many people who sincerely admit that they like programming. On the other hand, I found many people who do not like programming, for what reasons I cannot categorize them all.

People who do not like programming have one thing in common, and that is that they want to learn it badly. They wish we could inject them with all of the knowledge.

The problem that I found with beginners is that they tend to treat programming as a sequential concept. For example, let me learn all the keywords of a language, then I am going to program and if the meaning of one keyword is not clear then I cannot understand the rest.

A combination of time, experience, and ambition is the key to success. Programming is not a one shot learning process, but rather an incremental learning process and you must allow yourself time to work with it and grow.

In programming, like anything else, it is important to focus on what is important. It is like watching a movie; you do not have to see or hear everything; you can put the pieces together. Similarly, you do not have to know every single keyword and their functions to program; but your goal should be to know as much as you can, even the exceptional cases. Can you imagine if you focus 99% of your time on a subject that is only useful 1% of the time. Alternatively, you should spend most of your time on the topics that are most important.

If you can determine what is important and what is not, then learning becomes easier and more fun and you will not be easily overwhelmed or disappointed. My job throughout this book was to look at the subject matter critically from a learner's point of view and explain it through a learner's eye, sometimes with the cost of not giving complete details at the time, but explaining the concept further later on. I always tried to see if an idea could be represented in a better way. I want to encourage you to think critically as well as to look for a better way to represent the subject or a better way to solve a problem.

Looking back on my own experiences with programming, I appreciate the people who instilled the confidence in me to understand programming and I want you to know that if I can do it, you can to.

In this book I have expressed my views and opinions and many may not share them. We want you to express your feelings. The field of computer programming has not drastically changed since the beginning; some times it even went backwards rather than forwards. Is that good or bad? Obviously not incorporating new technology into programming for beginners is not good news, and something must be done cumulatively to standardize programming itself, not just a particular language like C/C++.

If you ask me what my advice would be to you if you are a beginner, stick to input/output, decision, loop, basics of file handling, functions, and arrays and with this set of tools you can solve any problem you desire from a financial application to the launching of a space shuttle.

We should remember that learning a language is learning how to program and solve problems; a language is a tool like a paintbrush and should not be a problem in itself. At your level, try to solve problems such as statistical problems (max, min, standard deviation), searching problems, and sorting problems. Knowledge of searching techniques is very important; it is one of the most important jobs of a computer today. Use the language as a tool to achieve the solution to a problem, it is not important to know every single language construct. Learn the object-oriented concept; in the beginning it may be tedious, but it will become easier and you will find many advantages as you apply it to problems such as not needing to pass parameters each time to the functions. As you progress through object-oriented programming, it becomes more involved and you will need to build more experience with it. With the emergence of the object-oriented programming paradigm as a topic added to languages, the time spent on problem solving has shrunk, and as a result we have programmers with more knowledge of programming languages but less experience with problem solving.

At an intermediate level, get accustomed to the concept of structure, class, object-oriented pillars, recursion, file handling, error checking, advanced functions (pass of parameters), strings, pointer manipulation, and more rigorous sorting and searching techniques.

At an advanced level you should focus more on objects, advanced pointers and linked lists as well as learning and programming a variety of data structures and analyzing different algorithms. Try to put your experience into building a large program with a software engineering approach, by collaborating with others and incorporating existing components. Optimization and algorithm complexity are ongoing topics that many researchers still focus on. The STL consists of containers, iterators, and algorithms and each of these components has room for expansion and improvement.

We are finishing the book that to me was a collection of many books and ideas that I have used in teaching my programming classes. I admit that I have learned from my students and my learning did not end as I progressed in writing this book.

For any problem, corrections, and comments please visit the site: www.DrEbrahimi.com and e-mail me at ebrahimi@juno.com.

SELF-TEST TRUE-FALSE CHAPTER 20 POTPOURRI

___1. C/C++ has the ability to perform low-level operations done by machine languages.

___2. The shift left operator is: variable<<n where n is the number of bits to be shifted.

___3. The complement operator: ~variable applies the 2's complement to the variable.

___4. Swapping two variables using bit-wise exclusive or (^) eliminates need for a temp variable.

___5. Command-line arguments allow you to create your own system commands.

___6. The typeid operator is useful to determine if two objects are of the same type.

___7. Enumeration is another integral data type like boolean.

___8. Namespace is used to create a scope for names.

___9. time( ) brings the number of seconds that have elapsed since midnight January 1, 1970.

___10. The keyword mutable allows a const member function to modify a data member.

___11. When a class contains another class, the relationship is known as Is-A.

___12. Friend functions can access member functions without being a member of the class.

___13. An array of objects can be used in the same way as an array of integers.

___14. Pointers cannot be used to point to objects.

___15. In the following: int * p=new int[500]; memory is allocated statically.

___16. The form of declaring a C file pointer is: FILE *a, *b;

___17. There is only one copy of a static data member that is shared by all objects of the class.

___18. HTML tags are enclosed in braces { } indicating the start and end of the tag.

___19. Anchor references can be to other pages or to anchors on your own page.

___20. A JavaScript program must be compiled before it is executed in the browser.

___21. A CGI takes information from forms on a Web page, processes it, and sends a response.

___22. A stream with two data is sent to a CGI in the following form: f=Alireza%f=Ebrahimi.

___23. There are two stages of compiling a Java program: compilation and interpretation.

___24. A Java .class file is bytecode that can be interpreted on many platforms.

___25. Dynamic Web pages can allow users to update databases located on a server.

CHAPTER 20 POTPOURRI ASSIGNMENTS

Q20a) Explain the following bit-wise operation symbols. & , ^ , << , >> , and ~.
For example, | is the bit-wise or operator.

Q20b) What would be the result of the following program?

```
#include<iostream>
using namespace std;
void main(){
        int x=3;
        x=x<<2;
        cout<<x;          }//MAIN
```

Q20c) Describe what is being done in the following program and give the output.

```
#include<iostream>
using namespace std;
void main(){
        char a='a',b='b';
        a=a^b;
        b=a^b;
        a=a^b;
        cout<<a<<" "<<b;}//MAIN
```

Q20d) Using command line arguments, write a program to search a file for a certain field of an employee's record and output the result. For example, typing "search name 012345" at the command line will give the name of the employee whose id is 012345. Remember, you must open a file containing the employee information.

Q20e) Create a file called employee.h that will include an employee class with necessary member data (e.g. id, name, telephone, address, salary) and member functions (e.g. display( ), search( ), update( )). Write a main program that makes use of this header file. Explain why the display( ) function of this employee class could be declared as const.

Q20f) Define an enumeration for a student's year in college (freshman, sophomore, junior, senior).

Q20g) Write a main program to make use of the following namespaces. Create two employee objects: one in the scope of the fulltime namespace, and the other in the scope of parttime.

```
namespace fulltime{
        class employee{
        public:  double salary;
                    double getgrosspay( ){ return salary;}  };  }
namespace parttime{
        class employee{
        public:  double hourlyrate;
                    int hoursworked;
                    double getgrosspay(){ return hourlyrate*hoursworked;}  };  }
```

Q20h) The keyword typedef is used to create an alias for an existing type. For example, the following statement creates a name that can be used to declare an STL stack of strings:

typedef stack<string> stackofstrings;

Use typedef to create an alias for an STL pair of strings.

Q20i) The #define directive is used to replace a name with its character sequence. For example, the name MAX_SALARY can be defined as the maximum number that can be entered for a salary. For what other constant values in a payroll program would it be useful to give a name with #define? Write a #define statement to give a name for the MENU or HEADER of a payroll program.

Q20j) Use #define to write a macro that will find the average of three numbers and write a main program to demonstrate it.

Q20k) The time( ) function is used to determine the time and date. Some trial software expires after a certain number of days; compare an expiration date with the date of the system and, if the software is expired, display a message to inform the user.

Q20l) What would be the output of the following program?

```
#include<iostream>
using namespace std;
int x=10;
void a( ){
        static int y=25;
        y*=2;
        cout<<y<<endl;}//a
int main( ){
        extern int x;
        cout<<x<<endl;
        a( );
        a( );
        a( );  }//MAIN
```

Q20m) What is the advantage of declaring a frequently used variable as register?

Q20n) Explain why the keyword mutable is useful for a data member such as salary in an employee class.

Q20o) A Has-A relationship is when one class is composed of another; an Is-A relationship is when one class is derived from another. In the following example, what is the relationship between the internship class and the student class? What is the relationship between gradstudent and student?

```
class internship{
public:  string department;
         float hourlyrate;
         int hoursworked;
         float getsalary(){ return hourlyrate*hoursworked;} };

class student{
public:  string fname, lname;
         int id, gpa;
         internship intern;};

class gradstudent: public student{
public:  string advisor;
         string thesis; };
```

Q20p) Friend functions are not part of a class but can access members of the class. Write a friend function for the student class above to overload the insertion operator to display the first and last name, id, and gpa of a student.

Q20q) Write a main program to use the student class from the question Q20o and the friend function from Q20p. Declare an array of 100 objects of the student class. Use a for loop to initialize the student information and display all students.

Q20r) Complete the following program to create a linked list of students. Write the function body for addstudent( ) to add a student to the list and displayall( ) to display all students in the list.

```
class student{
public:  string fname, lname;
         int id, gpa;
         student *next;  };

class studentlist{
private:
         student *first;
public:
         studentlist(){ first=NULL;}
         void addstudent();
         void displayall();     };

void studentlist::addstudent(){...}

void studentlist::displayall(){...}
```

Q20s) Write a C++ program that will dynamically allocate the memory for a linked list of students as they are added.

Q20t) Write a C program to make a copy of a file containing student id, name, and gpa. Remember, in C you must declare file pointers such as FILE *in, *out.

Q20u) Create a simple web page that contains information about you. The page can include a table, e-mail, hyperlinks, and forms.

Q20v) Write a JavaScript program that prompts the user to enter a username and password. The program checks if the password is correct and displays a message to say either access granted or denied. Hint: Use parallels arrays to store the usernames and passwords.

Q20w) Construct an HTML form with fields to take in an employee's name, hours worked, and hourly rate. Write a CGI program in C++ to calculate the gross pay and display it.

Q20x) Create a security page to restrict access to your website. Make an HTML page with a form for the user to enter their name and password. Write a CGI program that will open a file containing names and passwords, search the file to validate the password, and send an HTML page back to the user. The password file should be encrypted.

Q20y) Write a class for a general database called Dbase. This class contains an array of objects (persons), each with information such as first name, last name, id, etc. The database will have member functions to add a new person, search for an existing person, display all, etc. Using this class you can derive different classes such as employeeDbase or studentDbase.

Q20z) Write a Java program for a telephone operating system. Use the Cin class in Figure 20.39b for input.

CASE STUDY – PAYROLL SYSTEM PHASE 20: POTPOURRI

The objective of the final phase of the payroll system is to make your system accessible through the Internet by including web programming.

a) Make a web page as an interface for your system that uses a combination of HTML and JavaScript as a GUI. Include a menu with the options available on your system.
b) Use CGI to connect your interface with your payroll program.
c) You can try using other languages or environments to implement your system such as: .NET, Java Applets, Perl, etc.

GENERAL TESTS, PROJECTS, AND SOLUTIONS

THE FOLLOWING IS A SAMPLE OF SELF-TESTS THAT YOU CAN USE TO TEST YOUR ABILITIES. FOR ADDITIONAL TESTS, SEE THE BOOK WEBSITE: www.DrEbrahimi.com

PROGRAMMING 1 – TEST 1 (input/output, loop, and decision making)

Q1. a) For the following program, find ten syntax errors. Underline the errors and explain why. You may want to correct the syntax errors. (10 points)

```
#include <iostream.h \\THIS IS THE PAYROLL PROGRAM
using namespace std;
int viod main( )
const float TAXRATE=0.10;
int empid, hw,hr, ovh;
double regpy, ovp, gp ta, np;
char staus[20];
cout<<"ENTER EMP ID,  HW, HR, OVH, STATUS"<<ENDL;
while(cin>>hw>>hr>>status); {
if (hw> 40){ ovh=40-hw;
           ovp=ovh*hr*0.5;
regpay=40 * hr  }/*  OVERTIME PAY */
else  ovp=hw;
     reg=hw*hr;
     gp=reg-ovp;  }//NO OVERTIME
ta=gp*taxrate;
if(gp>500) taxrate=0.20;
else(gp>300) taxrate=0.30;
np=gp+ta;
cout<<Employee id is<<endl;
}//MAIN
cout<<"ENTER EMP ID,  HW, HR, OVH, STATUS"<<end;
cout<"OVERTIME PAY IS "<<ovp"<<"NETPAY "<<gp<<endl;}// return 0;
```

Q1. b) For the following program, find five logical errors. Underline the errors and explain why. You may want to correct the logical errors. (10 points)

```
#include <iostream.h \\THIS IS THE PAYROLL PROGRAM
using namespace std;
int viod main( )
const float TAXRATE=0.10;
int empid, hw,hr, ovh;
double regpy, ovp, gp ta, np;
char staus[20];
cout<<"ENTER EMP ID,  HW, HR, OVH, STATUS"<<ENDL;
while(cin>>hw>>hr>>status); {
if (hw> 40){ ovh=40-hw;
           ovp=ovh*hr*0.5;
     regpay=40 * hr  }/*  OVERTIME PAY */
```

```
else  ovp=hw;
      reg=hw*hr;
      gp=reg-ovp;  }//NO OVERTIME
ta=gp*taxrate;
if(gp>500)taxrate=0.20;
else(gp>300) taxrate=0.30;
np=gp+ta;
cout<<Employee id is<<endl;
}//MAIN
cout<<"ENTER EMP ID,  HW, HR, OVH, STATUS"<<end;
cout<"OVERTIME PAY IS "<<ovp"<<"NETPAY "<<gp<<endl;}// return 0;
```

Q2. Complete the following program by filling in the dots. The program computes students average and assigns a letter grade to each student.

```
...................<fstream.h>
main()
{
int stdid, assingscore, midscore, ...........................;
char ...................;
double averagescore;
ifstream  fin("studentgrades.in").........................
while(fin>>stdid>>...............>>midscore>>finscore)..........
sumscore=assingscore+midscore.........................finscore
averagesocre=sumscore/......................;
........... (averagescore>90)      grade='A';
else if(averagescore>80)...............='B';
......if (.....................>70)  grade='C';
else if(averagescore>......).............='D'
.........grade='F';
cout<<"STUDENTS ID IS: "<<<<.............................;
cout<<"STUDENTS AVERAGE GRADE IS: "<<..........................;
cout<<"STUDENT GRADE IS: "<<...............................<<endl;
.............................//WHILE
................
}//.......................
```

Q3. What would be the output of the following program?
Data entered as follows: 2 -1 5 0 3 12 HALT.
The word HALT (as a type mismatch) is used to terminate the loop.

```
#include <iostream.h>
main()
{int rday;
double rainfall,sumrain,maxrain;
rday=0;
maxrain=0;
sumrain=0;
cout<<"ENTER THE RAINFALL: ";

while (cin>>rainfall){
```

```
if (rainfall <0) cout<<"WRONG DATA - NEGATIVE"<<endl;
else if (rainfall > 10) cout<<"WRONG DATA- TOO HIGH"<<endl;
else if (rainfall == 0) cout<<" SUNNY"<<endl;
else {rday = rday +1;
     sumrain=sumrain + rainfall;
     cout<<"RAINDAY "<<rday<<endl;
     cout<<"TOTAL RAIN IS SO FAR: "<<sumrain<<endl;
   if (rainfall>maxrain) maxrain=rainfall; }//RAINY
cout<<"ENTER THE RAINFALL: ";
}//WHILE

cout<<"TOTAL RAINY DAY IS:"<<rday<<endl;
cout<<"TOTAL RAIN IS        :"<<sumrain<<endl;
cout<<"MAXIMUM RAIN IS   :"<<maxrain<<endl;
return 0;
}//MAIN
```

SHOW YOUR OUTPUT HERE (WHAT COMES ON THE COMPUTER SCREEN?):

Q4. a) Write an Invoice program. Program inputs are *item id, unit price, quantity,* and *sales tax,* which should be constant at 10%. Program should compute and print subtotal, tax amount, and total price.

Q4. b) Repeat the program for as many items as there are. You must also compute and print the grand total. Terminate the loop by pressing a control key.

Q4. c) Repeat the program using an existing data file that contains several different items. The name of the data file is "customer.in" which has the following format:

```
1234  100.99  4  0.10
3456  5.00    2  0.10
6789  2.50    6  0.10
```

Hint: *You may want to use the following statements in your program:*
```
grandtotal = 0;
subtotal = unitprice * quantity;
grandtotal = grandtotal + total;
```

Q5. a) Expand the above Invoice program to include discount rate. Compute the discount amount according to the following:
```
grandtotalprice > 500 discountrate = 0.30;
grandtotalprice > 200 discountrate = 0.20;
```

Q5. b) Expand the above Invoice program to include membership discount. Give additional 5% to gold members and 3% to silver members. The grand total includes: tax amount, price discount, and membership discount.
Hint: *Declare the membership status as a char variable with 'G' for gold member and 'S' for silver member.*

Q6. Answer any 5 of the following:
   a) What would be the output of each of the following two programs?
       Have #include<iostream.h> for each program
          1) void main(){ const int n=10; n=n+1; cout<<n;}

2) void main(){ int n=0; n=n+1; cout<<n;}
Hint: Are there any errors

b) List and explain two differences between C and C++. For example: comments, input/output, includes, new line.

c) List and explain two similarities between C and C++. For example: control structures, reserve words.

d) Explain three major steps in a search algorithm. What do you need to make a search program work?

e) Explain the concept of Object Oriented Programming.

f) Write a simple program that runs forever.

PROGRAMMING I – TEST 2 (SAMPLE1) (file, array, character, function, and search)

Q1. a) For the following program, find ten syntax errors. Underline the errors and explain why. You may want to correct the syntax errors. (10 points)

```
void main(){
int gp[100];np[1000];
double ta[100],tr[100];
character name[100] 4];
n=1;
while (fin>>hw[n]>>hr[n]) {n--; }//WHILE
for (i=0;i<n;i++){
if( hw[i]> 40 ){ovh=hw[I]-40;
            ovp[i]=ovh *hr[i] * 1.2;
            regp[i]=40* hr[i];
else if { ovp[i]=0.0;
        regp=hw[i]* hr[i]; }
}//OVP
for( i=o; i>n; i++){
gp[I]=reg[i] -ovp[n];}/ FOR
for (i=0;i<n;i++){
if gp[I]>500 then tr[I]=20.00
else if gp[]<200 tr[I]=.10;
else if gp[i]=0.50; }//TR
if (status=="M")&&(status==S) ta[I]=tr[I]+0.05;
for(i=0;i<n;i++) ta[i]=gp[i]*tr[i];
for(i=0;i<n;i++) np[i]=gp[i]+ta[i];
for(i=0;i<n;i++){cout<<setw(10)<<"NAME"<<setw(10)<<"GROSS PAY"
            <<"NET PAY"<<ENDL;
cout<< name[I]<<gp[I]<<ta[I]<<np[I[;}//OUTPUT
return;
}//End WHILE
{//MAIN
```

Q1. b) For the following program, find five logical errors. Underline the errors and explain why. You may want to correct the logical errors. (10 points)

```
void main(){
int gp[100];np[1000];
double ta[100],tr[100];
character name[100] 4];
```

```
n=1;
while (fin>>hw[n]>>hr[n]) {n--; }//WHILE
for (i=0;i<n;i++){
if( hw[i]> 40 ){ovh=hw[I]-40;
                ovp[i]=ovh *hr[i] * 1.2;
                regp[i]=40* hr[i];
else if { ovp[i]=0.0;
        regp=hw[i]* hr[i]; }
}//OVP
for( i=o; i>n; i++){
gp[I]=reg[i] -ovp[n];}/ FOR
for (i=0;i<n;i++){
if gp[I]>500 then tr[I]=20.00
else if gp[]<200 tr[I]=.10;
else if gp[i]=0.50; }//TR
if (status=="M")&&(status==S) ta[I]=tr[I]+0.05;
for(i=0;i<n;i++) ta[i]=gp[i]*tr[i];
for(i=0;i<n;i++) np[i]=gp[i]+ta[i];
for(i=0;i<n;i++){cout<<setw(10)<<"NAME"<<setw(10)<<"GROSS PAY"
                <<"NET PAY"<<ENDL;
cout<< name[I]<<gp[I]<<ta[I]<<np[I[;}//OUTPUT
return;
}//End WHILE
{//MAIN
```

Q2. a) Write a supermarket pricing program. Program inputs are: *itemid, itemname, unitprice, itemquantity* and *tax status*. Use 1 to indicate taxable items and 0 for non-taxable items, and the tax rate should be constant at 10%. Program should compute the subtotal for each item and add the sales tax if the item is taxable, then compute the grandtotal for the entire purchase. Program output should include itemid, itemname, subtotal, sales tax, and the total price for each item, then print the total sales tax and the grandtotal.
Sample data is stored in a data file, called *customer.in*

1234	shoes	25.00	2	1
9834	milk	1.99	1	0
1278	watches	60.00	1	1
9912	bread	1.00	3	0

Q2. b) Expand the above program to read the entire data (regardless of its size) into arrays and give total number of item purchased. For example, total item purchased from the above program is 4.

Q2. c) Compute the price for each group of items. A *for loop* is preferable to use.
        priceitems[i] = ...[i] * ...quantity[i];
Q2. d) Compute all the itemsalestax.
        If (taxable[i] == 1)
            itemsalestax[i] = priceitem[i] * 0.10;
        else.......... ;

Q2. e) Compute the total of all the items. Make sure initialize total to 0.
        total = total +......[i];

Q2. f) Compute the total sales tax of all items. Make sure to initialize totalsaletax = 0.

totalsalestax = ……. + itemsalestax[i]

Q2. g) Compute the grandtotal and display total, totalsalestax and grandtotal.

Q3. a) Expand the above supermarket pricing program, by using functions.

Q3. b) The main program of the supermarket pricing program consists of six functions for each of the above tasks. Write the main program with all the function calls. For example, computetotal( );

Q3. c) Write the function definition for one of the above functions.

Q3. d) Write the declaration of the variables and show where they are placed in the program.

Q3. e) Write one of the above function calls with the parameters.

Q4. Complete the following grading program by filling in the dots. The program will search by id. It computes students average and assigns a letter grade to each student. At the end the program, it will ask the user to enter the id and the program will display the grade.

```
…………………<fstream.h>
………….{…….. int MAXARRAY=25;
int stdid[MAXARRAY], assingscore[MAXARRAY], midscore[MAXARRAY],
………………………….., i,n;
char ………………..;
double averagescore[MAXARRAY];
ifstream  fin("studentgrades.in")……………………..
…..=0;
while(fin>>stdid[n]>>……………>>midscore[n]>>finscore[n]){……….}
for(i=0;i<n;i++){
sumscore[i]=assingscore[i]+midscore[i]………………………finscore[i]
averagesocre[i]=sumscore[i]/…………………..;
……….. (averagescore[i]>90)     grade[i]='A';
else if(averagescore[i]>80)……………..='B';
……if (…………………>70) grade[i]='C';
else if(averagescore[i]>……..)…………..='D'
……….grade[i]='F';}//COMPUTATION
…….<<" ENTER THE STUDENT ID ";
……..>>searched;
for(i=0;i<n;i++){
if(searched==………….[i]){
cout<<"STUDENTS ID IS: "<<<<…………………….;
cout<<"STUDENTS AVERAGE GRADE IS: "<<…..………………..;
cout<<"STUDENT GRADE IS: "<<……………………………<<endl;
break;…………//FOR
if (i== ……) cout<<" ……..FOUND "<<endl;
……………………
}//…………………….
```

Q5. What would be the output of the following program?

Data entered as follows: 5 -1 2 0 12 3 HALT

```
#include <iostream.h>
main()
{int rday;
double rainfall,sumrain,maxrain;
rday=0;
maxrain=0;
sumrain=0;
cout<<"ENTER THE RAINFALL: ";
while (cin>>rainfall){
if (rainfall <0) cout<<"WRONG DATA - NEGATIVE"<<endl;
else if (rainfall > 10) cout<<"WRONG DATA- TOO HIGH"<<endl;
else if (rainfall == 0) cout<<" SUNNY"<<endl;
else {rday = rday +1;
    sumrain=sumrain + rainfall;
    cout<<"RAINDAY "<<rday<<endl;
    cout<<"TOTAL RAIN IS SO FAR: "<<sumrain<<endl;
  if (rainfall>maxrain) maxrain=rainfall; }//RAINY
cout<<"ENTER THE RAINFALL: ";
}//WHILE

cout<<"TOTAL RAINY DAY IS:"<<rday<<endl;
cout<<"TOTAL RAIN IS          :"<<sumrain<<endl;
cout<<"MAXIMUM RAIN IS    :"<<maxrain<<endl;
return 0;
}//MAIN
```
SHOW YOUR OUTPUT HERE (WHAT COMES ON THE COMPUTER SCREEN?):

Q6. Answer any 5 from the following questions:
a) Write a simple program with a counter loop that runs forever.
b) Write the statement that converts a lower case marital status to upper case.
         e.g. ASCII for lower case 'a' is 97 and ASCII for 'A' is 65. char status;
c) Explain one advantage of using the C comment /* */ versus the C++ comment //.
d) Write a structured data type called goods for question Q2.
e) Write a class data type called goods for question Q2.
f) What is one disadvantage of defining external variables for functions?
g) Name three important elements of Object Oriented Programming.
h) What is a pointer?

PROGRAMMING 1 - TEST2 (SAMPLE 2)

Q1. Complete the following Payroll program by filling in the dots. This program will read in hours worked and hourly rate for each employee and computes the gross pay and net pay. Employee gets hour and a half overtime pay if they work more than 40 hours. The income tax rate varies base on employee's gross pay.

```
#include <............>
main()
{ int  empid, .............., hoursworked, ...............;
   float  hourlyrate , taxrate, regularpay, grosspay, taxamount , .............., netpay;
```

```
while(...........>>empid>>hoursworked>>hourlyrate)
.......
if( hoursworked >........) {
    overtimehour = hoursworked - ...........;
    overtimepay = overtimehour * hourlyrate * .......;
    regularpay = 40 * .............; }
else { overtimehour = ......;  overtimepay =0;
        regularpay = ........ * hourlyrate; }
        grosspay = regularpay + .............;
if ( grosspay > 400) ............ = 0.25;
else if ( .............. > 300) taxrate = 0.15;
.........  taxrate = 0.10;
taxamount = grosspay * .............;
netpay = ............ - taxamount;
cout<< "ID = "<<empid<<" HW = "<<hoursworked<< " HR = "<<..................<<endl;
cout<< "grosspay is "<<..............<<" net pay is "<<netpay;}//end loop
return 0; }
```

Q2. a) What would be the output of the following program with the given rainfall data:

2   4   3   0   8   1

```
#include <iostream.h>
main(){int n = 0, max;
int rainfall[10];
while (cin>>rainfall[n]) {n++; }
cout<<"THE RAINFALLS ARE "<<endl;
for ( int i = 0; i < n; i++) cout << "DAY = "<< i+1<<"   " <<rainfall[i]<<endl;
max = rainfall[0];
for ( int j = 0; j < n; j++)   if (rainfall[j] > max )  max = rainfall[j]; //end loop
cout <<"THE MAX IS "<<max;
return 0;}// end main
```
SHOW YOUR OUTPUT HERE (WHAT COMES ON THE COMPUTER SCREEN?):

Q2. b) What would be the output of the following program with the given rainfall data:

2   4   3   0   8   1

```
#include <iostream.h>
int rainfall[10], n, max, sum;
ReadRainfalls(){n = 0; while(cin>>rainfall[n]) n++; //end loop
cout<<"READING DONE "<<endl; return 0;}//end readrainfalls
FindMax(){ max = 0;
for ( int i = 0; i<n; i++)  if (rainfall[i]> rainfall[max] )  max = i; //end loop
cout<<"THE LOCATION OF MAX IS "<<max<<endl; return 0; }//end findmax
PrintAll() { for (int i = 0; i < n; i++) if  (i == max) cout << rainfall[i]<< "\t"<<" = MAX"
            <<endl;
                                else cout<<rainfall[i]<<endl;
cout <<"SUM IS "<<sum; return 0;}// end printall
ComputeSum(){ sum =0;
for(int i = 0; i < n; i++) sum = sum + rainfall[i]; //end loop
cout<<"end of the sum"<<endl;  }
void main()
{ cout << " ABOUT TO READ "<<endl;
```

732

```
        ReadRainfalls();
        FindMax();
        ComputeSum();
        PrintAll();
    }//end main
```
SHOW YOUR OUTPUT HERE (WHAT COMES ON THE COMPUTER SCREEN?):

Q3. You are to design a grading system from scratch for professor "T" to determine the grade for each student. The data file contains the following: STUDENTID, MIDTERM, FINAL, and ASSIGNMENT. Show your own data file.
  a) The program should read the data, compute the total score, compute the average, and print everything out. Run the program for one student.
  b) Expand the program to run for 5 students. In addition, include the student's name in the data file. Use different color if you do not want to rewrite the whole program over, make sure it is clear.
  c) Expand the program to run for as many students as there are in the data file. Show your data file.
  d) Expand the program again to assign a letter grade to each student according to the following :

$$\begin{array}{ll} \text{average} >= 90 & \text{grade} = \text{'A'} \\ \text{average} >= 80 & \text{grade} = \text{'B'} \\ \text{average} >= 70 & \text{grade} = \text{'C'} \\ \text{average} >= 60 & \text{grade} = \text{'D'} \\ \text{else} & \text{grade} = \text{'F'} \end{array}$$

Declare the variable grade as char.

Q4. a) Expand the above program Q3 to include arrays to store the student name, student's id, the score for midterm, final, assignment, the total and the average score, and the letter grade. You must use separate loops to read the data, compute grades, and print output.
   b) Expand the above program to include functions. Only write the main program and the body of the function PrintAll( ).

Q5. a) Write a program to show the menu and the function calls. The menu should have the following options:
                  1. Print
                  2. Search
                  3. Add
                  4. Delete
   b) Write the program for the search function only. The function asks the user to enter the student's name and then the program will search and display the information for that student including the grades.

*EXTRA CREDIT *
What is the difference between procedural and object-oriented programming? Define the following terms: Class, Derived class, Polymorphism, Operator Overloading, Function Overloading, Inheritance, and Virtual Function.

PROGRAMMING I – TEST 2 (SAMPLE3)

Q1. a) Find 10 syntax errors in the following program. Indicate the line number and explain why.

Q1. b) Find 5 logical errors in the following program. Answer Separately

```
1        # include <iostreem.h.>
2        /  / this is an assignment #4b written by John Doe */
3        void main( void  )
4         {char name[50][2];
5        long int empid[50];
6         int hw[50], ohw[50],i,n;
7         float  grosspay[50],taxamount[50], netpay[50];taxrate[50];
8         doubl  regularpay[50], overtimepay[50];
9        ifstream fin (payroll.in);
10       n==1;
11       while(fin>>empid[n]>>name[n]<<hoursworked[n]>>hourlyrate[n]){n++} //read all
12       For (i=0; i<=n; i++){    if (hoursworked[i] >40){
13                        ohw[i]=hw-40;
14                        overtimepay[n] = ohw[ i]* hourlyrate[i] * 0.5;
15                         regularpay[I]= hw[i] * hr[i]; // end overtime
16       elseif( <=40){
17                        ohw[i]=0;
18                        overtimepay[i]=0* taxrate[0]; ;
19                        regularpay[i]= hoursworked[i] * hourlyrate[i]; }
20       grosspay[i]=regularpay[i] + overtimepay[i];
21        }//end compute tax rate            /* end of else */
22        for(i=0; i<= n; i++){
23                if (grosspay[i] >500) taxrate[i]= 0.20;
24                 else if (grosspay[i] >400 ) taxrate[i]= 10.00;
25                  else  taxamount[n] =0;
26       grosspay[i]= regpay[i] - overtimepay[i];
27       axamount[i]= grossppay[i] X  taxrate[i];
28       netpay[i]=grosspay[i]- taxamount[i];}//
29        }//compute all netpay
30       cout<<setw(20)<<"NAME"<<setw(20)<<"GROSS PAY "<<setw(2)<<"NET
         PAY"<<endl;
31
32        for(i=0;i>n;i++){ cout<<setwidth(20)<<name[i]<<grosspay[I]<<netpay[i]<<endl;
33        }//end output
34
35       return o;}//end for loop
```

Q2. What is the output of the following programs given the following scores?
```
   a) #include <iostream.h>  // 100.0  90.0  80.0  50.0  100.0
        void main(){int n;
       float score, total=0,avg;
       cout<<"ENTER THE SCORE "<<endl;
       n=0;
       while (cin>>score) {
       total=total+score;
       n++;
```

```
cout<<"ENTER SCORE "<<endl;}//end loop
avg=total/n;
cout<<"TOTAL SCORE IS"<<total<<endl;
cout<<"AVERAGE SCORE IS "<<avg<<endl; }
```

b)
```
#include <iostream.h> // INPUT DATA IS THE SAME AS ABOVE
int n=0; //EXTERNAL VARIABLE
readAllScores(double scores[ ])
{n=0;
 while(cin>>scores[n] ) {n++;} //end loop
cout <<" Reading scores Done "<<endl;
return 0;}//end read
computeTotalScores(double scores[], int n) {double total=0;
for ( int i=0; i<n; i++)   {total= total + scores[i]; } //end loop
cout<<" TOTAL SCORES " <<total<<endl; return 0; }//end findsum
printAllScores(double scores[],int n){
for (int j=0; j<n;j++)
 { cout << scores[j]<<endl; }//end loop
cout<<" PRINTING DONE "<<endl;
}//end printAll

main()
{double scores[100];
cout << " READ ABOUT TO START "<<endl;
 readAllScores(scores);
  cout <<" AFTER READ "<<endl;
 computeTotalScores(scores,n);
  cout<<" AFTER TOTAL "<<endl;
 printAllScores(scores,n);
  cout<<" PRINT DONE "<<endl;
return 0;}//end main
```

Q3. You are to design a grading system from scratch for professor EBRAHIMI, in order to determine the grade for each student. The data file contains the following: studentId, midterm, final, homework, classwork, such as the following 1234567 80 100 90   100
   a) The program should read the data, compute the total score, compute the average, and print everything out. Run the program for one student.
   b) Expand the program to run for 5 students. In addition include the student's name in the data file. Use different color if you do not want to rewrite the whole program over.
   c) Expand the program to run for as many students as in the data file. Show your data file
   d) Expand the program again to assign a letter grade to each student according to the following :
         average >= 90 grade='A', average >= 80 grade= 'B', average >= 70 grade='C'
         average >= 60 grade='D', else   grade='F'
   Declare the variable grade as char grade.

Q4. Expand the above program Q3 to include arrays to store the student name, student's id, the score for midterm, final, assignment, class work, total and the average scores, and the letter grade. You must use separate loops to read the data, compute grades, and print output. Data is stored in a file called "studentgrade.in"

Q5. a) Expand the above program to include functions. Only write the main program and the body of the function ReadAllScoresl( ).

   b) Write the function SearchStudent() that searches for student id and displays name and grade

Q6. a) Expand above program to use either structure or class. Declare the user-defined type known as student.

   b) Write a menu in the main program to call the following functions:
         1. Print 2. Search 3. Add   4. Delete   5. Modify

   c) Write the function searchStudent() which returns index of found student.

EXTRA CREDIT (ANSWER ANY 4)

E1) What is the difference between char name[15] and char name[100][15]?

E2) What is the difference between procedural and object-oriented programming?

E3) What is object and what is class?

E4) Why do we need long integer instead of integer?

E5) What is a pointer, and how is a variable dynamically created and destroyed?

E6) Define the following terms: Data Abstraction, Polymorphism, and Inheritance.

PROGRAMMING I – SAMPLE PROJECT

The ultimate goal of these assignments is to develop a complete Payroll System Software or an Invoice System Software from scratch, going step by step. Upon completion of each assignment, name each program with your initials, and HW#.cpp. An example, if my name is Case Study, then my first program's name should be CSHW1.cpp

PART I:

Objectives- To use properly int, float, const float, cout, cin, and basic calculations

This program is INTERACTIVE. This means that the user is going to provide the input needed for computation. You, the programmer, have to think "ahead" and plan exactly how the program and the user are going to INTERACT (communicate with each other) and then write the program. Technique- In order to write the program you must consider:

1- The program should ask the user for Employee ID (The Employee ID should be a four digit number, such as the last four digits of the social security number), Hours worked, and Hourly rate. If you are going to work in Invoice, the program should ask for Product ID (also a four digit number), Quantity, and Unit price.

2- The next step for the program is to process the data and compute the Gross pay, Tax amount, and Net pay. The tax rate is a constant at 8% or 0.08, for Payroll as well as for Invoice. If you are working in Invoice, make sure that you calculate Subtotal, Tax amount, and Total.

3- The last step is display the results.

The results should display:

   a) Assignment number, Pay roll system or Invoice system, Dr. A. Ebrahimi, Your name

   b) Employee ID, Hours worked, Hourly rate, Gross pay, Tax amount deducted, Net pay.

   c) A message to the User.

PART II:

Objectives- To use control variable, counter, while loop and create a datafile.

This program SHOULD NOT be INTERACTIVE. The data needed for computation will be obtained from a data file that you have to create. Name the data file hw2data.in so you can

736

instruct the program where to get the data needed, when you run it. Once the program is executable, it will take the data incrementally (for computation) from the data file.

Technique- At this time, in order to write the program you must consider:

1- All the information required in Assignment 1.

2- This program is an expansion of the first one. Using the keyword while, in conjunction with a control variable, and a counter, you will make the program loop five times.

3- The program should display the results in almost the same manner that the first one.

4- If you have the program and data file, you can run the program in DOS or UNIX as follows:

CSHW2<hw2data.in

5- The last step in this assignment is to create an output file. Name it as hw2data.out. You could get it simply typing at the DOS prompt:

CSHW2<hw2data.in>hw2data.out

Do the above program interactively, if you encountered problem with your windows operating system.

PART III:

Objectives- The use of End Of File, fin in the while statement and some other calculations.

This Assignment is an expansion of Assignment 2. At this time, the program should loop as many times as it needs in order to satisfy the data file. If the data file has 10 items, the program should loop only 10 times, no more or less.

To accomplish this objective, the program SHOULD NOT use a CONTROL VARIABLE nor COUNTER. Now, we have to use EOF (End Of File), or fin, in the while statement.

Additionally, we are going to use the if statement to make decisions including or excluding parts of the program.

Technique- If you are working in Pay roll, you have to consider overtime if the hours worked are greater than 40. Also, for this program you have to consider:

if gross pay is over 500, tax rate is 0.25;

else

if gross pay is over 400, tax rate is 0.20;

else

if gross pay is over 200, tax rate is 0.10;

else tax rate is 0.00;

If you are working in Invoice, you have to consider variable tax rate (for different states,) then calculate subtotal and total:

if State is New York, tax rate is 0.085;

else

if State is New Jersey, tax rate is 0.07;

else

if State is Connecticut, tax rate is 0.08;

else tax rate is 0.00;

Print all, program, input and output.

PART IV:

Objectives- Become familiar with using searchname, searchid, string.h, fstream.h, array.

Part A Technique

1- Using all elements of the above programs write a program that will search for a specific item (employee or product).

If you are searching name, you could use if (!strcmp(searchname,employeename)) or if (strcmp(searchname,employeename)==0) . If you are searching numbers (such as ID,) you should use if (searchid==employeeid)

2- Additionally, THIS PROGRAM should call the data needed for computation from a data file accessed by the PROGRAM ITSELF using ifstream fin ("hw4data.in"), or ifstream fin (filename). Then this program should include a default system in the event the search item (employee or product) is not in the datafile. ("Employee/Product not found.")

Part B Technique

1- Using array within the program, create separate loops to read the datafile, calculate and print the output.

2- This program should display only the information pertaining to the searched item.

PART V:

Objectives- The use of functions

This assignment calls for functions. If you have in the assignment 4B separate loops for reading, calculating and printing the data, to accomplish the fifth assignment is a "cut and paste" assignment.

Technique

1- Create each component of your program under different names, with each component performing a different task, and place each component before the main. If you do this way, your function is also its prototype.

2- You will need one function for reading the data, one to calculate a specific task at the time, etc.

3- Now your program is easy to expand, as it is in any real SOFTWARE.

PART VI:

Objectives- Create and use of menu with structure or class

After the last assignment you will be able to build a real payroll/invoice interactive program

Technique

1- Create a menu for adding, modifying, deleting, searching, saving, and print. Each category should be a different function and let the user input interactively which option he/she wants to choose to manipulate your database.

2- Using if statements choose a function according to which option the user choose.

3- Use structured variables, so that you can always know which variables belong together, under one name. (As an example if you use ProductID, you immediately will know which is its unitprice. If you are using EmployeeID, you immediately know which is his/her hourlyrate.)

4- Finally, try to design a way to print out a check for the person/product you choose, or for the persons/products in your database.

PROGRAMMING II TEST 1 (SAMPLE 1)

Q1. a) What would be the output of the program? Run the program with 10 20 30 40.

Q1. b) What does the following program do?

```
#include <iostream.h>
main()
{ int table[10], n = 0, i, nko, upubm=0;
cout<<"ENTER THE DATA:"<<endl;
while(cin>>table[n]){ n++;}//while
for(i=0; i<n;i++) {cout<<" i is "<<i<<" table[i]="<<table[i]<<endl;}//for
nko = table[0];
for(i=1;i<n;i++)
{ if (table[i] < nko)
 nko = table[i];
}//for
   for(i=0;i<n;i++){
upubm = upubm + table[i];
}//for
  cout<<" THE NKO IS "<<nko<<endl;
  cout<<" THE UPUBM IS "<<upubm<<endl;
}//main
```

Q2. a) What is the output of the below program? Run the program with:

10.0 20.0 5.0 20.0

```
//function prototypes
int inputin(double itemp[]);
double comptot(double itemp[], int cnt);
double findmax (double itemp[], int cnt);
double compavg(double tot, int cnt);
void printdata(double itemp[],int cnt, double tot, double mx, double av);

#include<iostream.h>
void main(){
int cnt;
double itemp[100],av, tot,mx;
cout<<"CALLING INPUT "<<endl;
 cnt=inputin(itemp);
cout<<"CALLING TOTAL "<<endl;
tot= comptot(itemp, cnt);
cout<<"CALLING MAXIMUM "<<endl;
mx= findmax (itemp, cnt);
cout<<"CALLING AVERAGE "<<endl;
av= compavg(tot, cnt);
cout<<"CALLING PRINT OUT"<<endl;
 printdata(itemp, cnt, tot, mx, av);
}//end main
int inputin(double itemp[]){int cnt=0;
cout<<"ENTER THE ITEM: ";
   while(cin>>itemp[cnt]){cnt = cnt +1;
```

```
                    cout<<"ENTER THE ITEM: "; }//end while
return cnt;
}//end inputin
double comptot(double itemp[], int cnt){
double tot=0;
for (int i=0; i<cnt; i++){
        tot = tot + itemp[i]; }//end for
cout <<"TOTAL: "<<tot<<endl;
return tot;
}//end comptot
double findmax (double itemp[], int cnt){ double mx;
mx=itemp[0];
for (int i=0; i<cnt; i++){
        if (itemp[i]>mx){ mx=itemp[i];  }//end if
 }//end for
return mx; }
double compavg(double tot, int cnt){
double av;
av=tot/cnt; return av;}
void printdata(double itemp[],int cnt, double tot, double mx, double av){
for (int i=0; i<cnt; i++){cout<<itemp[i]<<endl; }//end for
cout<<"CNT IS: "<<cnt<<" TOT IS: "<<tot<<endl;
cout<<" AV IS:"<<av<<" MX IS : "<<mx<<endl; }//end print
```

Q3. a) Complete the following Search program

```
main()
{......... int MAXSIZE=6;
long int accountnumber[]=
{123490, 569876,543689,107412,111111,............};
double accountbalance........={230.90,789.00,99.99,986.54,1.00,340.44};
long int ...................;
cout<<"PLEASE ENTER THE....................: ";
cin>>searchaccountnumber;
for(int i=0; i<MAXSIZE;......){
    ......... (......................... [....] = =searchaccountnumber){
                    cout<<"BALANCE IS :"<<..................<<endl;
                                    ......... 1;
                                    }//end if
}//end for
cout<<.......................................
...................;}//end main
```

Q3. b) Complete the following selection sort program. Program each time finds the minimum
value and place it at the beginning location.

```
        const ...... n =100;
        int tbl[.....], minloc,pass, i;
        for  (pass=0; pass<n-1,pass........){
        minloc=pass;
        for (i=pass +1; i<n; i++){
                if tbl[i]<tbl[..........]) {minloc=i;}//end for ...................
```

```
int temp=tbl[minloc];
tbl[..........]=tbl[I]
tbl[i]=temp;
}//end for ....................
```

Q4. Design a simple database "Grading System" for Professor Ebrahimi with the following functions: append( ), display( ), search( ), modify( ) and delete( )
   a) Show the main menu.
   b) Show the function insert.
   c) Show the function modify.

Q5. How can the grading system be improved using different data structures such as arrays and random access files? What is the problem with modification and deletion?
   a) Show the insertion function.
   b) Show the deletion function.
   c) Indicate one advantage and one disadvantage for each method versus the other.

Q6. a) Declare the user data type called *Student* using a structure or class.
   b) Show the insertion function for the above.
   c) Show the structure using a linked list.
   d) Show display function using linked list.

PROGRAMMING II – TEST 1 (SAMPLE 2)

Q1. Given the program below, with the following data:
```
          10 20 30 40  50
#include <iostream.h>
main()
{ int table[10], n = 0,  i, nko, upubm;
while(cin>>table[n]){ n++;}//while
for(i=0; i<n;i++) {cout<<" i is "<<i<<" table[i]="<<table[i]<<endl;}//for
nko = table[0];
for(i=1;i<n;i++)
{ if (table[i] < nko)
 nko = table[i];
}//for
for(i=0;i<n;i++){
 upubm = upubm + table[i];
 }//for
cout<<" THE NKO IS "<<nko<<endl;
cout<<" THE UPUBM IS "<<upubm<<endl;
 }//main
```

   a) What would be the output of the program?
   b) What does program do?

Q2. a) Convert the above program using function with external variables.
   b) Convert the above program using pass of parameter and return value as needed.

741

Q3. For the following data: 5   14   12   7   1
   a) Explain and show each pass for one of the below sorting algorithms: Selection, Exchange, and Insertion.
   b) Compare two of the above sorts. Indicate one advantage and one disadvantage of each sort.
   c) Write an Exchange SORT function using the following variables: table[], pass, swap(&tbl[i], &tbl[i+1]), i

Q4. a) What is the advantage of the linear search and binary search? Show how many comparisons it takes to search for number 12 from the data set: 5 14 12 7 1 using linear search and binary search. How should the given data be arranged when using binary search?

Q4. b) Complete the following binary search function:

```
binsearch(table,first,last,lookup)  int  table[ ],.....,.....,....... ;
{ int mid;
  while (......... <= last) {
  mid = (........) / 2;
  if (lookup == .......)  return (mid);
  if (.......<table[....])  ....... = mid - 1;
  else  last = ............. ;
   }
}
```

Q4. c) Write a recursive program for the above binary search.

Q5. a)What does the following function do?
```
        void TRCSYP(char str2[], char str1[]){
        int i=0;
        while (str1[i]!=NULL){ str2[i]=str1[i]; i++;}
        }//TRCSYP
```

Q5. b) Write the function EBSTRCMP(str1, str2) where two strings are compared character by character. If the strings are identical return 1, otherwise return 0.

Q6. There are two files, FileA and FileB; each file contains sorted data. Output FileC should be a sorted file resulting from merging FileA and FileB. If the numbers are identical, only the numbers from FileA will be copied to FileC. Show your data and command.

Q7. Write a program for a payroll system using object oriented features such as class, derived class, polymorphism, and inheritance. Show the data members as well as member functions. employee class, parttimer, manager. Program should compute, search, and display.

Q8. a) Create two nodes, nodep and nodeq. Connect nodep to nodeq using self-referential structure. Write the code.
   b) Build a list called LIST pointing to the beginning of the list. nodep will be the previous node, and nodeq will be the new node. Write the code.
   c) Write a function to search and print the through the LIST.

PROGRAMMING II - SAMPLE PROJECT 1

BUILDING A SIMPLE DATABASE:

<u>PHASE I</u>:
Separate programs to:
      Create a file
      Display the file
      Search the file

<u>PHASE II</u>:
Put all the separate programs (making them functions) into 1 unit

<u>PHASE III</u>:
Passing of parameters
Include modify and delete functions in the menu
To start duplicate the field into new file and display it

Hints: to modify a field, copy entire record until the record search succeeds, get modification request – copy the modification and copy the rest of the file

> *Delete the original file and rename the new file with the original name using system commands in the <stdlib>*
>   *system("del directory.in");*
>   *system("rename newdir.in directory.in");*

This is not an efficient way for a large file; however, other assignments will explore and enhance this.

<u>PHASE IV</u>:
Change program using array
Load entire file into arrays at the beginning before menu
Store into the file upon exit

** Take advantage of the return feature if you choose for extra credit, also write the search function such a way that it can be shared with modify and delete.

<u>Special note</u>: to make sure all of your functions work, i.e. add, modify, delete, etc. write them as a separate program and work them along with your already existing file before you combine them, it should cut down on a good number of errors.

PROGRAMMING II - SAMPLE PROJECT 2

<u>PART I</u>: (Do not use array)
1.   Read a series of rainfalls
2.   Compute the Sum of rainfalls
3.   Compute average rainfall
4.   Find the Maximum rainfalls
5.   Find the minimum (do not consider 0 as a minimum)
6.   Print sum, average, minimum and maximum rainfall

Hint: Program should check for invalid data entry such as negative numbers and any number greater then 50. Invalid data should be rejected and program should ask for next entry.

A: Loop for 7 days

B.   Loop with a given number of days (e.g. n)

C.   Program should terminate with a sentinel value (dummy value) such as 999

EXTRA CREDIT

E1. Run program using EOF interactively (e.g. ctrl/z or ctrl/d in Linux)

E2. Run program using Data file (no interaction)

Challenge:

Make the program bulletproof, checking for any invalid entries including characters

      a.   Count the number of rainy days

      b.   Count the number of sunny days (days where rain = 0)

Please note:

Each assignment should be well documented.

Progress should be shown incrementally.

PART II: Using arrays, structures, or classes

1.   Read the valid rainfall into an array (the program should check for invalid rainfall and reject any invalid information)

2.   The maximum array size is 365 (remember that an array is a consecutive, contiguous memory location that is assigned by a complier for you)

3.   Use variable "n" as size of valid data

4.   Use a separate loop to fill the array

(the following loop will not check for the validity of the railfall)

      e.g.:   n=0;

                         while (cin>>rainfall [n]){

                         n++;   }

5.   Compute the sum by going through the array:

      e.g.:   for (d=0;d<n;d++)

6.   Compute the average rainfall (hint: do not divide by zero)

7.   Find the maximum by using array again

      e.g.:   max = rain[0];

             for (d=1; ...)

8.   Find the minimum similarly using separate loop again

9.   Sort the rainfall by using either maximum or minimum

Hint: (Algorithm) find the next minimum and swap it with the next first and repeat it "n" times.

      e.g.   for (pass=0;pass<n;pass++){

             find min location

             for (day=pass+1;day<n;day++)

             swap   }

EXTRA CREDIT

Ebrahimi Sort

      To speed up the algorithm take advantage of finding the min and max on each pass. The program should sort faster.

PROGRAMMING II - SAMPLE PROJECT 3

The object of this project is to design a simple supermarket pricing system.

PART I:
Write a program that will be used by a supermarket in which the barcode, the name, and the price of an item can be inputted. The program must have a menu to insert and display the items.

PART II:
Add a search function to the menu. The program should be able to search by barcode or name. Once the item is found, the price should be displayed.

PART III:
Convert the previous program to arrays. Load all the items into the appropriate arrays before the menu. Before exiting the program, store all the data from the arrays to the file.

PART IV:
Add a function that will modify the price. Also, add a delete function to the menu.

PART V:
Add a sort function that sorts the items by the name.

PART VI:
Convert the program to a structure. Apply binary search on the name.

PART VII:
Convert the program by using object-oriented programming paradigm: class, polymorphism, and inheritance.

PART VIII:
Instead of array, use linked list. All data manipulations are done by insertion and deletion.

PART IX:
Add customer sale by allowing the item barcode numbers to be entered. The program for each barcode will display the price. At the end, the subtotal and the total with tax should be displayed.

EXTRA CREDIT
The program should be divided into 2 separate parts: users (customer sale) and administrators. The administration part should only be accessible with a password.
The program should include your own features such as membership by providing customers discount on the next purchase. Set your own regulations.

DATA STRUCTURES – TEST 1 (SAMPLE 1)

Q1. ANSWER 4 OUT OF 5
   a) Define the data structures.
   b) Name three major data structures and an application for each of the three data structures.
   c) Give one example of static and one example of dynamic data structures.
   d) What is recursion and why is it important? Give an example.
   e) What would be the order of notation for: Bubble sort, quicksort, linear search, binarysearch, and hashing?

Q2. Write a simple hash function for the social security number: int hashfun(int ssn)

Q3. a) Sort the following data slot[]={8,3,1,5,7,10,4}
   b) According to a bubble sort, show the steps and movement of data.
   c) According to the straight selection sort, show the steps and movement of data.
   d) Indicate one advantage of bubble sort and one advantage of selection sort that is taken into consideration in EXSEL sort.
   e) Write the function for either the bubble sort or the straight selection using the following variables: int tbl[10], i, j, mloc. Swap( ) already exists and you don't have to write it.

Q4. a) Apply the linear search with the following data tbl[]={8,3,1,5,7,10,4}, looking for the number 7. Show the steps and the process.
   b) Apply the binary search with the following data tbl[]={1,3,5,7,8,10,12,13}, looking for the number 7. Show the steps and the process.
   c) Write a linear search function using int linearsearch(int tbl[], int n, int searchkey)
   d) Write a recursive binary search using int binsearch(int tbl[],low,high,searchkey)

Q5. a) Build a stack program with a menu using only the following variables: X, option, mystack[50], and mytop. Write the main program. The menu's options are as follows:
   1 to push
   2 to pop
   3 to check if stack is empty
   3 to check if stack is full

Q5. b) Write the push(int mystack[],int &mytop, int x) function.
   c) Write the function int pop(int mystack[], int &mytop).
   d) Write the function bool empty(int mytop)
   e) Write the function bool full(int mytop)

Q6. a) Build a queue program with a menu using only the following variables x, option,myqueue[100],rear and front
   1 to enqueue
   2 to dequeue
   3 to check if queue is empty
   3 to check if queue is full

Q6. b) Write the function enqueue(int myqueue[],int &rear,int x)
   c) Write the function int dequeue(int myqueue[],int front)
   d) Write the function bool empty(int counter)
   e) Write the function bool full(int counter).

Q7. a) Convert the following infix notation to postfix notation: 9 - 3 * 2

  b) Evaluate the following 9 3 2 * - , by using a stack.

  c) Write a function to evaluate postfix: int evaluate(char postfix[]). String postfix contains the postfix expression. Assume the following function are already existed: push,pop,empty, isfull, isoperator, operand() and eval()

Q8. You are to simulate an Airport with two queues; assume all the following functions and variables exist: rand, departure queue, arrival queue, dequeue, enqueue, isempty, and isfull.

DATA STRUCTURES – TEST 1 (SAMPLE 2)

Q1. Answer 5 out 7

  a) What are data structures?

  b) Give three examples of data structures and one application for each.

  c) What are pointers and give one example where pointers are used in data structures.

  d) What would be the disadvantage of static data structures versus dynamic data structures.

Q2. a) By drawing, demonstrate the following stack and queue statically.

  b) Write the following function definitions for a static stack using array structures and queue

    using: push(mystack,x)

         x=pop(mystack)

         enqueue(myqueue,x)

         x=dequeue(myqueue)

Q3. a) By drawing, illustrate the following stack and queue dynamically:

       push(mystacktop,5); push(mystacktop,7);

       x=pop(mystacktop);

       push(mystacktop,10);

       enqueue(myqueuerear,5); enqueue(myqueuerear,7);

       x=dequeue(myqueuefront);

       enqueue(myqueuerear,10);

Q3. b) Write the following function definitions for a static stack using array and queue using

    structures. push(mystacktop,x)

         x=pop(mystacktop)

         enqueue(myqueuerear,x)

         x=dequeue(myqueuefront)

Q4. a) Illustrate the evaluation of a postfix notation for the following expression 2 3 * 10 +

  b) Explain the algorithm for postfix evaluation

  c) Write the program for postfix evaluation using the following functions isdigit(), isoperator() , push () , pop (), and evaluate () . *Hint: you do not have to write code for the indicated functions.*

Q5. Simulate an airport for arriving and departing planes.

  a) Show your menu with random number generator (1 arrival 2 departure)

  b) Show the submenu for enqueue and dequeue (1 enqueue 2 dequeue)

  c) Maximum size of queue is 10, no enqueue after 10.

  d) Show the main program

Q6. a) Explain pass of parameter mechanism by reference and by pointer using swap(....) function.

b) What would the order or notation for a bubble sort. What would be an order of notation for a fast search program.

c) Use template to write a generic swap function

Q7. a) What is object oriented programming? Explain three element of OOP

b) What is STL and give some example either for stack or string

c) Write the stackempty() and stackfull() functions.

d) Write the queuefull() and queueempty() functions.

Q8. a) Show three different ways in passing parameters. Use the swap function.

b) Use template to swap two variables of different types

DATA STRUCTURE – TEST 2 (SAMPLE 1)

Q1. Answer any four
   a) What are Data Structures, Give thee examples and explain one application (usage)for each of the data structures.
   b) Give one advantage and one disadvantage of static data structures versus dynamic data structures.
   c) By an example (code or declaration) for each, define three components of object oriented programming.
   d) What would be the order of notation for a bubble sort, quick sort, sequential search, binary search, and hashing (choose only four).
   e) What is recursion, and why is it important? Give an example.
   f) What is STL? How can it be used in Data structures? Give an example.

Q2. Using Structure or Class implement a stack called STACK and build a stack's object (variable) called thestack. The Class stack consists of stkinfo[MAXSIZE] and stktop. The member function of STACK are stkpush( ), stkpop( ), stkempty( ) and stkfull( ).
   a) Show STACK data structures. (declaration)
   b) Stkfull( ) return true or 1 if stack is full, else return false or 0
   c) Stkempty( ) return true or 1 if stack is empty, else return false or 0
   d) Write the code for function stkpush( ). The function stkfull( ) will be called inside the function to whether push the x.
   e) Write the code for the pop

Q3. Implement the queue using a single linked list
   a) Show the Queue Data Structure.
   b) quefull( ) return true or 1 if queue is full, else return false or 0
   c) queempty( ) return true or 1 if queue is empty, else return false or 0
   d) queinsert( ) insert at rear, querear is the pointer to the rear of the queue
   e) queremove( ) remove from front, quefront is the pointer to the front of queue

Q4. a) Explain how the following infix expression is converted to postfix 2 + 3 * 4
   b) Explain how the postfix expression (above after conversion) is evaluated
   c) Write a high level program (using the functions only) to convert infix to postfix.
   d) Write a high level program (using the functions only) to evaluate the postfix. The following functions are already available:
      push( ) push either operator or operand into the stack
      pop( ), return the top of the stack
      ishigher(stktop,operator) true if top of stack is higher than the current operator
      evaluate(operandl,operand2, operator) return the numeric result after the applying the operator

Q5. You are to buld an Insertion Sort using double linked list with the following: insertatbegining( ), insertatmiddle( ), and insertatend( ).
   a) Write the function insertatbeginning(node *q, node *p) { //insert p at beginning of list}
   b) Write the function insertatmiddle(node *q, node *p) { //insert p into list }
   c) Write the function insertatend(node *q, node *p) { //insert p at end of list}
   d) Write an insertion sort function that calls proper function upon the decision of where x is to be inserted.

Q6. a) What is hashing and what does a hash function do?
   b) Give two ways to hash social securities

Q6. c) What would be the problem with hashing?
    d) Write a hash function for SSN. The Size of hash table is 100.

Q7. a) Build a binary search tree for the following data 20 45 10 8 25 12
    b) Write the data structure (BTS) using info, 1child and rchild .
    c) Write a recursive function for binsearchtree(root,x), looking for x.
    d) By traversing the tree, how many comparisons are needed to search for 12?
    e) Build a B tree with a maximum of two data per node for above data.

Q8. You are to network five computers known as A, B, C, D, and E accordingly. The Computer
    A is connected to All computers in both ways (bidirectional). Each computer is connected
    to its adjacent computer (letter wise).
    a) Show the Graph
    b) Show the Adjacency Matrix
    c) Show the data structure representing the matrix
    d) Show the data structure using the linked list (array of pointers)
    e) Show three ways a message can be sent from Computer B to all the computers (according
    to above Graph). Which path is the fastest? Why? Assuming the cost of a message is
    the difference between the two letters (A is 1, B is 2, C is 3, D is 4 and E is 5). A cost of
    message from A to D (4 - 1) will be 3 and cost of message from B to C is 1 (3 - 2).

DATA STRUCTURES – TEST 2 (SAMPLE 2)

Q1. Answer 5 of the following question
    a) What is data structures all about? Give 4 examples with one application for each.
    b) What is Static data and what is Dynamic data structures. By Example give one advantage of
    each.
    c) What Abstraction Data Type give an example.
    d) What would be the order of notation for : linear search, bubble sort, quicksort, binarysearch
    e) What is recursion, why is important, Give an example (Fibonacci,or Towers of Honoi)
    f) Give some example of STL for either string or stack.
    g) What is graph? Show its data structure. (Use matrix or linked list)

Q2. a) Build a stack program with the following menu and the variables X, option,
    stackitem[100], and top.
    1 to push   2 to pop 3 to check if stack is empty 4 to check if stack is full.
    Show your data structure

Q2. b) Write the push() function.
    c) Write the the function pop().
    d) Write the function empty()
    e) Write the function full()

Q3. a) Build a queue program with the following menu and the variables X, option,
    queueitem[100], rear, and top.
    Show your data structure (either use structure or class)
    1 to enqueue 2 to dequeue 3 to check if queue is empty 4 to check if queue is full

Q3. b) Write the queue( ) function.
    c) Write the the dequeue( ) function.
    d) Write the function empty()
    e) Write the function full().

Q4. a) Convert the following infix notation to postfix notation: 2 * 3 + 8 * 2
   b) Evaluate the following: 4 3 * 5 2 –*
   c) Write a program that evaluates a postfix notation
      Assume all the functions such as push, pop, empty, full, isoperator, operand( ), and evaluate( ) already exist.

Q4. d) By the use of a stack show how the above infix expression is converted into postfix notation.

Q5. You are to build an insertion sort using linked list (single or double)for the following numbers:
      20 10 45 8 25 12.
   a) Build the sorted list after arrival of each input data.
   b) The beginning node of the list is called sortlst, and new node is called p, show and write the code for the proper insertion.
   c) Write the code for general insertion. (use sortlst, p as a auxiliary node, q as the new node, x as input, hint: use loop)

Q6. a) Build a binary search for the following data 10 8   45 25 5 12 1.
      How many comparisons are needed to search for input 45.
   b) Write the data structure called BINTREE with leftchild and rightchid.
   c) Write the function btreesearch (BINTREE *root, int x)
   d) Build a B Tree with a maximum of two data per node.

Q7. a) What is hashing, and what does a hash function do?
   b) Write a fast hash function to hash C/C++ reserved words. Table size is 211.
   c) What would be the problem with the hashing and how can it be resolved?
   d) How would you improve your hash function?

DATA STRUCTURE - SOLUTION TEST 1 (SAMPLE 1)

Q1. a) Define the data structures: simply it's a way to organize data. They are ways in which data is arranged or organized in your computer's memory (or stored on a disk). They contain algorithms, which are procedures a program uses to manipulate the data in these structures.

Q1. b) Name 3 major data structures and an application of each:
   - STACK –Provides last in first out access. examples – Polish calculator, stack of plates in a cafeteria, windows, e-mail, and answering service.
   - QUEUE -   provides first in first out access. examples – line of people in a bank, the lineup of jobs waiting to print in a printer spool, planes arriving and departing from an airport runway, e-mail, and answering service.
   - HASH – a fast search program of a known element. Hashing goes right to the location of the element without having to scan the entire array. Example— Three way folding of SSN.
Q1. c) Static - array - contains memory already known and size is determined when the program is compiled.
      Dynamic - Linked list - size is determined when the program is actually running - uses memory during execution time.

751

Q1. d) Recursion - is when a function calls itself. It is important in designing certain algorithms. It's short and can make some problem solving simpler than doing it iteratively (looping). Example: the most common example is Factorial Numbers or power() calculations:

```
double power ( double x, int n)
{
    if (n==0) return 1.0;  //any number  x to the 0 power = 1
    else return power (x, n-1) * x;}
```

Q1. e) Order of notation for the following:
bubblesort (exchange sort) = $O(N^2)$
quicksort (exchange sort) = $O(Nlog_2N)$
linear search = $O(N)$
binary Search = $O(log_2N)$
hash search = $O(1)$ order of one – fastest –if no collision

Order of preference from fastest -> slowest: $O(1) - O(logN) - O(N) - O(N^2)$

Q1. f) Write a simple hash function for hashfun(int ssn)

```
int hashfun (int ssn){
int ssn;
return ssn %10000; }
```

This allows for collisions, but it's a simple hash function using module to make the number within the hash table range.

Q3. Sort the following: slot[] = {8,3,1,5,7,10,4}

a) bubblesort

8	3	1	5	7	10	4
3	8	1	5	7	10	4
3	1	8	5	7	10	4
3	1	5	8	7	10	4
3	1	5	7	8	10	4
3	1	5	7	8	10	4
3	1	5	7	8	4	10
1	3	5	7	8	4	10
1	3	5	7	4	8	10
1	3	5	4	7	8	10
1	3	4	5	7	8	10
1	3	4	5	7	8	10

b) Straight Selection sort:

8	3	1	5	7	10	4
1	3	8	5	7	10	4
1	3	8	5	7	10	4
1	3	4	5	7	10	8
1	3	4	5	7	10	8
1	3	4	5	7	10	8
1	3	4	5	7	8	10

c) Advantage of bubble sort and selection sort in relation to EXSEL sort:
advantage of bubble sort - if there is no swap in one pass, the data is sorted.
advantage of selection sort - can place the smallest numbers no matter where they are in the beginning of the data (SEE chap11).

d) function for bubblesort using tbl[10],i,j,n

```
void bubblesort (int tbl[], int n)
{
        int  i, scan, pass;
        for (pass=1; pass<n; pass++){
            for (scan = 0; scan<n-pass; scan++){
                if(tbl[scan]>tbl[scan+1]){
                    swap (tbl, scan, scan+1);}
            }//end for scan loop
        }//end for pass loop
}//end bubblesort function
```

Q4. a) Apply linear search to the following looking for 7:
$$tbl[]=\{8,3,1,5,7,10,4\}$$
Compare 7 to each element of the array in a loop until it is found or the end of the array is reached

Q4. b) Apply the binary search by comparing the key to the middle element of the array. If it is not in the middle, either it is on the left of the middle or right of middle. As long as lo is less than hi, continue.

Q4. c) Complete program as follows:

```
#include<iostream.h>
linearsearch(int tbl[ ],int searchkey, int n){
    for(int i=0; i<n;i++){
        if (searchkey==tbl[i]) return i; }//FOR
    return -1; }//end linearsearch
main(){
    int tbl[]={8,3,1,5,7,10,4}, n=7;
    int searchkey,chosen;
    cout<<"Enter the number you want to search for: ";
    cin>>searchkey;
    chosen=linearsearch(tbl,searchkey,n);
    if (chosen== -1){
        cout <<"That number you entered " << searchkey << " " << "is not found. \n";
        cout << "Please try again." << endl;    }
        else  cout<<"The number you entered " << searchkey << " " <<"was found." <<endl;
    return 0;  }//end main
```

Q4. d) - binary search function:

```
int binsearch (int tbl[], int low, int high, int searchkey){
        int mid;
        if (low > high)  return -1;
        mid = (low + high)/2;
        if (searchkey == tbl[mid]) return mid;
        else if ( searchkey < tbl[mid])
        binsearch (tbl, low, mid-1, searchkey);
```

753

else binsearch (tbl, mid+1, high, searchkey); }//binsearch function

Q5. a)
```
#include <iostream.h>
void main(){
        const int MAXSIZE = 5;
        int mystack[MAXSIZE];
        int mytop;
        int x;
        mytop = 0;
        char option;
        do{     cout << "This is a stack program.\n";
                cout <<"Please choose from one of the following options:\n";
                cout << "1=PUSH\n2=POP\n3=ISFULL\n4=ISEMPTY\n";
                cout << "Please enter your option: ";
                cin >> option;
        switch (option){
        case '1': cout << "Enter a number to be pushed: ";
                cin >> x ;
                push (mystack, mytop, x);
                break;
        case '2': cout << "Number popped: \n"<< pop( mystack,  mytop);
                cout<<endl;
                break;
        case '3': if(isfull(mytop, MAXSIZE)==1)  cout << "Stack is full."<< endl;
                else cout<< "Stack is not full."<< endl;
                break;
        case '4': if (isempty(mytop)==1)         //return true for empty
                cout << "Stack is empty. Go away!" << endl;
                else cout <<"Stack isn't empty yet." << endl;
                break;
        case 'q': cout <<"Thank you for playing, menu game is now over. BYE!\n";
                cout<< endl;
                break;
        default: cout <<"\nInvalid option entered."
                        <<"\nYour options are from 1 - 4 only."
                        <<"\nPlease enter correct options." << endl; }//end switch
        }while (option != 'q' || option != 'Q');
}//main
```

Q5. b)
```
void push (int mystack[], int &mytop, int x){
        mystack[mytop] = x;
        mytop++;}//push function
```

Q5. c)
```
int pop (int mystack[], int &mytop){
        mytop --;
         return mystack[mytop];}//pop function
```

Q5. d)
```
bool empty(int mytop){
        if (mytop = = 0) return true;
        else return false;}//empty function
```

Q5. e)
```
bool full(int mytop, const int MAXSIZE){
    if (mytop = = MAXSIZE) return true;
    else return false;}//full function
```

Q6. a)
```
//An example of a Queue Program
#include <iostream.h>
void main(){
    const int MAXSIZE = 5;
    int myqueue[MAXSIZE];
    int rear, front, counter;
    int x;
    rear = 0;
    char option;
    do{     cout << "This is a QUEUE program.\n";
            cout <<"Please choose from one of the following options:\n";
            cout << "1=Enqueue\n2=Dequeue\n3=Empty\n4=Full\n";
            cout << "Please enter your option: ";
            cin >> option;
            switch (option){
            case '1': cout << "Enter a number Enqueue: ";
                    cin >> x ;
                    enqueue(myqueue, rear, x);
                    break;
            case '2': cout << "Number Dequeued: \n"<< dequeue( myqueue,  front);
                    cout<< endl;
                    break;
            case '3': if (isempty(counter)==1) cout << "Queue is empty." << endl;
                    else cout <<"Queue has more room." << endl;
                    break;
            case '4': if (isfull(counter, MAXSIZE)==1)
                            cout<< "Queue is full."<< endl;
                    else    cout<< "Queue is not full."<< endl;
                    break;
            case 'q':
            cout <<"Thank you for playing, menu game is now over. BYE!\n";
                    break;
            default: cout <<"\nInvalid option entered."
                    <<"\nYour options are from 1 - 4 only."
                    <<"\nPlease enter correct options." << endl; }
        }while ((option != 'q') || (option != 'Q'));
    cout <<"Please choose from one of the following options:\n";
    cout << "1=Enqueue\n2=dequeue\n3=ISEMPTY\n4=ISFULL"
        <<" (enter q or Q to quit)\n";
    cin >> option;    }//main
```

```
/*
This is a QUEUE program.
Please choose from one of the following options:
1=Enqueue
2=Dequeue
3=Empty
```

```
                4=Full
                Please enter your option: 3
                Queue has more room.
                This is a QUEUE program.
                Please choose from one of the following options:
                1=Enqueue
                2=Dequeue
                3=Empty
                4=Full
                Please enter your option:  */
```

Q6. b) int enqueue (int myqeue[], int &rear, int x){
            myqueue[rear] = x;
            rear ++;}

Q6. c) int dequeue (int myqueue[], int &front){
            front -- ;
            return myqueue[front] ; }

Q6. d) bool empty (int counter) {
        if (counter = =0) return true;
        else return false; }

Q6. e) bool full (int counter, int MAXSIZE) {
        if (counter = = MAXSIZE) return true;
        else return false; }

INTERNET AND WEB PROGRAMMING - SAMPLE TEST

Q1. a) Explain the following perl program in terms of c++. What does it do?

```
1.    open (PAYROLL,"payroll.dat") || die "cant't open the file $_";
2.    while <PAYROLL>{
3.    ($name, $hw, $hr) = split (/, /);
4.    $gp = $hw * hr;
5.    if ($gp> 500) {$tr=0.30; }
6.    elsif ($gp > 300) {$tr=0.20; }
7.    else { $tr=0.0; }
8.    if ($name = ~ I$ |i$| E$|e$/) {print "name=$name  tr=$tr   gp=$gp\n";}
9.    } #end while
```

Q1. b) Run the above program with the following datafile (payroll.dat).

> Alireza Ebrahimi, 40, 100.00
> Joe Smith, 3, 25.00
> Jean Doe, 10, 10.00

Q2. a) Design a form for the following e-business "pizzareza.com". The form consists of customer's name, address, telephone number, email, and a text area, where customers can leave details of the order such as please make it spicy.
Use the Input tag with different types, a table with three rows and three columns with following headers:

> pizza TYPE(small, medium, large) PRICE 5.00, 8.00, 12.00 and quantity
> radiobox cheese topping by default (extra cost 1.00)
> checkbox Other topping (anchovies, vegetable, sausage).

Q2. b) Write the html tags for the above form.

Q3. Write the CGI program that computes the cost of the above order including 8% sales tax and let the customer know the total cost and time of the delivery.
You may use the following CGI.PM

> use CGI qw(:standard);
> print header();
> print start_html(" PIZZAREZA ");
> print(" THANK YOU FOR ORDERING PIZZA

 \n";
> my ($....,$......,$......)= (param ("......."), (........), (......))
> at the end use the following time function
> print scalar (localtime())
> print"</body> </html>";

Q4. a) Explain the following JavaScript program

```
1.    <html>
2.    <head>
3.    <title> Figure it out </title>
4.    <script language = "Javascript>
5.    var person = [1234, 9807,  3456, 9845, 3275];
6.    function buttonPressed ()
7.    {
```

```
8.    var searchKey= searchForm.inputVal.value;
9.   var index= tosearch(person, parseInt(searchKey));
10. if (index!=-1)
11.    search.result.value= "Found value in location " + index;
12. else
13.    searchform.result.value= " Match not found ";
14. }// end buttonPressed
15. function tosearch (person,searchKey)
16. {
17.   for (var i = 0; i <person.length; i++)
18.   {
19.     if (person[i] = =searchKey)
20.            return i;
21.    }//loop
22.   return -1;
23. }// end tosearch
24. </script>
25. </head>
26. <body>
27. <form name="searchForm"> <p> ENTER THE PERSON'S ID <br>
28. <input name "inputVal" type = "text">
29. <input name = "search" type = "button" value = "tosearch"
30.    onclick = buttonPressed()"><br> </p>
31. <p> Result <br>
32. <input name = "result" type = "text"  size = "30" > </p>
33. </form>
34. </body>
35. </html>
```

Q4. b) Show the output of the above program with one interaction.

Q5. a) Convert the above program to a C++ or to a Perl program
      b) Write a C++ or a Perl program which search an item from the data file.

Q6. Write a small data base (telephone directory) with the following functions: append, display, search, modify, and delete.
    a) Show the menu with the function calls.
    b) Show the function that appends a record.
    c) Show the function that modifies the telephone number

Q7. a) Indicate three reasons why Perl or C++ is chosen as a language of choice for Web Programming.
    b) Write the detailed steps in getting the domain name, etc. to execute a cgi program. You may want to use pizzaonline.com
    c) Indicate one advantage and one disadvantage of JavaScript in comparison to either C++ or Perl.

VISUAL C++ - TEST 1

The following test was intended for Visual Basic, however you can use your own self-learning skill to apply it to VISUAL C++. It is a little more work than VB.

Q1. a) Show a form with the required controls (text boxes, labels, and commands) for a payroll system. Input consists of employee's name, hours worked, hourly rate, and tax rate. Output consists of gross pay, tax amount and net pay.
  b) Write a subprogram for the compute command.
  c) How is possible to compute for entering different tax rate without re-entering the other input entries. Show the subprogram.

Q2. Extend the above program to include the following (Show your form)
  a) Display overtime hours and overtime pay. Show the code
  b) Set variable tax rate for each computed gross pay. Tax rate for gross pay more than 500 is 20%, for more than 300 is 15% and 10% for the rest. Compute tax amount. For Single employees additional 5% will be added to the tax rate. You may want to use option box for marital status and check list for different tax rates and a frame.

Q3. Extend the above program as follows:
  a) Write (save) every employee's data including the computed data into a file called personnel.txt. Create a command box and show the code.
  b) Create a command box called append which add any future entry to the file. Show the code as well as the button.
  c) Test the entries for blanks before writing it to the file. Show the code.

Q4. Extend the above program as follows:
  a) Display all the data from the personel.txt to a picture box. Show the code and the command.
  b) Create a Search command that search for an employee name. Show the code and the command.

Q5. Extend the above program as follows:
  a) Delete an employee's record. *Hint: you may want to read all data into an array or create a new file and filecopy the new file to personel.txt and then kill the new file after the filecopy.*
  b) Modify a textbox through an input box dialogue. You need to search for each of the above first.

Q6. a) Give an example of control arrays
  b) What would be the advantage of having data control (data bound)? Explain some of the features.

VISUAL C++ - TEST2

The following test was intended for Visual Basic, However use your own self- learning skill to apply it to VISUAL C++. It is a little more work than VB.

Q1. You are to design an invoice system for a small company called MailOrder Enterprise.
  a) Show the named form, with the required controls and buttons (text boxes, labels and the command). The data entries include invoice number, item's name, item's price and item's quantity. The Output consists of subtotal, tax amount, and total (Tax rate is 8.5%).
  b) Write a subprogram for the compute command.

c) How is possible to compute for different tax rate without re-entering the other input data. Show the subprogram.

Q2. Extend the above program to include the following (Show your form).
  a) Compute the discount based on the following: 20% for the total greater than $500, and 10% for the total greater than $200. Otherwise there will be no discount.
  b) Set variable tax rate depend on the shipping destination (NY 8.5% NJ 7% and other States 0%)
  c) Extra credit question: Use a list or combo list to list all the states and tax rates.) You may want to use option boxes for state tax rate and discount rates in a frame.

Q3. Extend the above program as follows:
  a) Save every data entry to a file including the computed data into a file called customer.txt. Create a command box and show the code.
  b) Test the entries for blanks before writing it to the file and echo a message explaining why. Show the code.

Q4. Extend the above program by adding two command boxes: Display all and Search.
  a) Display all the data from the customer.txt to a picture box. Show the code and the command
  b) Create a Search command that search for a customer name or invoice number. Show the program for search by name and for search by invoice just show the function call.

Q5. Extend the above program to include two more command boxes: CANCEL and MODIFY.
  a) CANCEL will delete an entire invoice record. *Hint: you may want to read all data into an array or create a new file called custemp.txt. Use filecopy to copy the custemp.txt to customer.txt and then kill the file custemp.txt after the file copy.*
  b) Modify an invoice record. (You need to search for each of the above commands. Use the same search function for the CANCEL and MODIFY.)
  c) Apply Sort: There are fifty states with their tax rates, show how can they be sorted.

Q6. Explain the steps in using a database(Access) in your project.
  a) Show the connection and properties.
  b) Show the code for adding a new record.
  c) Show the code for deleting and editing a record.
  d) Show your data base sample.

EXTRA CREDIT
How your project can be enhanced by the following inclusion:
E1. timer
E2. SQL
E3. Horizontal and vertical scroll bars
E4. Images and pictures
E5. Random Access files
E6. OLE, ACTIVE X

LANGUAGES AND TRANSLATORS – TEST 1 (SAMPLE 1)

Q1. Explain in detail the important phases of a compiler.

Q2. What is the difference between a compiler and an interpreter?

Q3. Show by an example how a symbol table is implemented.

Q4. Write a lexical analyzer that will recognize variables (reserved, non-reserved), digits (numbers), operators and delimiters.

Q5. Write a recursive descent parser for the following:

> if *condition* then *statement*
> else *statement*

Q6. Parse top down and bottom up the following sentence given the following grammar:

> Grammar: S --> aXYe   X --> Xbc | b   Y --> dY| f | null
> Sentence: abbcdfdfe

LANGUAGES & TRANSLATORS – TEST 1 (SAMPLE 2)

Q1. Answer any three questions.

a) What is the difference between a compiler and an interpreter? Indicate one advantage and one disadvantage of interpreter.

b) What does Code optimization do give an example?

c) Give one method that compiler handles and recovers errors.

d) What is LEX and what is YACC?

e) Explain three major phases of a compiler.

Q2. Give a brief history on three of the following languages. One of the languages should be of your project. In your explanation answer the following:

a) Design purpose (how, when, who, where, why answer at least three)

b) Strength of each language

c) Weakness of the language (your opinion counts)

> Java, C++, C#, Perl, JavaScript
> Algol, Pascal, Smalltalk, FORTRAN, Visual Basic, Prolog
> Visual C++, Ada, B

Q3. Write a sample program in the following languages:

> e.g. find the average of series of valid scores (0-100)

a) Java   b) Lisp

Q4. Write a lexical analyzer to recognize the following tokens:

a) Identifiers: each identifier starts and ends with a $ except reserved word which ends with:

b) Numbers: All numbers start with zero

c) Operators are +, -, x , ÷ , = and ≠.

d) No punctuation allowed except blank space

Q5. Consider the following grammar for arithmetic expression:

> EXP→ EXP - TERM | EXP – EXP | TERM
> TERM→ TERM * FACTOR | FACTOR
> FACTOR→(EXP) | digit

a) Generate the following expression (2 * 5) - (3 * 5)

b) Is grammar ambiguous? How can the ambiguity be resolved?

c) Write a high level parser to recognize the above expression.

Q6. a) Generate code for the following statements z=x-y ; if (z > 0) max =x; else max =y

b) Draw structure of a symbol table using pointers. Show some sample entries.

LANGUAGES AND TRANSLATORS – TEST 2

Q1. a) Why is an interpreter is slower than a compiler?

b) How can a long expression with common expressions be optimized?

c) What is wrong with some of the error strategies in most of the compilers?

d) Write a regular expression for C/C++ identifier.

e) Show the four phases of a complier for the statement p= regpay+ 0verpay *2, where the variables are float.

Q2. Briefly explain your programming language project. In your explanation answer the following:

a) Design purpose (how, when, who, where, why answer at least three)

b) Strength of the language

c) Weakness of the language.

d) Write a sample program using major features of the language.

Q3. Write a lexical analyzer based on the state transition diagram to recognize the following tokens according to the following states.

a) Operator: start from 0 and ends at state 8. The states 2, 3, 4 , 5, 7, and 8 are the terminal states for each operators (>=, >, ==,!=,<=,<)

b) Identifiers: Starts from state 9 and ends at states 11. Identifier starts with a letter follows to another states which is either letter or digit any other char will leads to state 11.

c) Numbers: Starts from state 12 and ends at state 16. Only fixed decimal numbers are allowed. A char of digit will leads to state 13 where one or more digits are expected. A period will lead to state 14 and finally any other char will lead to state 16.

Q4. Consider the following grammar for arithmetic expression:

$$E \rightarrow E - T \mid E + T \mid T$$
$$T \rightarrow T * F \mid T / F \mid F$$
$$F \rightarrow (E) \mid digit$$

a) Is the expression   1 * (2 + 3) legal? Show the Bottom-up parsing.

b) Is grammar ambiguous? Why?

c) Write a high level parser to recognize the above expression.

Q5.a) Write the assembly equivalent for each of the following statements.

     I) p= i + r

     II) if (a != b) flag=0; else flag =1;

b) Write a program that generates assembly code for above statements upon the recognition. Assume there would not any syntax errors in above statements

Q5. c) How can it be possible to simulate an interpreter to recognize an instruction. Each instruction has 16 bit where the first 4 bits represent the operation and the rest indicate the address. All operations are done in register R1.

Q6. a) What is the role of symbol table in a compiler design? Show one implementation.

b) Write a fast hash function for a symbol table's entries.

c) Write a pseudo code for the symbol table insertion.

SYSTEM DESIGN AND IMPLEMENTATION CRITERIA AND EVALUATION

- Do you have a System?
- What is your system about? Is it unique? If yes, in what way.
- Is your system running?
- What language(s) are you using?
- How do you implement your database (Flat File, Access, Oracle, DB2, SQL)?
- How many databases (data controls) do you have?
- How many tables do you have?
- How many fields are in your tables?
- Check your system functions:
- Insert (add, append)
- Search (wild, partial, smart)
- Modify (update, edit)
- Deletion (remove, purge)
- Report (print out, display, statistics)   How many?
- Does your system validation (input, computation, output)? If yes explain.
- Do you have any security such as password (user, administrator) and encryption in your system? Describe.
- Is your system GUI and friendly (graphic user interface, multimedia)? Explain.
- Is your system Web Oriented (HTML, JavaScript, C++/CGI, Perl/CGI, ASP, JSP, JavaServlet)?
- How many forms do you have?
- What is your domain name(website address, URL)?
- Do you have documentation of your system (1 page summary, Detailed Manual)?
- Does your system have a HELP section?
- List your resources and references.
- Is your system extendible (expandable, maintainable, modifiable)?

SAMPLE CASE STUDY

PAYROLL SYSTEM DESIGN

The following are the steps in designing and implementing a simple payroll system from scratch in several phases according to the following. The layout and code for the 7 phases are shown below and the rest are for you do on your own and assistance can be found on the book web site. Note this payroll system can be used as a guideline in designing other system such as invoice, supermarket pricing, weather forecasting, or student grading system.

PHASE 1 INPUT/OUTPUT

1A) COMPUTE THE GROSS PAY FOR AN EMPLOYEE BY ENTERING INTERACTIVELY HOURS WORKED AND HOURLY RATE.

SAMPLE INPUT AND OUTPUT PHASE 1A:

```
ENTER EMPLOYEE ID: 5678
ENTER HOURS WORKED: 40
ENTER HOURLY RATE: 15.00

YOUR ID IS: 5678
YOUR HOURS WORKED IS: 40
YOUR HOURLY RATE IS: $15.00
YOUR GROSS PAY IS: $600.00
```

```cpp
#include<iostream.h>
//phase1a payroll
main( ){
        int employeeId, hoursWorked;
            float hourlyRate, grossPay, taxAmount, netPay;
          float const TAXRATE=(float).30;
        cout<<"Please Enter The Employee Id:";
        cin>>employeeId;
        cout<<"Please Enter The Hours Worked:";
        cin>>hoursWorked;
        cout<<"Please Enter The Hourly Rate:";
        cin>>hourlyRate;
        grossPay=hoursWorked*hourlyRate;
        taxAmount=grossPay*TAXRATE;
        netPay=grossPay-taxAmount;
        cout<<"Employee Id is        "<<employeeId<<endl;
        cout<<"The hours Worked are    "<<hoursWorked<<endl;
        cout<<"The Hourly rate is      "<<hourlyRate<<endl;
        cout<<"The Gross pay is        "<<grossPay<<endl;
return 0;
}//MAIN
```

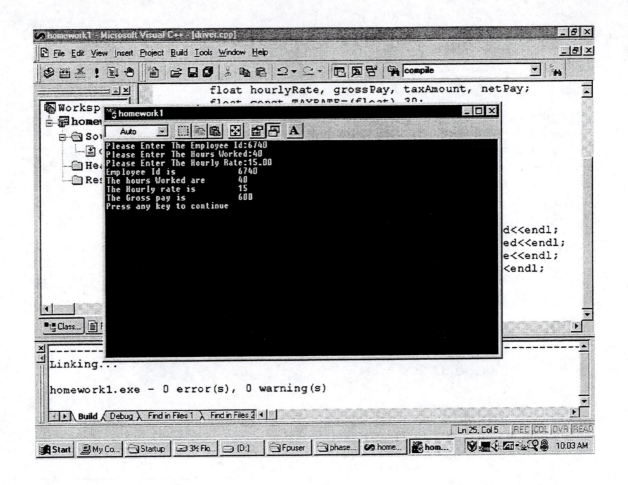

1B) COMPUTE THE NET PAY BY APPLYING A FIXED TAX RATE OF 10%. EMPLOYEE IDS SHOULD BE ENTERED (ENTER ONLY LAST FOUR DIGITAL SS# AT THIS TIME.)

PURPOSE OF PHASE 1: INPUT, ARITHMETIC EXPRESSIONS, OUTPUT.

SAMPLE INPUT AND OUTPUT PHASE 1B:

```
ENTER EMPLOYEE ID: 5678
ENTER HOURS WORKED: 40
ENTER HOURLY RATE: 15.00

YOUR ID IS: 5678
YOUR HOURS WORKED IS: 40
YOUR HOURLY RATE IS: $15.00
YOUR GROSS PAY IS: $600.00
YOUR TAX RATE IS: 0.10
YOUR TAX AMOUNT IS: $60.00
YOUR NET PAY IS: $540.00
```

766

```cpp
#include<iostream.h>
//phase1b payroll
main(){
        int employeeId, hoursWorked;
        float hourlyRate, grossPay, taxAmount, netPay;
        float const TAXRATE=(float).30;
        cout<<"Please Enter The Employee Id:";
        cin>>employeeId;
        cout<<"Please Enter The Hours Worked:";
        cin>>hoursWorked;
        cout<<"Please Enter The Hourly Rate:";
        cin>>hourlyRate;
        grossPay=hoursWorked*hourlyRate;
        taxAmount=grossPay*TAXRATE;
        netPay=grossPay-taxAmount;
        cout<<"Your Id is          "<<employeeId<<endl;
        cout<<"Your hours Worked are  "<<hoursWorked<<endl;
        cout<<"Your Hourly rate is   "<<hourlyRate<<endl;
        cout<<"Your Gross pay is     "<<grossPay<<endl;
        cout<<"Your Tax rate is      "<<TAXRATE<<endl;
        cout<<"The Tax amount is     "<<taxAmount<<endl;
        cout<<"The Net pay is        "<<netPay<<endl;
return 0;
}//MAIN
```

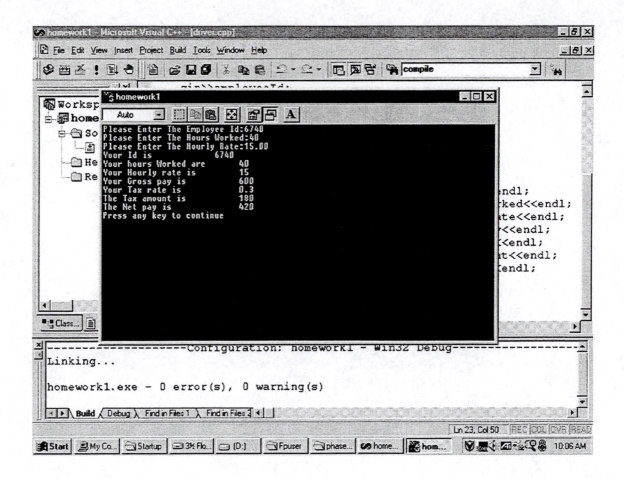

The main purpose for this phase is to get accustomed to the repetition of program using a loop, reading data interactively as well from an external file.

HINT: Use a while loop

PHASE 2: LOOP

2a) Extend Payroll program (phase 1b) to repeat interactively for 5 employees.

Example:	Enter Employee Id	6740
	Enter Hours Worked	40
	Enter Hourly Rate	$ 10
	Employee Id is	6740
	The hours Worked are	40
	The hourly rate is	$10
	The gross pay is	$400

The tax is	0.30
The net pay is	$280

Enter Employee Id	3578
Enter Hours Worked	30
Enter Hourly Rate	10

Employee Id is	3578

…………..

```cpp
#include<iostream.h>
//phase2a payroll
int main(){
        int employeeId, hoursWorked, myNumber  ;
        float hourlyRate, grossPay, taxAmount, netPay;
        float const TAXRATE=(float).30;
        myNumber = 1;
        while(myNumber <=  5){
        cout<<"Please Enter The Employee Id:";
        cin>>employeeId;
        cout<<"Please Enter The Hours Worked:";
        cin>>hoursWorked;
        cout<<"Please Enter The Hourly Rate:";
        cin>>hourlyRate;
        grossPay=hoursWorked*hourlyRate;
        taxAmount=grossPay*TAXRATE;
        netPay=grossPay-taxAmount;
        cout<<"Your Id is   "<<employeeId<<endl;
        cout<<"Your hours Worked are "<<hoursWorked<<endl;
        cout<<"Your Hourly rate is    "<<hourlyRate<<endl;
                cout<<"Your Gross pay is "<<grossPay<<endl;
                cout<<"Your Tax rate is  "<<TAXRATE<<endl;
                cout<<"The Tax amount is "<<taxAmount<<endl;
                cout<<"The Net pay is   "<<netPay<<endl;

                myNumber = myNumber + 1;
        }//repeats 5 times
return 0;
}//MAIN
```

```cpp
#include<iostream.h>
//phase2a payroll
int main(){
        int employeeId, hoursWorked, myNumber  ;
        float hourlyRate, grossPay, taxAmount, netPay;
        float const TAXRATE=(float).30;
    myNumber = 1;
    while(myNumber <=  5)
        {
cout<<"Please Enter The Employee Id:";
cin>>employeeId;
cout<<"Please Enter The Hours Worked:";
cin>>hoursWorked;
cout<<"Please Enter The Hourly Rate:";
cin>>hourlyRate;
grossPay=hoursWorked*hourlyRate;
taxAmount=grossPay*TAXRATE;
netPay=grossPay-taxAmount;
cout<<"Your Id is            "<<employeeId<<endl;
cout<<"Your hours Worked are     "<<hoursWorked<<endl;
cout<<"Your Hourly rate is     "<<hourlyRate<<endl;
cout<<"Your Gross pay is      "<<grossPay<<endl;
cout<<"Your Tax rate is        "<<TAXRATE<<endl;
cout<<"The Tax amount is       "<<taxAmount<<endl;
cout<<"The Net pay is         "<<netPay<<endl;
myNumber = myNumber + 1;
}//repeats 5 times
return 0;
}//MAIN
```

2b) Extend payroll phase 1b to repeat for 5 employees from an input file.

Data typed and saved under employee.in

#include <fstream.h> instead of <iostream.h>

Use ifstream fin("employee.in")

Use the same while loop as 2a

```cpp
#include<iostream.h>
#include<fstream.h>
//phase2b payroll


int main()
{

        int employeeId, hoursWorked, myNumber ;
        float hourlyRate, grossPay, taxAmount, netPay;
```

771

```cpp
        float const TAXRATE=(float).30;
    myNumber = 1;

        ifstream inFile; //file object
        inFile.open("employeedata.in");//open file and connect to inFile object
    while(myNumber <= 5)//start loop
        {
                cout<<"Please Enter The Employee Id:";
                inFile>>employeeId;
                cout<<"Please Enter The Hours Worked:";
                inFile>>hoursWorked;
                cout<<"Please Enter The Hourly Rate:";
                inFile>>hourlyRate;
                grossPay=hoursWorked*hourlyRate;
                taxAmount=grossPay*TAXRATE;
                netPay=grossPay-taxAmount;
                cout<<"Your Id is              "<<employeeId<<endl;
                cout<<"Your hours Worked are      "<<hoursWorked<<endl;
                cout<<"Your Hourly rate is      "<<hourlyRate<<endl;
                cout<<"Your Gross pay is        "<<grossPay<<endl;
                cout<<"Your Tax rate is         "<<TAXRATE<<endl;
                cout<<"The Tax amount is          "<<taxAmount<<endl;
                cout<<"The Net pay is           "<<netPay<<endl;

                myNumber = myNumber + 1;//increment counter
        }//end loop
        inFile.close();//close the file we are connected

//repeats 5 times
        //repeat 5 times from data file
    return 0;
    }
```

2c) Extend payroll phase 1b to repeat for as many employees entered interactively.

No loop counter needed.

cout <<"enter employeeid";

while(cin>>employeeid) {…

…..

cout<<"enter employeeid";

} //end while loop

 having cin>> in loop enables user to exit loop by pressing ctrl/z

```
#include<iostream.h>
//phase2c payroll


int main()
{
        int employeeId, hoursWorked ;
```

```cpp
        float hourlyRate, grossPay, taxAmount, netPay;
        float const TAXRATE=(float).30;
cout<<"enter employeeId:";
while(cin>>employeeId)
        {

                cout<<"Please Enter The Hours Worked:";
                cin>>hoursWorked;
                cout<<"Please Enter The Hourly Rate:";
                cin>>hourlyRate;
                grossPay=hoursWorked*hourlyRate;
                taxAmount=grossPay*TAXRATE;
                netPay=grossPay-taxAmount;
                cout<<"Your Id is          "<<employeeId<<endl;
                cout<<"Your hours Worked are     "<<hoursWorked<<endl;
                cout<<"Your Hourly rate is    "<<hourlyRate<<endl;
                cout<<"Your Gross pay is     $"<<grossPay<<endl;
                cout<<"Your Tax rate is      $"<<TAXRATE<<endl;
                cout<<"The Tax amount is      $"<<taxAmount<<endl;
                cout<<"The Net pay is      $"<<netPay<<endl;
                cout<<"enter employeeId:";

        }//end loop



        //repeat for as many employees entered interactively
return 0;
}
```

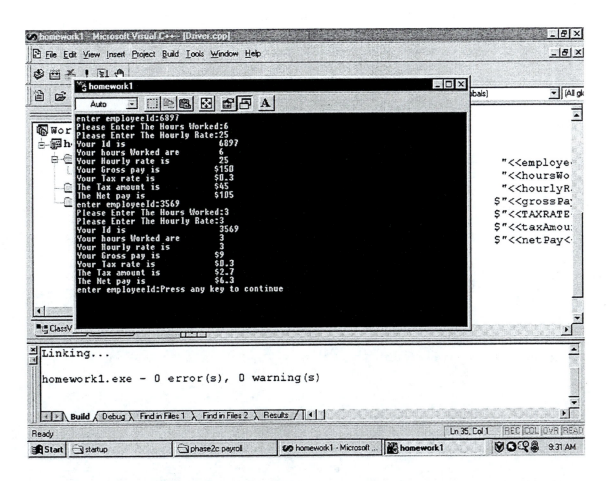

2d) Extend payroll phase 1b to repeat for as many employees from an input file.

Enter more than 5 employee's in employee.in

while(fin>>employeeid){...your program.....}//end loop

No loop counter needed

No interaction need

```cpp
#include<iostream.h>
#include<fstream.h>
//phase2d payroll


int main()
{

        int employeeId, hoursWorked;
        float hourlyRate, grossPay, taxAmount, netPay;
        float const TAXRATE=(float).30;


        ifstream inFile; //file object
        inFile.open("employeedata.in");//open file and connect to inFile object
    while(inFile>>employeeId)//start loop
```

```
    {
            cout<<"Reading The Employee Id:"<<endl;
            cout<<"Reading The Hours Worked:"<<endl;
            inFile>>hoursWorked;
            cout<<"Reading The Hourly Rate:"<<endl;
            inFile>>hourlyRate;
            grossPay=hoursWorked*hourlyRate;
            taxAmount=grossPay*TAXRATE;
            netPay=grossPay-taxAmount;
            cout<<"Your Id is            "<<employeeId<<endl;
            cout<<"Your hours Worked are     "<<hoursWorked<<endl;
            cout<<"Your Hourly rate is    $"<<hourlyRate<<endl;
            cout<<"Your Gross pay is      $"<<grossPay<<endl;
            cout<<"Your Tax rate is       $"<<TAXRATE<<endl;
            cout<<"The Tax amount is       $"<<taxAmount<<endl;
            cout<<"The Net pay is         $"<<netPay<<endl;


    }//end loop
    inFile.close();//close the file we are connected

//repeats for as many employees from input file
return 0;
}
```

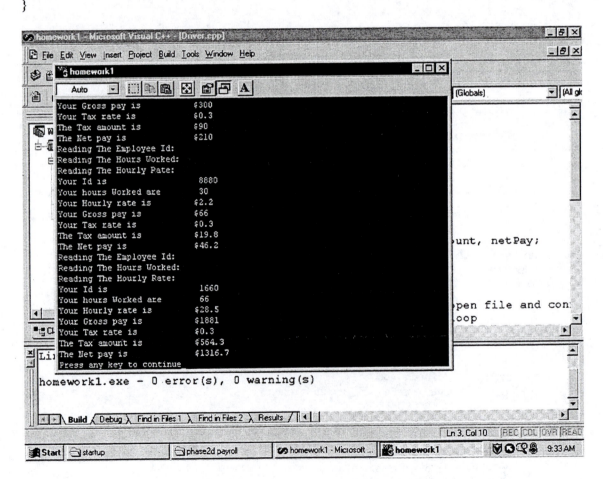

PHASE 3: EXPAND PHASE OF PAYROLL SYSTEM TO INCLUDE VARIABLE
TAXRATE ACCORDING TO THE FOLLOWING:

If gross pay >$500 then taxrate = 30%
If gross pay > $200 then taxrate = 20%
Else taxrate = 10%

```
#include<iostream.h>
#include<fstream.h>
//phase3a payroll

int main(){

        int employeeId, hoursWorked;
        float hourlyRate, grossPay, taxAmount, netPay;
        float TAXRATE;


                cout<<"Enter The Employee Id:";
                cin>>employeeId;
                cout<<"Enter The Hours Worked:";
                cin>>hoursWorked;
                cout<<"Reading The Hourly Rate:";
                cin>>hourlyRate;
                grossPay=hoursWorked*hourlyRate;

        if(grossPay>500)
                TAXRATE=.30f;
        else if(grossPay>200)
                TAXRATE=.20f;
        else TAXRATE=.10f;

                taxAmount=grossPay*TAXRATE;
                netPay=grossPay-taxAmount;
                cout<<"Your Id is          "<<employeeId<<endl;
                cout<<"Your hours Worked are   "<<hoursWorked<<endl;
                cout<<"Your Hourly rate is    $"<<hourlyRate<<endl;
                cout<<"Your Gross pay is      $"<<grossPay<<endl;
                cout<<"Your Tax rate is       $"<<TAXRATE<<endl;
                cout<<"The Tax amount is      $"<<taxAmount<<endl;
                cout<<"The Net pay is         $"<<netPay<<endl;

return 0;
}//MAIN
```

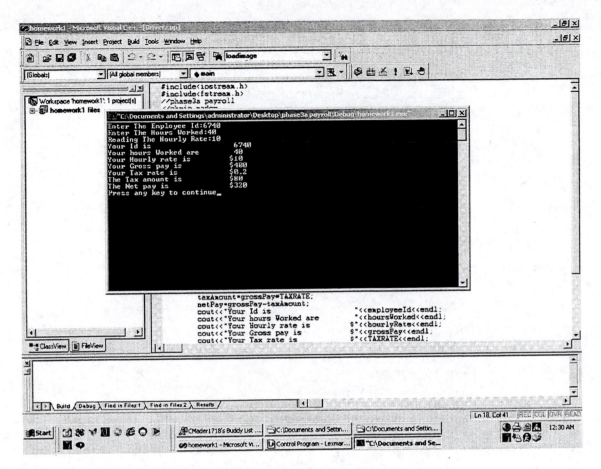

Overtime: Greater than 40 hours = time and a half
- Find overtime hour and overtime pay   (hourlyrate * 1.5)

```cpp
#include<iostream.h>
#include<fstream.h>
//phase3b payroll
int main(){
        float overTime, overtimePay, regPay, overtimepayCalc, hoursWorked;
        int employeeId;
        float hourlyRate, grossPay, taxAmount, netPay;
        float TAXRATE;
        overTime=0;
        overtimePay=0;

                cout<<"Enter The Employee Id:";
                cin>>employeeId;
                cout<<"Enter The Hours Worked:";
                cin>>hoursWorked;
                cout<<"Reading The Hourly Rate:";
                cin>>hourlyRate;
                grossPay=hoursWorked*hourlyRate;

                if(hoursWorked>40){
                        overTime=hoursWorked-40;
                        regPay=40*hourlyRate;
```

```
                    overtimepayCalc=hourlyRate*1.5f;
                    overtimePay=overTime*overtimepayCalc;
                    grossPay=overtimePay+regPay;
        }//IF >40
        if(grossPay>500)
                TAXRATE=.30f;
        else if(grossPay>200)
                TAXRATE=.20f;
        else
                TAXRATE=.10f;

        taxAmount=grossPay*TAXRATE;
        netPay=grossPay-taxAmount;
        cout<<"Your Id is            "<<employeeId<<endl;
        cout<<"Your hours Worked are   "<<hoursWorked<<endl;
        cout<<"Your over time hours are  "<<overTime<<endl;
        cout<<"Your Hourly rate is     $"<<hourlyRate<<endl;
        cout<<"Your over time pay is   $"<<overtimePay<<endl;
        cout<<"Your Gross pay is       $"<<grossPay<<endl;
        cout<<"Your Tax rate is        $"<<TAXRATE<<endl;
        cout<<"The Tax amount is       $"<<taxAmount<<endl;
        cout<<"The Net pay is          $"<<netPay<<endl;


return 0;
}//MAIN
```

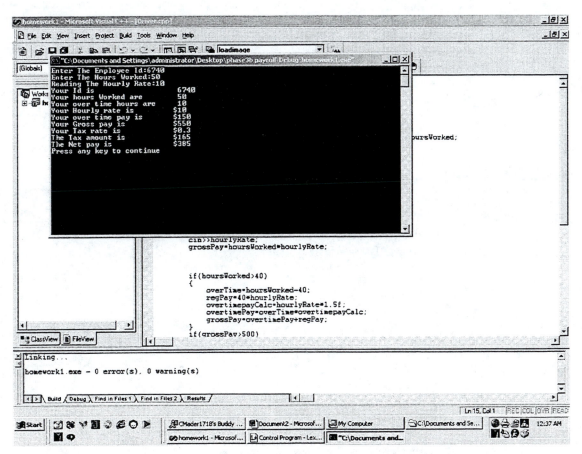

Include marital status for taxrate :
1) single = 1   married=2   Head of Household = 3 (USE INTEGER)
additional 5% will be added to the tax rate of a single person
subtract 5% if Head of Household.

```cpp
#include<iostream.h>
#include<fstream.h>
//phase3c1 payroll

int main(){
float overTime, overtimePay, regPay, overtimepayCalc, hoursWorked;
        int employeeId,single, married, headofhouse, answer;
        float hourlyRate, grossPay, taxAmount, netPay;
        float TAXRATE;
                overTime=0;
                overtimePay=0;
                single=0;
                married=0;
                headofhouse=0;

        {

                cout<<"Enter The Employee Id:";
                cin>>employeeId;
                cout<<"Enter The Hours Worked:";
                cin>>hoursWorked;
                cout<<"Reading The Hourly Rate:";
                cin>>hourlyRate;
                cout<<"Enter 1 if Single, 2 if Married, 3 if Head of House:";
                cin>>answer;


                grossPay=hoursWorked*hourlyRate;

                if(hoursWorked>40)
                {
                        overTime=hoursWorked-40;
                        regPay=40*hourlyRate;
                        overtimepayCalc=hourlyRate*1.5f;
                        overtimePay=overTime*overtimepayCalc;
                        grossPay=overtimePay+regPay;
                }
                if(grossPay>500)
                        TAXRATE=.30f;
                else if(grossPay>200)
                        TAXRATE=.20f;
                else
                        TAXRATE=.10f;

                if(answer==1)
                        TAXRATE=TAXRATE*1.05F;
                else if(answer==3)
                        TAXRATE=TAXRATE*.95F;
                taxAmount=grossPay*TAXRATE;
                netPay=grossPay-taxAmount;
```

```cpp
        cout<<"Your Id is              "<<employeeId<<endl;
        cout<<"Your hours Worked are       "<<hoursWorked<<endl;
        cout<<"Your over time hours are    "<<overTime<<endl;
        cout<<"Your Hourly rate is        $"<<hourlyRate<<endl;
        cout<<"Your over time pay is      $"<<overtimePay<<endl;
        cout<<"Your Gross pay is          $"<<grossPay<<endl;
        cout<<"Your Tax rate is           $"<<TAXRATE<<endl;
        cout<<"The Tax amount is          $"<<taxAmount<<endl;
        cout<<"The Net pay is             $"<<netPay<<endl;


    }//WHILE
return 0;
}//MAIN
```

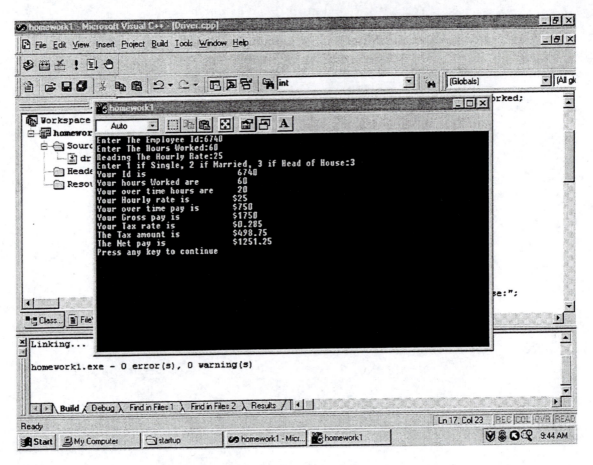

2) USE CHARACTER marital status (1 or 2 M or S)

3) Accept both upper or lower case (e.g. accept M or m)

Purpose of Phase 3: Decision Making, use of character and integer.

PHASE 4: OUTPUT FORMAT , USE OF ARRAYS

EXPAND PHASE 3C TO INCLUDE THE FOLLOWING
A) DISPLAY COMPANY TITLE AND A HEADER WHICH LABELS THE
   OUTPUT IN A TABULAR FORM
INPUT FIRST NAME AND LAST NAME OF EMPLOYEE.
char firstname[10], lastname[15]
HINTS: YOU MAY WANT TO USE THE FOLLOWING I/O MANIPULATORS
 #include <iomanip.h>, setw(15), setprecision(2)
setiosflags(ios::fixed|ios::showpoint|ios::left),

Dr. EBRAHIMI PAYROLL INSTITUTE
106 EASY STREET,
PLEASANTVILLE, N.Y. 11068

(header line double underlined):

FIRST NAME	LAST NAME	STAT	SSN	HW	HR	OTH	OTP	REGP	GROSS	TAX	NET
JOHN	SMITH	M	113	50	20	10	300	800	1100	385	715
JANE	DOE	M	223	45	15	5	112..5	675	787.5	275	512.5

B) CONVERT THE PROGRAM AS IT IS TO ARRAYS. SET MAXSIZE OF ARRAY
TO 100.   int hw[100],empid[100]

C) TAKE ADVANTAGE OF ARRAY BY BREAKING PROGRAMS INTO
SEPARATE UNITS. EACH SHOULD HAVE A SEPARATE LOOP.
- READ ALL DATA INTO ARRAY.
- COMPUTE ALL THE OVERTIMEPAY.
- COMPUTE ALL THE GROSSPAY.
- COMPUTE ALL THE TAXRATES.
- COMPUTE ALL THE NETPAY.
- DISPLAY ALL ARRAYS.

D) INCLUDE A SEARCH BY EMPLOYEE ID. (EXTRA CREDIT)
E) INCLUDE A SEARCH BY EMPLOYEE NAME (EXTRA CREDIT).
F) SORT THE DATA EITHER BY EMPLOYEES ID OR BY EMPLOYEE NAME.

```cpp
#include<iostream.h>
#include<fstream.h>
#include<iomanip.h>

//phase4a payroll
main(){

        char maritalstatus, firstName[10], lastName[15];
        float overTime, overtimePay, regPay, overtimepayCalc, hoursWorked;
        int employeeId;
        float hourlyRate, grossPay, taxAmount, netPay;
        float TAXRATE;
            overTime=0;
            overtimePay=0;
            regPay=0;
            cout<<"Enter your First name: ";
            cin>>firstName;
            cout<<"Enter your Last name: ";
            cin>>lastName;
            cout<<"Enter The Employee Id:";
            cin>>employeeId;
            cout<<"Enter The Hours Worked:";
            cin>>hoursWorked;
            cout<<"Reading The Hourly Rate:";
            cin>>hourlyRate;
            cout<<"Enter s if Single, m if Married, h if Head of House:"<<endl<<endl;
            cin>>maritalstatus;

            grossPay=hoursWorked*hourlyRate;

            if(hoursWorked>40){
                    overTime=hoursWorked-40;
                    regPay=40*hourlyRate;
                    overtimepayCalc=hourlyRate*1.5f;
                    overtimePay=overTime*overtimepayCalc;
                    grossPay=overtimePay+regPay;
            }//IF >40
            if(grossPay>500)
                    TAXRATE=.30f;
            else if(grossPay>200)
                    TAXRATE=.20f;
            else
                    TAXRATE=.10f;

            if(maritalstatus=='s')
                    TAXRATE=TAXRATE*1.05F;
            else if(maritalstatus=='m')
                    TAXRATE=TAXRATE*.85f;
            else if(maritalstatus=='h')
                    TAXRATE=TAXRATE*.95F;
            taxAmount=grossPay*TAXRATE;
            netPay=grossPay-taxAmount;

            cout<<"         Dr. Ebrahimi Payroll Institute"<<endl;
            cout<<"              106 Easy Street"<<endl;
```

```cpp
                cout<<"            Pleasantville, N.Y. 11068"<<endl<<endl;


cout<<"First Name  Last Name Stat  ssn   HW  OTH  OTP  REGP  GROSS  TAX    NET"<<endl;
cout<<"==========  ========= ====  ====  ==  ===  ===  ====  =====  ===    ==="<<endl;
setprecision(2);

cout<<setiosflags(ios::left)<<setw(12)<<firstName
        <<setiosflags(ios::left)<<setw(10)<<lastName
        <<setiosflags(ios::left)<<setw(6)<<maritalstatus
        <<setiosflags(ios::left)<<setw(6)<<employeeId
        <<setiosflags(ios::left)<<setw(4)<<hoursWorked
        <<setiosflags(ios::left)<<setw(5)<<overTime
        <<setiosflags(ios::left)<<setw(5)<<overtimePay
        <<setiosflags(ios::left)<<setw(6)<<regPay
        <<setiosflags(ios::left)<<setw(7)<<grossPay
        <<setw(8)<<taxAmount
        <<setiosflags(ios::left)<<setw(7)<<netPay<<endl<<endl;
return 0;
}//MAIN
```

Enter your First name: chris
Enter your Last name: mader
Enter The Employee Id:6878
Enter The Hours Worked:44
Reading The Hourly Rate:10
Enter s if Single, m if Married, h if Head of House:

s

            Dr. Ebrahini Payroll Institute
                106 Easy Street
            Pleasantville, N.Y. 11068

First Name	Last Name	Stat	ssn	HW	OTH	OTP	REGP	GROSS	TAX	NET
chris	mader	s	6878	44	4	60	400	460	96.6	363.4

Press any key to continue_

F) Convert the program as it is to arrays. Set MAXSIZE of array to 100.
int hw[100],empid[100]

#include<iostream.h>

```
#include<fstream.h>
#include<iomanip.h>

//phase4b payroll
main(){
    char maritalstatus[100], firstName[100][10], lastName[100][15];
    float overTime, overtimePay, regPay, overtimepayCalc, hoursWorked[100];
    int employeeId[100],myNumber,aNumber;
    float hourlyRate[100], grossPay, taxAmount, netPay;
    float TAXRATE;
        overTime=0;
        overtimePay=0;
        regPay=0;
        myNumber=0;
        aNumber=0;

        cout<<"Enter your First name: ";
while(cin>>firstName[myNumber]&&myNumber<100){
        cout<<"Enter your Last name: ";
        cin>>lastName[myNumber];
        cout<<"Enter The Employee Id:";
        cin>>employeeId[myNumber];
        cout<<"Enter The Hours Worked:";
        cin>>hoursWorked[myNumber];
        cout<<"Reading The Hourly Rate:";
        cin>>hourlyRate[myNumber];
        cout<<"Enter s if Single, m if Married, h if Head of House:"<<endl;
        cin>>maritalstatus[myNumber];
        cout<<"Enter your First name: ";
                myNumber=myNumber+1;
    }//end of loop

        cout<<"        Dr. Ebrahimi Payroll Institute"<<endl;
        cout<<"            106 Easy Street"<<endl;
        cout<<"        Pleasantville, N.Y. 11068"<<endl<<endl;


cout<<"First Name  Last Name Stat  ssn   HW  OTH  OTP  REGP  GROSS  TAX    NET"<<endl;
cout<<"=========  ========= ==== ==== == === == ==== ===== ===   ==="<<endl;

while(aNumber<myNumber)
{

        grossPay=hoursWorked[aNumber]*hourlyRate[aNumber];

        if(hoursWorked[aNumber]>40)
        {
                overTime=hoursWorked[aNumber]-40;
                regPay=40*hourlyRate[aNumber];
                overtimepayCalc=hourlyRate[aNumber]*1.5f;
                overtimePay=overTime*overtimepayCalc;
                grossPay=overtimePay+regPay;
        }
        if(grossPay>500)
                TAXRATE=.30f;
        else if(grossPay>200)
```

```
                TAXRATE=.20f;
        else
                TAXRATE=.10f;

        if(maritalstatus[aNumber]=='s')
                TAXRATE=TAXRATE*1.05F;
        else if(maritalstatus[aNumber]=='m')
                TAXRATE=TAXRATE*.85f;
        else if(maritalstatus[aNumber]=='h')
                TAXRATE=TAXRATE*.95F;
        taxAmount=grossPay*TAXRATE;
        netPay=grossPay-taxAmount;


setprecision(2);

cout<<setiosflags(ios::left)<<setw(12)<<firstName[aNumber]
    <<setiosflags(ios::left)<<setw(10)<<lastName[aNumber]
    <<setiosflags(ios::left)<<setw(6)<<maritalstatus[aNumber]
    <<setiosflags(ios::left)<<setw(6)<<employeeId[aNumber]
    <<setiosflags(ios::left)<<setw(4)<<hoursWorked[aNumber]
    <<setiosflags(ios::left)<<setw(5)<<overTime
    <<setiosflags(ios::left)<<setw(5)<<overtimePay
    <<setiosflags(ios::left)<<setw(6)<<regPay
    <<setiosflags(ios::left)<<setw(7)<<grossPay
    <<setw(8)<<taxAmount
    <<setiosflags(ios::left)<<setw(7)<<netPay<<endl;

aNumber=aNumber+1;
}//WHILE
return 0;
}//MAIN
```

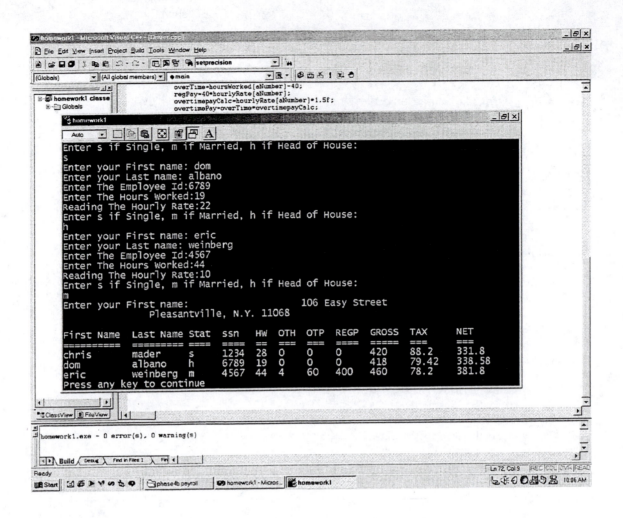

PHASE 5: FUNCTIONS EXTERNAL VARIABLES, PASS OF PARAMETERS
FUNCTIONS WITH EXTERNAL VARIABLES (GLOBAL VARIABLES)
PLACE ALL THE SHARED VARIABLES OUTSIDE THE MAIN AND
FUNCTIONS
A) FUNCTIONS WITH PASS OF PARAMETERS AND PROTOTYPES
C) FUNCTIONS WITH RETURN VALUES

```
char nempname[100][20], int hw[100], n;
double hr[100];//…………..
//………
readalldata(){
while(fin<<empname[n]<<hw[n]<<hr[n]<<status[n]){
n++;
}//end while
```

788

```
        }//end readalldata


        computeovertime(){
        for(i=0;i<n; i++){
        //......
        }//end for
        }//end of computeovertime pay

        void main()
        {
        readalldata();
        computeovertimepay();
        computeregpay();
        computegrosspay();
        //............
        searchbyid();
        displaytitleheader();
        displayalloutput();}//end main



#include<iostream.h>
#include<fstream.h>
#include<iomanip.h>

//phase5a payroll

//funtions

        char maritalstatus[100], firstName[100][10], lastName[100][15];
        float overTime[100], overtimePay[100], regPay[100], overtimepayCalc, hoursWorked[100];
        int employeeId[100],myNumber,counter;
        float hourlyRate[100], grossPay[100], taxAmount[100], netPay[100];
        float TAXRATE;
          //myNumber=0;
              //counter=0;
getuserinfo(){
        cout<<"Enter your First name: ";
   while(cin>>firstName[myNumber]&&myNumber<100)
        {
                cout<<"Enter your Last name: ";
                cin>>lastName[myNumber];
                cout<<"Enter The Employee Id:";
                cin>>employeeId[myNumber];
                cout<<"Enter The Hours Worked:";
                cin>>hoursWorked[myNumber];
                cout<<"Reading The Hourly Rate:";
                cin>>hourlyRate[myNumber];
                cout<<"Enter s if Single, m if Married, h if Head of House:"<<endl;
                cin>>maritalstatus[myNumber];
                cout<<"Enter your First name: ";
                        myNumber=myNumber+1;
```

```
        }//WHILE

}//GETUSERINFO

outputheader(){
    cout<<endl<<endl<<endl<<"          Dr. Ebrahini Payroll Institute"<<endl;
                cout<<"              106 Easy Street"<<endl;
                cout<<"          Pleasantville, N.Y. 11068"<<endl<<endl;


    cout<<"First Name  Last Name Stat  ssn  HW  OTH OTP   REGP  GROSS TAX    NET"<<endl;
    cout<<"========= ========= ==== ==== == === ===  ==== ===== ===   ==="<<endl;

}//OUTPUTHEADER

grosspay(){
        counter = 0;
    while(counter<myNumber){

                grossPay[counter]=hoursWorked[counter]*hourlyRate[counter];
                counter=counter+1;
    }//WHILE
}//GROSSPAY

overtimepay(){
    counter = 0;
    while(counter<myNumber)
        {
                overTime[counter]=0;
                if(hoursWorked[counter]>40)
                overTime[counter]=hoursWorked[counter]-40;
                overtimepayCalc=hourlyRate[counter]*1.5f;
                overtimePay[counter]=overTime[counter]*overtimepayCalc;
                counter=counter+1;
        }//WHILE
}//OVERTIMEPAY

calregpay(){
 counter=0;
while(counter<myNumber){
        regPay[counter]=40*hourlyRate[counter];
        counter++;
        }
}//CALREGPAY

calgrosspay(){
 counter = 0;
while(counter<myNumber){
                grossPay[counter]=overtimePay[counter]+regPay[counter];
                counter=counter+1;
        }//WHILE

}//CALGROSSPAY

tax(){
  counter = 0;
```

```
while(counter<myNumber){
                `if(grossPay[counter]>500)
                        TAXRATE=.30f;
                else if(grossPay[counter]>200)
                        TAXRATE=.20f;
                else
                        TAXRATE=.10f;

                if(maritalstatus[counter]=='s')
                        TAXRATE=TAXRATE*1.05F;
                else if(maritalstatus[counter]=='m')
                        TAXRATE=TAXRATE*.85f;
                else if(maritalstatus[counter]=='h')
                        TAXRATE=TAXRATE*.95F;
                taxAmount[counter]=grossPay[counter]*TAXRATE;
counter=counter+1;
}//WHILE
}//TAX

netpay(){
  counter = 0;
while(counter<myNumber){
                netPay[counter]=grossPay[counter]-taxAmount[counter];
                counter=counter+1;
        }//WHILE
}//NETPAY

output(){
setprecision(2);
counter = 0;
while(counter < myNumber){
        cout<<setiosflags(ios::left)<<setw(12)<<firstName[counter]
                <<setiosflags(ios::left)<<setw(10)<<lastName[counter]
                <<setiosflags(ios::left)<<setw(6)<<maritalstatus[counter]
                <<setiosflags(ios::left)<<setw(6)<<employeeId[counter]
                <<setiosflags(ios::left)<<setw(4)<<hoursWorked[counter]
                <<setiosflags(ios::left)<<setw(5)<<overTime[counter]
                <<setiosflags(ios::left)<<setw(7)<<overtimePay[counter]
                <<setiosflags(ios::left)<<setw(6)<<regPay[counter]
                <<setiosflags(ios::left)<<setw(7)<<grossPay[counter]
                <<setw(8)<<taxAmount[counter]
                <<setiosflags(ios::left)<<setw(7)<<netPay[counter]<<endl;

                counter++;
        }//WHILE
counter = 0;
}//OUTPUT

main(){
getuserinfo();
outputheader();
grosspay();
overtimepay();
calregpay();
calgrosspay();
tax();
```

```
netpay();
output();
}//MAIN
```

B) FUNCTIONS WITH PASS OF PARAMETERS AND PROTOTYPES

```
//prototype
void readalldat(char [], int,double,char,int &);
 //..........

void main()
{
int n;
readalldata(empname,hw,hr,status,n);
computeovertimepay(hw,hr,overtimepay);
computeregpay(hw,hr,regpay);
computegrosspay(overtomepay,regpay,grosspay);
//...................
searchbyid();
displaytitleheader();
displayalloutput();
}//end main

readalldata(char empname[], int hw, double hr,char int &n){
while(fin<<empname[n]<<hw[n]<<hr[n]<<status[n]){
n++;
}//end while
}//end readalldata

computeovertimepay(int hw,double hr, double overtimepay){
//.....
}

//.......
```

C) FUNCTIONS WITH RETURN VALUES

```
double computeovertimepay(int hourlywage,double hourlrate)
{double extrapay;


return extrapay;
}//end overtime pay

main()
{int n;
```

```
n=readalldata(empname,hw,hr,status);

for {i=0; i<n;i++)
{
ovetimepay[i] =computeovertimepay(hw[i],hr[i]);

//…..
}//for loop

i=searchid();
if (i ==-1) cout<<" name not listed"
else {//…..

}//end main
```

PHASE 6: STRUCTURE AND CLASS
   A) EXPAND THE PAYROLL PROGRAM TO INCLUDE STRUCTURE FOR THE
      EMPLOYEE DATA BY USING STRUCT.
   B) CREATE A MENU TO DISPLAY DATA, SEARCH BY ID OR BY NAME
   C) CONVERT THE STRUCTURE TO A CLASS

```
# include <iostream.h>
#include <fstream.h>
int n;
class employee {
public:
char name[100][15];
int hoursworked[100];
double hourlyrate[100];
double grosspay[100];
double netpay[100];
void readdata();
};

employee professor;
void employee::readdata(){
ifstream fin ("payroll.in");

while (fin>>name[n]>>hoursworked[n]>>hourlyrate[n]){
        n++;
}//WHILE
}//READATA

main(){
professor.readdata();
cout<< "THE NUMBER OF EMPLOYEES ARE  "<<n<<endl;
return 0;
}//MAIN
```

PHASE 7: FILE HANDLING
BUILD A SIMPLE DATA BASE WITH FOLLOWING MENU OPTIONS
A) ACCESS THE DATA DIRECTLY FROM FILE
   CREATE, DISPLAY, SEARCH, MODIFY, AND DELETE.
B) DOWNLOAD THE FILE INTO AN ARRAY
   SAVE THE ARRAY TO THE FILE
   ADD, SEARCH, MODIFY, AND DELETE IS DONE WITH THE ARRAY.
   APPLY BINARY SEARCH INSTEAD OF LINEAR SEARCH

C) USE RANDOM ACCESS MEMORY
D) MAKE YOUR RANDOM ACCESS EFFICIENT
E) USE HASHING TO SPEED UP PROCESS

PHASE 8: CLASS INHERITANCE AND POLYMORPHISM
RECONSTRUCT THE EMPLOYEE CLASS AS BASE CLASS TO INCLUDE
FIRST NAME LAST NAME, STREET ADDRESS, CITY, STATE, ZIPCODE ,
DEPTID, LEVEL, AND ITS ACCESSOR FUNCTIONS. USE THE PRINT
FUNCTION AS A VIRTUAL FUNCTION. CREATE DERIVED CLASSES SUCH
AS FULLTIMEEMPLOYEE, PARTTIMEEMPLOYEE, CONSULTANT, AND
COMMISSIONEDEMPLOYEE
EMPLOYEES ALSO CAN BE CATEGORIZED AS HOURLYPAID OR
SALARIED.

PHASE 9: DYNAMIC MEMORY ALLOCATION AND ALGORITHM
A) DESIGN YOUR PAYROLL SYSTEM TO INPUT THE DATA INTO A
LINKED LIST
ALL THE FUNCTIONS MANIPULATE THE LIST SUCH AS SEARCH,
MODIFICATION, AND DELETION
B) USE DOUBLE LINKED LIST
C) USE TREE STRUCTURE FOR YOUR PAYROLL SYSTEM
D) USE SEARCH, INSERTION, AND DELETION WITH BINARY SEARCH
   TREE

PHASE 10: STANDARD TEMPLATE LIBRARY
REDESIGN YOUR PAYROLL SYSTEM ONLY USING STL DATA
STRUCTURES AND ALGORITHMS. DRAW THE PAYCHECK AND WRITE
OUT THE WORDING OF THE AMOUNT ON THE CHECK USING STL STRING
MANIPILATION.

PHASE 11: PUBLISH YOUR PAYROLL WEB SYSTEM
USE HTML AND JAVASCRIPT FOR INTERFACE AND INPUT AND OUTPUT
INTERACTION AND USE CGI FOR INTERNAL PROCESSING.

INDEX